OFFICIALS AND STAFF
INDIANAPOLIS MOTOR SPEEDWAY CORPORATION

BOARD OF DIRECTORS

Mari H. George
Chairman

Anton H. "Tony" George
President & Chief Executive Officer

M. Josephine George
Nancy L. George

Katherine M. George
Jack R. Snyder

EXECUTIVE STAFF

Jeffrey G. Belskus
Executive Vice President &
Chief Operating Officer

John Newcomb
Vice President, Sales
& Marketing

Leo Mehl
Vice President & Executive
Director of the Pep Boys
Indy Racing League

W. Curtis Brighton
Vice President &
General Counsel

Fred J. Nation
Vice President, Corporate
Communications & Public
Relations

Peggy Swalls
Vice President, Administration

Laura George
Staff Advisor

Kenneth T. Ungar
Chief of Staff

SPEEDWAY STAFF

Don Bailey
Vehicle Coordinator
Dawn Bair
Manager of Creative Services
Ellen Bireley
Manager of Museum Services
Dr. Henry Bock
Director of Medical Services
Martha Briggs
Manager of Accounting
Jeff Chapman
Director of Marketing & Branding
Randy Clark
Manager of Food & Beverage
Sean Clayton
Manager of Market Research
Derek Decker
Manager of Corporate Hospitality
Nancy Doan
Manager of Public Relations
Chuck Ferguson
Director of Information Services &
Telecommunications

Kevin Forbes
Director of Engineering & Construction
Lee Gardner
Director of Automotive Partnerships
Lynn Greggs
Director of Accounting &
Administration
Mel Harder
Director of Facility Operations
Pat Hayes
Manager of Contract Administration
Marty Hunt
Manager of Track Racing Operations
John Kesler
Manager of Sales
Jeff Kleiber
Manager of Event Operations
Patricia Kuhn
Director of Human Resources
John Lewis
Manager of Facilities
Kent Liffick
Director of Sponsorship Development

Mai Lindstrom
Director of Public Relations
Bruce Lynch
Director of Retail Sales & Operations
Buddy McAtee
Director of Sales
Matt McCartin
Manager of Marketing
Richard McComb
Director of Finance
Robert McInteer
Director of Safety
Ron McQueeney
Director of Photography
David Moroknek
Director of Licensing
& Consumer Products
Gloria Novotney
Director of Credentials
Dan Petty
Manager of Retail Merchandising
Lisa Sommers
Manager of Public Relations,
Special Events

PEP BOYS INDY RACING LEAGUE STAFF

Brian Barnhart
Director of Racing Operations
Mark Bridges
Technical Manager
Phil Casey
Technical Director
Joie Chitwood
Manager of Administration

Ron Green
Manager of Media Relations
Andy Hall
Director of Corporate &
Sponsor Relations
Les Mactaggart
Technical Consultant
John Pierce
Safety Consultant

Jim Reynolds
Manager of Fuel Services
Johnny Rutherford
Special Projects
Al Unser
Driver Coach & Consultant
Chuck Whetsel
Manager of Timing & Scoring

RACE
FOR
HEROES

CONTENTS

First published in 1999 by MBI Publishing Company, 729 Prospect Avenue, PO Box 1, Osceola, WI 54020-0001 USA

© IMS Corporation, 2000

All rights reserved. With the exception of quoting brief passages for the purposes of review,
no part of this publication may be reproduced without prior written permission from the Publisher.

The information in this book is true and complete to the best of our knowledge. All recommendations are made without any guarantee on the part of the author or Publisher,
who also disclaim any liability incurred in connection with the use of this data or specific details.

We recognize that some words, model names and designations, for example, mentioned herein are the property of the trademark holder.
We use them for identification purposes only. This is not an official publication.

MBI Publishing Company books are also available at discounts in bulk quantity for industrial or sales-promotional use. For details write to Special Sales Manager at
Motorbooks International Wholesalers & Distributors, 729 Prospect Avenue, PO Box 1, Osceola, WI 54020-0001 USA.

Designed by Tom Heffron

Editorial Contributors: Tim Tuttle, Jonathan Ingram, Jan Shaffer, John Sturbin, and Donald Davidson   Photography Contributions by Roger Bedwell, Dan Boyd, Matt Griffith,
Michael Haley, Jim Haines, Walt Kuhn, Jerry Lawrence, Linda McQueeney, Ron McQueeney, Jef Richards, Sam Scott, Steve Snoddy, Leigh Spargur, and Ken Truett

Printed in Hong Kong   ISBN 0-7603-0774-1

Thank You

The 1999 Indianapolis 500 was very special. With the sun shining, the presence of nearly 100 recipients of the Congressional Medal of Honor toured the track to the cheers and tears of a capacity crowd. With Lee Greenwood singing, "Proud to be an American.," the Rev. Billy Graham delivering the prayer, Jim Nabors' stirring "Back Home Again in Indiana," and the B-2 Stealth Bomber flying close overhead, the crowd was ready for a great race.

And a great race it was. It was Arie Luyendyk's finale, Robby McGehee's Rookie of the Year run, and Kenny Brack's steady race-winning performance taking the checkered flag as Robby Gordon faltered in the final laps.

It was a race true to the tradition of the Indianapolis 500, and this edition of the Indy Review tells the whole story of the month of May and the Pep Boys Indy Racing League season in words and pictures.

We are about to enter a new millennium, and the Indianapolis Motor Speedway will be celebrating it with a third event added to our schedule, the United States Grand Prix at Indianapolis. The face of the Speedway is changing, improving, and evolving as it has since 1909. There is one consistent thread: spirited competition among men and machines producing the Greatest Spectacle in Racing at the Racing Capital of the World.

On behalf of my family, our staff at the Indianapolis Motor Speedway and the Pep Boys Indy Racing League, and all of the drivers who compete on our track, thanks to all of you for making us a success.

Sincerely,

Tony George

Tony George
President
Indianapolis Motor Speedway

1999 IRL Pep Boys Championship Series

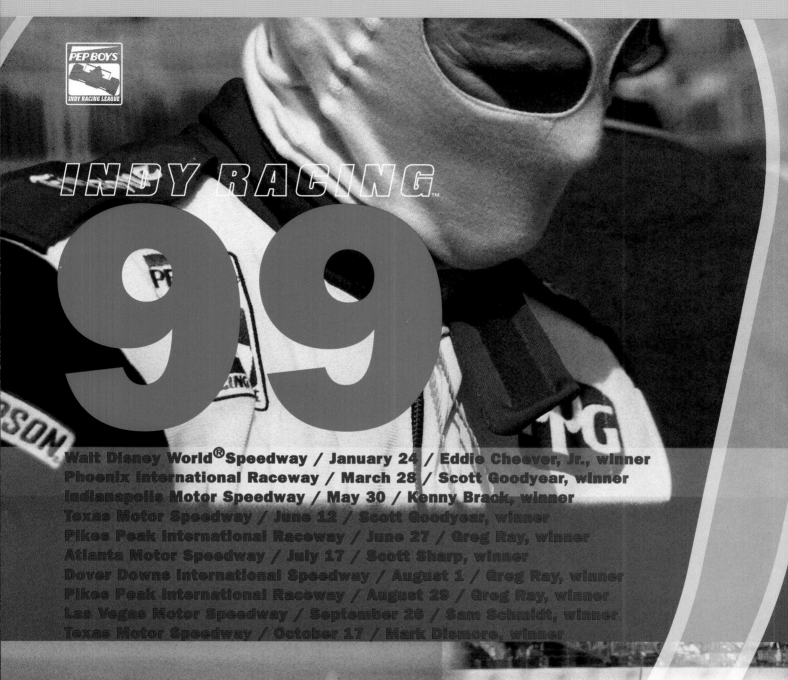

INDY RACING™

99

Walt Disney World® Speedway / January 24 / Eddie Cheever, Jr., winner
Phoenix International Raceway / March 28 / Scott Goodyear, winner
Indianapolis Motor Speedway / May 30 / Kenny Brack, winner
Texas Motor Speedway / June 12 / Scott Goodyear, winner
Pikes Peak International Raceway / June 27 / Greg Ray, winner
Atlanta Motor Speedway / July 17 / Scott Sharp, winner
Dover Downs International Speedway / August 1 / Greg Ray, winner
Pikes Peak International Raceway / August 29 / Greg Ray, winner
Las Vegas Motor Speedway / September 26 / Sam Schmidt, winner
Texas Motor Speedway / October 17 / Mark Dismore, winner

Be sure to visit the official IRL website at www.indyracingleague.com

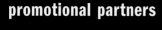

Dèjá Vu for Steady Eddie

Inset: A consolidated and strengthened Team Cheever produced a 'spot-on' race-day setup that served race winner Eddie Cheever well. "I was flat out the whole way," he said. "We had a problem in qualifications, but the car was impeccable today."

Team Cheever Returns to Disney Winner's Circle

by Tim Tuttle

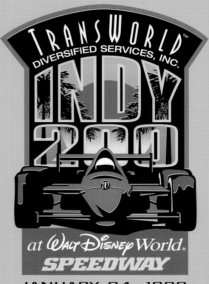

TransWORLD™ DIVERSIFIED SERVICES, INC.

INDY 200

at WALT DISNEY World. SPEEDWAY

JANUARY 24, 1999

PEP BOYS®

INDY RACING LEAGUE

For virtually his entire career, Eddie Cheever has been known more for his ability to get hired to drive race cars in premier series than for any distinguishing achievements. But, after forming his own team, Cheever won the 1998 Indianapolis 500. It was something, Cheever said, "that I can finally hang my hat on, something that I can be known for."

Team Cheever's other major accomplishment in 1998 was expanding to a two-car team and helping Robby Unser become the Indy Racing League's Rookie of the Year. The rest of Cheever's season following Indy wasn't anything to write home about: He had just one podium, a 3rd at the second Texas race, and was 9th in the overall points. It appeared that Cheever was being swallowed up into the sea of mediocrity again.

The team struggled after the season concluded. Over the winter the budget to run Unser for the 1999 season never materialized. The forced consolidation of the team's energy into

Starting from the 13th position on the grid, Eddie Cheever (51) charged hard and worked his way through the pack. He powered into the lead on Lap 142, took his last pitstop on Lap 174, regained the lead on Lap 193, and held on to the checkered flag on Lap 200. Because of radio trouble, he was unaware of his lead. "I thought I had finished second."

5

Bright Florida sunshine and a hard-charging field of IRL race cars made it a great day for the big crowd attending the TransWorld Diversified Services, Inc. Indy 200 at Walt Disney World

a one-car team turned out to be a blessing in disguise. Former crew chief Owen Snyder assumed an engineering and development role—a move Cheever could afford to make because of the presence of Dane Harte, who had proven to be a highly capable crew chief for Unser, and because team manager Dick Caron, a veteran of many Indy car campaigns, was still there to oversee the operation.

The new combination clicked for Cheever immediately. In the Indy Racing League's opener at Walt Disney World Speedway, Cheever's Dallara-Oldsmobile Aurora bolted to an impressive victory. He started 13th on the unforgiving tri-oval, which has only one good passing zone. Cheever won by 5.148 seconds over Panther Racing's

Scott Goodyear, and a heads-up drive by Jeff Ward captured 3rd place for ISM Racing's G Force-Aurora driver.

The victory was the third of Cheever's IRL career. His first, at Disney in 1997, had been—even he will admit—a fluke. The 1997 race had been decided by blown engines for leaders Buzz Calkins and Tony Stewart, followed by rain that caused the race to be shortened. And Cheever was at the right place, at the right time when the checkered flag fell. Cheever won without having led a green flag lap.

How Cheever won in 1999 at Disney was important to him. He carved his way through the pack, serving notice that, at age 39, he had the commitment and will to challenge for the championship.

"I had the best team and the best car," Cheever said. "That doesn't happen very often."

Snyder's new role as engineer was key to Cheever's victory. With Harte in charge of making sure the Dallara was mechanically sound, Snyder developed a strong setup for racing conditions. Snyder spent a decade with Galles Racing working with Al Unser Jr., famous for his charges from the back. "I have never liked qualifying," Cheever said. "I work on race setups in practice. I have Owen Snyder, and from his days with Al Unser Jr., that's what he likes and what we do. The race pays a lot more than qualifying."

Cheever began charging from the 13th qualifying position when the green flag dropped and was 10th by Lap 10. From that point on, Cheever methodically marched through the field. He reached 4th place by Lap 78 and 3rd place on Lap 109. Goodyear had taken the lead from polesitter Scott Sharp six laps before.

Fast work by the Cheever team moved him up to second during a yellow-flag pit stop with 110 laps completed. It was during this

Jeff Ward posted a second-place finish at Orlando in 1998 and backed it with a third-place finish in this year's race. The ISM Racing Thermo Tech G Force/Aurora/Goodyear driver avoided a collision between Buddy Lazier and Scott Sharp during his third-place drive and was 8.5 seconds behind Scott Goodyear at the finish.

Despite battling the lingering effects of pneumonia, Scott Goodyear finished second in the Pennzoil Panther G Force/Aurora/Goodyear. Lack of grip in the last stint of the race relegated Goodyear to a runner-up finish. It was the fourth runner-up finish of his IRL career as he remained winless on the circuit.

Jeff Ward sent Mark Dismore (28) into a spin, yet Dismore finished sixth and noted: "I came into the pits because the car was shaking so bad. It felt like a basketball, but we finished up strong."

pit stop that the brain trust of Snyder, Caron, and Harte decided to make subtle changes to the Dallara.

"We didn't want to get carried away," Caron explained. "The car was good. We changed the front wing angle a little, the front tire pressures, and put a different compound (IRL rules allow for two) on the right front." Cheever found the adjustments to his liking. "We changed some things on the second stop that made the car strongest at the end," he said. "My car also got better as more rubber went down on the track." With the lead in sight, Cheever began stalking Goodyear relentlessly. "Eddie will stand on the gas," Snyder said, "and he has no fear."

Cheever was presented with an opportunity to take the lead on Lap 142 that required decisive action, and he went for it. Goodyear came upon Stephan Gregoire's lapped G Force entering Turn 2, the circuit's fastest section and best passing area. Cheever didn't hesitate, powering down the inside to overtake both cars. He began pulling away from Goodyear and was in front by 6.8 seconds on Lap 170. Cheever was the first among the leaders to make his final pit stop, on Lap 174, and he cycled back to the front by Lap 193. Of the final 58 laps, Cheever led 40.

Goodyear chased Cheever to the checkered flag but was forced to settle for the runner-up position, his fourth in his IRL career. The Canadian had desperately wanted his and the team's first IRL triumph. "Eddie [Cheever] got his car working better than mine when he needed to," Goodyear said. "You always prefer to win, so you're disappointed when you don't. I'll take second for sure."

After qualifying fourth, Goodyear's consistent and slightly conservative driving style kept his G Force-Aurora in contention during the first half of the race. Scott Sharp dominated the initial 102 laps, leading 100 laps and giving up the point only once while making a

Raul Boesel (30) looked like a sure bet to win his first IRL race as he held the lead entering the final 10 laps. But he had to stop for a splash of fuel, pushing him back to fifth place.

Pit crews were fast and efficient in seemingly mid-season form at the season opener that featured a 28-car field and 20 cars running at the finish. Pit strategy and fuel mileage played a crucial role in determining the outcome of the race.

pit stop. Goodyear—a cautious and precise driver who is not afraid to take risks that are worth the rewards—had maneuvered himself up to second. With a chance to take the lead, Goodyear challenged Sharp in Turn 3—a tight and usually one-groove corner. Briefly, the opening became wider and Goodyear's G Force dived to the inside. "I didn't know if you could pass there," Goodyear said. "It's tight. He [Sharp] gave me room and I got inside. We raced to the next turn [1] and I had the line."

After Goodyear's second pit stop, under caution on Lap 109, he maintained the lead. But as soon as the race went green, Goodyear knew the car wasn't performing at the same level as prior to the pit stop. "We lost the car in the second segment," he said. "It was all over the road. We really didn't have any grip. You don't have to look at the lap times on the dash to know you aren't going fast enough. You know you don't have your foot on the throttle long enough. It's a tough situation." Goodyear found running in traffic even more difficult. "Our car was particularly nervous in traffic," he said.

The polesitter, Scott Sharp, had roared away at the start. He guided his Kelley Racing Dallara-Aurora into a 3.5-second advantage over Goodyear after 80 laps. "It was almost too good to be true," Sharp said. "I felt if we didn't do anything wrong, we'd be in good shape. All the way up to halfway, I felt like I was cruising. The car

was so awesome. All of a sudden, something happened in the handling of the car, and it went away in a large way."

Sharp's Dallara wasn't terrible to drive, but it developed a handling flaw that turned traffic into a time-consuming obstruction. "Scott had high-speed understeer [push]," Kelley Technical Director David Cripps said, "and the problem here is if you have high-speed understeer, you can't pass in traffic." Sharp tenaciously defended third place for the majority of the race's second half. He was 12.6 seconds behind Cheever and 5.8 seconds behind Goodyear when the third and final round of scheduled pit stops approached.

Cheever was the first of the group to pit, followed by Goodyear. Sharp inherited the lead on Lap 178 and pitted three laps later. The pit stop went smoothly, but as Sharp returned to the action, Rookie John Hollansworth made light contact with the outside wall in Turn 2. The yellow caution light came on, and Sharp went one lap down.

During the pit stop Cripps had adjusted Sharp's Dallara, and it bounced back into the competitive form it had been in during the first half of the race. On Lap 195 Sharp logged in the race's fastest lap (166.121 miles per hour). "We had changed the wing and the tire pressures and got the car back," Cripps said. "If we hadn't caught the yellow and lost a lap, nobody would have touched us. Scott would have gone around the outside of everybody. But that's

the way oval racing is, catching yellows at the wrong time. It's an occupational hazard."

The yellow may have been bad luck for Sharp, but it was just what the doctor ordered for Raul Boesel. He needed those fuel-saving caution laps to reach the finish. If he had stayed on the lead lap, Boesel and McCormack Motorsports would have snared their first IRL victory.

Boesel started in third position and stayed in the top five for nearly the entire race. Team owner Dennis McCormack decided upon a two-stop pit strategy when the caution came out on Lap 110. As the top four cars—Goodyear, Buddy Lazier, Cheever, and Sharp—pitted, Boesel took the lead for several laps before coming in at the end of the caution for fuel. Pitting cost Boesel's G Force-Aurora track position, but opened up the possibility of going the race distance without another stop.

IRL cars typically have a maximum green-flag range of 70 miles; Boesel was trying to go 82. But the fuel mileage improves dramatically under caution. When Sharp made his final stop, Boesel took the lead on Lap 181 and the team was confident he could reach the finish with the fuel he had on board. Boesel had 6 laps under caution earlier on this fuel load; the Hollansworth wall-brushing incident provided him with 11 more.

Boesel had a buffer of four lapped cars to Cheever for the Lap 189 restart. It appeared everything was in place for an unchallenged dash to the checkered flag. But when the race went green, Boesel's car was sluggish. Sharp, directly behind Boesel, blasted past to regain the lead lap. Cheever overhauled both Sharp and Boesel to take the lead. Boesel coasted around to the pits, certainly an agonizing journey.

The team's post-race inspection of Boesel's car uncovered a fuel cell malfunction that didn't allow it to fill to its full 35-gallon capacity. "We were getting good enough fuel mileage," McCormack said. "We thought we were cutting it thin, but we thought that if we were going to run out, it would be on the last lap. Our telemetry said we had 3 or 3 1/2 gallons left." The primary sponsor on Boesel's car, TransWorld Diversified Services, was also the title sponsor of the race. "I was optimistic," Boesel said. "I thought it was the great script. The race is sponsored by our sponsor and it

was going to be my first win and Dennis' first win. That's a dream race. It was a disappointment when the car started to cough, but fifth place shows our strength as a team."

Jeff Ward survived an eventful race to finish third in ISM Racing's G Force-Aurora. He was in sixth during a wild restart on Lap 121 in which Lazier, who was fourth, tried to pass Sharp for third on the inside of Turn 1. They ran out of real estate and Lazier's right-front tire touched the left sidepod of Sharp's Dallara. Sharp bounced off and kept going; Lazier spun and lost two laps before getting restarted.

"I had a great run on him [Sharp]," Lazier said. "There was somebody in front of Scott, and I saw him coming down. I couldn't get any lower on the race track. I didn't want to touch wheels and slowed down as much as I could. Boom, we hit."

Kelley Racing's Mark Dismore was directly behind the Lazier/Sharp contact, and Ward was directly behind Dismore. "When Scott and Buddy got together, I was right behind them," Dismore said. "I got out of the gas and touched the brake. Ward drilled me in the crash bumper, the attenuator. I did a 360 and didn't touch anything. I must be living right."

Ward's contact with Dismore knocked off Ward's front wing. But with the yellow out, he was able to pit and have the entire nose section replaced without losing a lap. "I was lucky to drive through that mess," Ward said. "We shouldn't have finished this race, and we did. I had the front wings knocked off. I banged wheels with [Team Menard's] Greg Ray. I think I hit just about everybody out there. I feel good about [finishing third] . . . we've got to be happy."

Cheever took the checkered flag without knowing he'd won. His radio

had failed with about 60 laps remaining and, with the cautions and pit stops, Cheever didn't know where he was running. Cheever thought that Sharp, who was fourth and on the end of the lead lap after passing the slowing Boesel on the final start, was probably the leader. Cheever thought he might be in second.

"I took the attitude that anybody in front of me was bad and that I wanted to keep everybody else behind me," Cheever explained.

"I passed a lot of cars. I thought that Sharp was the leader and I was second. They [IRL officials] said to go to start/finish and when I got there, somebody said that I had won.

"It was a very important victory for our team, one that we can use to build our momentum for the season." And useful for this reason, too: Nobody will ever be able to get away with accusing Eddie Cheever of being a one-race wonder.

OFFICIAL BOX SCORE
PEP BOYS INDY RACING LEAGUE
Indy 200 at Walt Disney World Speedway
Sunday, January 24, 1999

FP	SP	Car	Driver	Car Name	C/E/T	Laps Comp.	Running/ Reason Out	IRL Pts.	Total IRL Pts.	IRL Standings	IRL Awards	Designated Awards	Total Awards
1	13	51	Eddie Cheever, Jr.	Rachel's Gourmet Potato Chips/ Children's Beverage Group/Dallara	D/A/G	200	Running	50	50	1	$91,900	$35,000	$126,900
2	4	4	Scott Goodyear	Pennzoil Panther G Force	G/A/G	200	Running	40	40	2	76,900	1,150	78,050
3	6	35	Jeff Ward	Thermo Tech/Ceasefire/ ISM Racing Goodyear Aurora	G/A/G	200	Running	35	35	4	65,500	5,050	70,550
4	1	8	Scott Sharp	Delphi Automotive Systems	D/A/G	200	Running	37	37	3	54,100	35,000	89,100
5	3	30	Raul Boesel	TransWorld Racing/ McCormackMotorsports	G/A/F	199	Running	31	31	5	49,900	10,000	59,900
6	10	28	Mark Dismore	MCI WorldCom	D/A/G	199	Running	28	28	6	44,800	100	44,900
7	17	18	Steve Knapp	Earls Performance Products	G/A/G	198	Running	26	26	7	43,700	100	43,800
8	20	9	Davey Hamilton	#9 Galles Racing/ G Force/Aurora/Goodyear	G/A/G	198	Running	24	24	8	42,700	100	42,800
9	14	11	Billy Boat	AJ Foyt Enterprises	D/A/G	198	Running	22	22	9	42,700	0	42,700
10	8	91	Buddy Lazier	Delta Faucet/Coors Light/Hemelgarn Racing	D/A/G	198	Running	20	20	10	41,700	600	42,300
11	19	10	John Paul Jr.	Jonathan Byrd's/VisionAire/Firestone	G/A/F	197	Running	19	19	11	40,600	0	40,600
12	9	20	Tyce Carlson	Blueprint-Immke Racing Grene Lefe Resort Firestone	D/A/F	197	Running	18	18	12	39,600	0	39,600
13	12	50	Roberto Guerrero	Cobb Racing/ G Force/Infiniti/Firestone	G/I/F	197	Running	17	17	13	38,600	5,000	43,600
14	24	33	Brian Tyler	Truscelli Team Racing	G/A/G	195	Running	16	16	14	15,500	0	15,500
15	21	81	Robby Unser	Team Pelfrey/Enginetics	D/A/F	195	Running	15	15	15	14,500	0	14,500
16	25	7	Stephan Gregoire	Mexmil/Tokheim	G/A/F	194	Running	14	14	16	13,500	0	13,500
17	11	12	Buzz Calkins	Bradley Foodmarts/Sav-O-Mat	G/A/F	194	Running	13	13	17	34,400	0	34,400
18	27	3	Andy Michner	Brant Racing R & S MKV	R/A/G	191	Running	12	12	18	12,400	0	12,400
19	18	42	John Hollansworth Jr.	Lycos/Pcsave.com/ Feed the Children/Dallara	D/A/F	179	Accident	11	11	19	33,400	0	33,400
20	26	44	Robbie Buhl	Sit Down Connection	D/I/F	175	Running	10	10	21	10,400	0	10,400
21	2	2	Greg Ray	Glidden Menard	D/A/F	163	Gearbox	11	11	19	32,400	0	32,400
22	5	14	Kenny Brack	AJ Foyt PowerTeam Racing	D/A/G	106	Accident	8	8	22	32,400	0	32,400
23	23	22	Gualter Salles	TECO Energy	D/A/F	91	Accident	7	7	23	10,400	0	10,400
24	16	19	Stan Wattles	Metro Racing Systems/NCLD	R/A/G	54	Running	6	6	24	32,400	0	32,400
25	28	66	Scott Harrington	Harrington Motorsports	D/I/F	49	Engine	5	5	25	10,400	0	10,400
26	22	98	Donnie Beechler	Cahill Racing/Firestone/ Oldsmobile Special	D/A/F	15	Suspension	4	4	26	10,400	0	10,400
27	7	99	Sam Schmidt	Sprint PCS	G/A/F	14	Accident	3	3	27	32,400	0	32,400
28	15	5	Jason Leffler	Treadway Racing	GAF	2	Accident	2	2	28	32,400	0	32,400

Time of Race: 1:41:14.800   Margin of Victory: 5.148 seconds   Fastest Lap: #8 Scott Sharp (Lap 195, 166.121)   Average Speed: 118.538
PPG Pole Winner: Scott Sharp   PPG Team Pole Award: Kelly Racing   Coors Light Pit Stop Contest: Raul Boesel (1:24.848)   MBNA America Lap Leader: Scott Sharp
MCI WorldCom Long Distance Award: Eddie Cheever   Delphi "Leader At Halfway" Award: Scott Sharp
Chassis Legend: D-Dallara; G-G Force; R-Riley&Scott   Engine Legend: A-Oldsmobile Aurora; I-Nissan Infiniti   Tire Legend: F-Firestone; G-Goodyear

Caution Flags:
3-9   #5 Leffler, Accident T1
15-21 #99 Schmidt, Accident T1
27-28 #98 Beechler, Spin T1
53-60 #66 Harrington, Tow In
       #14 Brack, #22 Salles, Acc.
108-119 T3
       #10 Paul, #91 Lazier, Spin
121-125 T1
       #42 Hollansworth, Accident
182-188 T2

Lap Leaders:
1-55	#8 Scott Sharp	Scott Sharp	3	103
56-57	#20 Tyce Carlson	Eddie Cheever Jr.	2	40
58-102	#8 Scott Sharp	Scott Goodyear	3	36
103-110	#4 Scott Goodyear	Raul Boesel	2	19
111-117	#30 Raul Boesel	Tyce Carlson	1	2
118-141	#4 Scott Goodyear			
142-173	#51 Eddie Cheever Jr.			
174-177	#4 Scott Goodyear			
178-180	#8 Scott Sharp			
181-192	#30 Raul Boesel			
193-200	#51 Eddie Cheever Jr.			

ALERO™

INTRIGUE®

BRAVADA®

AURORA

SILHOUETTE®

START
BELIEVING YOUR EYES

The new Oldsmobiles. Five vehicles designed with one philosophy in mind.
The perfect combination of sophisticated design and ultimate driver control.
The driving experience will open your eyes.

OLDSMOBILE®

START
SOMETHING™

Scott Goodyear Turns Up the Heat

Inset: Scott Goodyear led the final 51 laps, but had to survive a late-race restart to earn his first-ever IRL victory in the Pennzoil Panther G Force/Aurora

Goodyear and Panther Racing Score First IRL Win

by Tim Tuttle

Panther Racing, a high-profile team, was born in the fall of 1997. Veteran Indy car team manager John Barnes compiled an ownership group consisting of NFL quarterback Jim Harbaugh, television motorsports producer Terry Lingner, Indianapolis auto dealer Gary Pedigo, and himself, and convinced Pennzoil to paint its famous yellow on their cars. Panther's promise of committed and knowledgeable leadership and a substantial budget enticed Scott Goodyear, one of the Pep Boys Indy Racing League's most established drivers, to leave powerful Treadway Racing and join the new operation for the 1998 season.

Their initial campaign together wasn't a bust, but it didn't satisfy Panther's expectations, either. Goodyear was seventh in the 1998 championship, with quasi-highlights of second- and third-place finishes. Goodyear was to the point when he explained Panther's objectives prior to the 1999 season. He simply stated, "We're racing for only one reason—to win races."

There is a self-applied pressure in a win-or-nothing ambition, and Panther responded to it decisively with its first victory in the

Today was the day! Scott Goodyear (4) swept past Greg Ray (2) en route to his first-ever IRL win, a victory he savored after having posted four second-place finishes in his IRL career. Goodyear's patience paid off in the waning stages of the race. He avoided a wreck between race leaders Eddie Cheever and Buddy Lazier, swept into the lead position, and held it to the finish.

One of the day's hard chargers was Robbie Buhl, who improved from 17th to 3rd in the Dreyer & Reinbold Racing Dallara/Infiniti/Firestone. It was the second-best finish for an Infiniti engine in IRL competition.

MCI WorldCom 200 at Phoenix International Raceway. "We've now matured as a team and little things start to make the difference," said Goodyear, who led 134 of the 200 laps and won by 4.738 seconds over Pagan Racing's Jeff Ward on the 1-mile speedway. Robbie Buhl, using Nissan Infiniti power, finished third and gave the company its second podium finish in 4 years of IRL competition. Goodyear's victory was worth $139,600 (prize money) and a priceless contribution towards Panther's pursuit of the championship. It was a drama-filled, tumultuous day of competition, 14 of the 27 starters were running at the finish.

Panther fine-tuned its operation for 1999. It stayed with the G Force/Oldsmobile Aurora/Goodyear equipment combination. The hiring of Andy Brown as chief engineer was its only major change. The Goodyear/Brown relationship, vital to success, blossomed virtually overnight. "Andy and I had a rapport immediately," Goodyear said. "It was almost like we'd been together for years."

Goodyear knew he and Brown were on the same wavelength in the opener at Orlando, where they finished a frustrated second. "At Orlando, I was calling in and telling them what tire pressures and wing adjustments I wanted and he [Brown] called back and said that was exactly what he had ready for the car," Goodyear said. "He knew what I wanted."

The Orlando result served to increase Panther's motivation.

"After we were second, people kept coming up and saying, 'Good job, good job,' but we didn't feel that way," Goodyear explained. "There was not a person on our race team that went back to the race shop on Monday [following Orlando] and was happy, I can tell you that. We came here to win. Nothing else would have been enough to please us."

At the Phoenix International Raceway, Goodyear's balanced mixture of aggressive and conservative driving—making the right move at the right time—carried him to his first IRL triumph in 21 starts. The 39-year-old Canadian had started third and moved into the lead by passing Kelley Racing's Mark Dismore inside during Turn 1 of Lap 15. Goodyear held the front for 81 straight laps until pitting, along with the other leaders, under caution.

Eddie Cheever had masterfully sliced-and-diced through the traffic to advance from 18th on the grid to second. The Team Cheever crew slapped on four tires and replenished fuel on the Dallara-Aurora with an efficiency that elevated it past Goodyear. The lead, because they didn't pit, belonged to Billy Boat and TeamExtreme rookie John Hollansworth. When Boat ran out of laps and was forced to stop 29 laps later under green, Cheever swept past into the lead.

Kelley Racing's Mark Dismore started second in the MCI WorldCom 200 Dallara/Aurora/Goodyear and led for the first 14 laps. He battled handling problems, though, and finished one lap down in seventh place.

Buddy Lazier had overtaken Goodyear on Lap 108, and was menacing Cheever, never an easy driver to pass. Their swords were drawn, in full cut-and-thrust mode. Goodyear, in third, could see the battle raging and had no intention of getting too close to the action. It was a decision that likely saved him from a DNF. With 52 laps remaining, Lazier took his Dallara-Aurora to the outside of Cheever while exiting Turn 2. Lazier was less than a car length behind and to the right of Cheever as they went down the dogleg. Traffic and trouble awaited them entering Turn 3.

"There were cars filling every lane that was there," Goodyear said. "I'd never seen it like that [at Phoenix]. You had a guy [Cheever] up there who uses all the track and then some and a guy [Lazier] who uses half the track. I wanted to be far enough back there because I thought it might be like the Fourth of July."

There were, indeed, fireworks.

Cheever went inside in Turn 3. Two cars ahead, Scott Sharp's Dallara-Aurora ran out of fuel and slowed. It touched off an explosive chain reaction. Scott Harrington tapped Sharp, nudging him into Cheever, whose left front touched Harrington's right rear. That sent Cheever to the outside, and Lazier's nose hit Cheever's right rear, and both went hard into the outside wall.

"It was incredibly tight," Cheever said. "Buddy and I were going at it. It's just something that happens when you are competing that heavily. You have to take risks. This is flat-out racing and Buddy and I were going for broke. That's what it's all about." Lazier classified his abrupt exit as "a racing incident." "I was totally committed to the outside," he said. "Going down the back straight, Eddie went

A restart on Lap 196 gave Jeff Ward (21) in the Pagan Racing Dallara/Aurora/Goodyear one last shot at leader Scott Goodyear, but Goodyear got a good jump and left Ward as the runner-up.

high and low and then low. He and Harrington got together, Eddie popped out, and we got together."

Goodyear darted his way through the debris, took the lead, and went unchallenged to the checkered flag. Ward's second place in his debut with Pagan was positive proof that he and crew chief/engineer Mitch Davis are quick studies in chassis setup. Davis and Ward had been together since 1997, when Ward's third at the

A crew member adjusts the front wing on the Truscelli Team Racing G Force/Aurora/Goodyear of Roberto Moreno, who spun off the track on Lap 193, yet finished sixth just one lap down.

Indianapolis 500 earned him Rookie of the Year honors for the event. They moved to ISM Racing in 1998 and stayed there through the 1999 opener at Disney.

But, 10 days prior to the start of the Phoenix event, Davis and ISM parted company. He had been unhappy with ISM's lack of testing and other budgetary constraints. Ward had also expressed serious concerns about the team's financial condition and decided to follow Davis out the door a few days later.

Davis and Ward had competed exclusively with a G Force chassis and wanted to switch to Dallara. Pagan, idle since the 1998 Charlotte race, had a pair of them available, and they formed an alliance. The team supplied the Dallara-Aurora and Davis and Ward funded the running expense (typically about $70,000) for Phoenix. Davis put together the crew, mostly former ISMers.

"Things happened quickly and we decided we needed to be here," Ward said. "I had to get to Phoenix to get points. When you don't have points and you're not in the championship, it doesn't look good when you're trying to attract sponsorship."

Ward had never driven a Dallara prior to Friday's opening practice.

He qualified fifth and was running fourth prior to the Cheever/Lazier crash, which moved him up to second. Robbie Buhl passed Ward on a restart on Lap 168. "Hollansworth's transmission went out, and I almost hit him," Ward explained. "I had to go down to the pit lane exit to avoid him, and Buhl got by me."

Ward passed Buhl on Lap 179 by going inside in Turn 1 and completing the pass while exiting Turn 2. But second place (worth

$64,950, defraying much of the expenses) would have to do. "I didn't have anything for Goodyear," Ward said. Pagan's Aurora was built to a mid-1998 specification, and was an estimated 20-30 horsepower down compared to the updated powerplants. "Goodyear beat us only [because] he had the latest spec motor," Davis said. "Other than being down a little horsepower, the car was a rocketship. Jeff is awesome. He comes into traffic and never gives up. Nobody thought we could change teams a week ago and do this."

Buhl's third-place finish represented a breakthrough for Nissan's Infiniti, which was on the podium for only the second time. It was arguably, however, the Infiniti's most competitive IRL race. When Mike Groff finished second with Infiniti-power at Disney in 1997, he had the good fortune of catching a race-ending rainstorm at a very opportune time.

"We never had quite the race car we wanted, but we were patient and it paid off," Buhl said. Third was also the best IRL result for Sinden Racing Services, a lower budget team owned by Jeff Sinden and Joe Kennedy. "It feels good to race [competitively] again," Kennedy said. "The engine has the potential to win. We're chasing the setup. We're just learning to work with Robbie. We really didn't get to work with him [in the opener] at Disney because we had brake problems. Robbie is so awesome, so consistent and he keeps it out of trouble."

The close confines and high speeds of Phoenix contributed its typical carnage. In addition to Cheever and Lazier, Greg Ray,

Steve Knapp (35) and Kenny Brack (14) went out on Lap 47 with this collision in Turn 1. Buzz Calkins (12) and Tyce Carlson (20) avoided the mishap, which also involved Raul Boesel (not pictured).

Kenny Brack, Robby Unser, Steve Knapp, Roberto Guerrero, and John Paul Jr. also were eliminated in wall-banging incidents. None were injured.

Team Menard's Ray had taken his first IRL pole with a 177.139 mile-per-hour lap. No. 2 qualifier Mark Dismore passed Ray on the outside of Turn 1 at the start. Goodyear had passed them both, but Ray regained second place on Lap 16. Ray's Dallara-Aurora was still running second on Lap 94, and Cheever was bearing down. Entering Turn 1, with traffic again playing a critical role, Goodyear went low to lap Paul's G Force-Aurora.

Paul, two laps down, moved up the track to give Goodyear room and went into the slick, gray-surfaced outside. That forced Paul to slow in order to turn the car and avoid hitting the wall. Ray roared around the corner and they collided, putting them into the outside wall.

LOWE'S MOTOR SPEEDWAY VISIONAIRE 500
BY JONATHAN INGRAM

Following an accident in which three spectators were killed and eight injured, the third round of the Pep Boys Indy Racing League season at the Lowe's Motor Speedway was canceled after 79 laps had been run. No points and no prize money were awarded to participants, reducing the season's schedule to 10 events.

The mutual decision by track president H.A. "Humpy" Wheeler, IRL founder Tony George, and Executive Vice President Leo Mehl to end the race came within minutes after a red flag halted the race. It was an emotional Wheeler who announced to fans that the race would be canceled due to the fatalities and refunds would be issued for the tickets.

The decision to halt the race was met with approval from the competitors. "Our hearts and prayers go out to everyone affected by this terrible tragedy," said Greg Ray, who started on the pole and was the leader at the time the race ended. "I think Humpy Wheeler and [track chairman] Bruton Smith are gentlemen in every sense of the word," said Ray. "They have a great love of motorsports, but they have an even greater love of family. They did the right thing."

Rookie Scott Harrington endured contact with several cars and showed poise with his drive to a fifth-place finish in the Harrington Motorsports Dallara/Infiniti/Firestone.

If you build it, they will race it. Greg Ray (left) and Scott Sharp don't care if there's no purse or trophy at stake, they're hard-core racers and will compete on anything they can find.

"I was turning in as normal and he [Paul] was high," Ray said. "He was slow coming back out of the gray. I couldn't get to the brakes quick enough. I had nowhere to go. It's my nature to be aggressive, but I was taking it easy. We were faster than Scott Goodyear. I was in no big hurry to make a move."

Paul was trying to give the leaders room to pass. "Goodyear pushed me up into the marbles, and I had it under control," Paul said. "I was as far out of the way as you can get. Ray didn't check up and ran into the side of me. I did everything that I could do to stay out of the way."

Brack, the defending IRL champion, had started a disappointing 21st in AJ Foyt's Dallara-Aurora and was up to eighth for a Lap 47 restart. ISM's Knapp missed a shift and Brack, in avoidance, darted to the left. "While I was turning the car, I missed a shift and got hit," Brack said. Raul Boesel, charging on the inside, center-punched Brack's left-rear wheel with his G

Force's nose. Brack was twisted to the right and Knapp plowed into him.

Brack had also been eliminated in a crash sequence and didn't start the first race of the season at Walt Disney World. "This is two races in a row [where] freak things have happened and it's frustrating," said the Swede, who left Phoenix ranked 27th in the championship.

Boat, Brack's Foyt teammate, wasn't directly involved in the crash, but it affected his race. Boat had been 10th, directly behind Boesel, and was forced to lock up the brakes to avoid hitting Brack. "We barely missed Kenny's crash, but we flat-spotted the tires staying out of it and had to pit," Boat said. "That put us back in line." Having lost track position, Foyt decided to keep Boat out when most of the field pitted on Lap 96. Boat took the lead but was forced to pit under green on Lap 126. "We gambled on getting track position," Boat said, "and it backfired." Boat rallied to finish fourth. "We had a competitive race car, and things didn't fall our way. But, considering we started 23rd, I'm pretty happy."

Harrington, in the second race with his family-owned team, drove his Dallara-Infiniti to fifth. "This team didn't exist until January 1," Harrington said. "We probably have the lowest budget out there." Veteran Roberto Moreno enjoyed an impressive IRL debut. The Brazilian brought Truscelli Racing's G Force-Aurora home in sixth. Moreno qualified third and ran competitively throughout. He was on the lead lap until a spin, which didn't do any harm to the car, with several laps remaining put Moreno one lap down.

Kelley Racing's Dismore and Sharp were seventh and eighth, respectively. Dismore slipped slowly backwards after his strong start, and Sharp never had the speed to get to the front. "It was a frustrating day," Dismore said. "At first, it was real strong, but it started to go away and was very hard to control. First, it was

overster and then it was understeer. It was nothing I could really tell the team what to fix." Sharp had started fifth. "The car was really poor in traffic," Sharp said. "That was the biggest thing. It's really not acceptable."

The Desert Mile proved to be a formidable test for the teams and drivers. Only 14 cars made it to the finish, but the show was simply spectacular and uncharacteristic for the Phoenix track. Known as a one groove oval, cars went three wide in the corners dicing for position. Although every position is crucial, collecting early season points is vital in quest of the championship.

Defending IRL Champion Kenny Brack failed to finish the first two races, and reigning Indy 500 Champion and Disney winner Eddie Cheever didn't collect any points at Phoenix.

After two races Goodyear led the total points with a second place at Disney and a win in the Desert Mile. Jeff Ward was second in points with a third in the first round and second in this race. And the Kelley Racing Team remained close to the front: Driver Scott Sharp recorded a fourth at Disney and eighth at Phoenix and Mark Dismore grabbed sixth- and seventh-place finishes in the first two rounds.

OFFICIAL BOX SCORE
PEP BOYS INDY RACING LEAGUE
MCI WorldCom 200 at Phoenix International Raceway
Sunday, March 28, 1999

FP	SP	Car	Driver	Car Name	C/E/T	Laps Comp.	Running Reason Out	IRL Pts.	Total IRL Pts.	IRL Standings	IRL Awards	Designated Awards	Total Awards
1	3	4	Scott Goodyear	Pennzoil Panther G Force	G/A/G	200	Running	53	93	1	$97,600	$42,000	$139,600
2	5	21	Jeff Ward	Pagan Racing Dallara	D/A/G	200	Running	40	75	2	59,200	5,750	64,950
3	17	44	Robbie Buhl	Oldsmobile Dreyer & Reinbold	D/I/F	200	Running	35	45	7	46,900	7,850	54,750
4	23	11	Billy Boat	AJ Foyt Racing	D/A/G	200	Running	32	54	6	56,600	15,100	71,700
5	8	66 R	Scott Harrington	Harrington Motorsports	D/I/F	200	Running	30	35	9	30,100	100	30,200
6	4	33	Roberto Moreno	Truscelli Team Racing	G/A/G	199	Running	28	28	16	46,600	100	46,700
7	2	28	Mark Dismore	MCI WorldCom	D/A/G	199	Running	28	56	5	45,400	100	45,500
8	6	8	Scott Sharp	Delphi Automotive Systems	D/A/G	198	Running	24	61	4	44,300	44,300	44,300
9	20	99	Sam Schmidt	Sprint PCS	G/A/F	198	Running	22	25	20	22,300	22,300	22,300
10	19	7	Stephan Gregoire	Mexmil/Tokheim/Viking Air	G/A/F	198	Running	20	34	10	43,200	600	43,800
11	7	98	Donnie Beechler	Cahill Racing	D/A/F	197	Running	19	23	22	20,100	20,100	20,100
12	22	16	Marco Greco	Phoenix Racing	G/A/F	195	Running	18	18	25	19,000	19,000	19,000
13	26	3	Andy Michner	Brant Racing R&S MKV	R/A/G	187	Running	17	29	14	39,900	39,900	39,000
14	12	12	Buzz Calkins	Bradley Food Marts/Sav-O-Mat	D/A/F	187	Running	16	29	14	38,700	38,700	38,700
15	16	42 R	John Hollansworth Jr.	Pcsave.com/Lycos/ Feed the Children/Dallara	D/A/F	166	Gearbox	15	26	19	37,600	10,000	47,600
16	11	50	Roberto Guerrero	#50 Cobb Racing Infiniti	G/I/F	160	Accident	14	31	12	36,600	0	36,600
17	18	51	Eddie Cheever Jr.	Team Cheever/Children's Beverage Group	D/A/G	148	Accident	13	63	3	35,400	0	35,400
18	15	91	Buddy Lazier	Delta Faucet/Coors Light/ Hemelgarn Racing	D/A/G	148	Accident	12	32	11	35,400	0	35,400
19	10	30	Raul Boesel	TransWorld Racing/ McCormack Motorsports	G/A/F	147	Oil pressure	11	42	8	34,300	0	34,300
20	14	6	Eliseo Salazar	Nienhouse Motorsports Racing Special	G/A/F	107	Electrical	10	10	28	11,200	0	11,200
21	1	2	Greg Ray	Glidden/Menards	D/A/F	93	Accident	12	23	22	33,200	12,500	45,700
22	25	10	John Paul Jr.	Jonathan Byrds/VisionAire/Firestone	G/A/F	91	Accident	8	27	17	33,200	0	33,200
23	9	20	Tyce Carlson	Blueprint-Immke Racing	D/A/F	65	Accident	7	25	20	33,200	0	33,200
24	21	14	Kenny Brack	AJ Foyt PowerTeam Racing	D/A/G	46	Accident	6	14	27	11,200	0	11,200
25	24	35	Steve Knapp	Thermo Tech ISM Racing	G/A/G	45	Accident	5	31	12	33,200	0	33,200
26	13	81	Robby Unser	Team Pelfrey/Enginetics	D/A/F	35	Accident	4	19	24	33,200	0	33,200
27	27	25	Davey Hamilton	Barnhart Motorsports/Spinal Victory	D/A/G	31	Handling	3	27	17	11,200	0	11,200
28	28	15 R	Jaques Lazier	Tivoli Lodge G Force	G/I/G	0	Did not start	2	2	31	11,200	0	11,200

Time of Race: 1:56:40.052 Avg Speed: 102.856 mph Margin of Victory: 4.738 seconds Fastest Lap: #4 Goodyear (Lap 175, 167.528 mph)
PPG Pole Winner: Greg Ray (177.139 mph) PPG Team Pole Award: Glidden/Menards
MBNA America Lap Leader: Scott Goodyear MCI WorldCom Long Distance Award: Billy Boat
Firestone First At 99 Award: John Hollansworth Jr. Delphi ""Leader At Halfway" Award: Billy Boat Coors Light Pit Stop Contest: Scott Goodyear"
Chassis Legend: D-Dallara; G- G Force; R-Riley&Scott Engine Legend: A-Oldsmobile Aurora; I-Nissan Infiniti Tire Legend: F-Firestone; G-Goodyear

LAP LEADERS
1-14 28 Mark Dismore
15-96 4 Scott Goodyear
97-97 98 Donnie Beechler
98-126 11 Billy Boat
127-148 51 Eddie Cheever, Jr.
149-200 4 Scott Goodyear
LEADER SUMMARY
134 4 Scott Goodyear
29 11 Billy Boat
22 51 Eddie Cheever, Jr.
14 28 Mark Dismore
1 98 Donnie Beechler

CAUTION FLAGS
1:21-23 3 0:02:41
2:37-45 9 0:09:10
3:47-58 12 0:13:12
4:67-75 9 0:09:43
5:94-101 8 0:08:45
6:149-160 12 0:12:55
7:163-167 5 0:06:06
8:193-195 3 0:02:56
TOTAL LAPS:61 1:05:28

Racing teams arriving at IMS were met with new track facilities rising out of the on-going construction in preparation for the United States Grand Prix at the Indianapolis Motor Speedway. A new Pagoda-style control tower had started taking shape, its elevator shafts visible and in place. In addition, Tokheim and the Indianapolis Motor Speedway unveiled a new fueling station for the teams in Gasoline Alley. Construction of a road course for the new 2000 Formula One race was also underway. Seven huge video screens had been placed around the track to allow fans to see all the action on Race Day.

The eyes of Eddie Cheever Jr. reflect the gravity of his situation. Serving as both car owner and driver, he shoulders double the pressure of a typical racer preparing to qualify.

Eddie Cheever Jr., came out of the gate fast in the No. 51 Team Cheever/The Children's Beverage Group entry, posting a lap at 221.888 miles per hour using Infiniti Indy V-8 power for the first time just 1 hour and 3 minutes into practice. Before the day ended, though, Cheever was eighth fastest, and Greg Ray gained the top spot at 225.887 miles per hour in the No. 2T Glidden/Menards machine (the 21st time a Team Menard car had turned the fastest practice speed of a day since 1994). He was followed by two-time Indy 500 winner Arie Luyendyk at 225.163 mph in the No. 5 Sprint PCS/Meijer car and Scott Goodyear at 224.405 mph in the No. 4T Pennzoil Panther G Force entry.

Ray stopped early in his primary car because of an engine malfunction. "We had a very high-mileage engine but it wasn't a catastrophic failure," he said. "But we don't know for sure. The track conditions were real greasy so we were just mating our setup to the conditions." Later, he took out his backup and less than two hours later, turned the day's fastest lap. He was asked if he got a "tow." "No, that was a clean lap," Ray said. "The 227 [at the April open test] was also a clean lap. In fact, we were looking for dance partners today."

Luyendyk, who announced his retirement from open-wheel racing before the event, felt comfortable during his last appearance at Indy. "In the cockpit, it's all the same," Luyendyk said. "The adrenaline is the same. The aggression is there. In fact, I was probably too aggressive for the first day. I was second quickest the first day last year and we almost didn't qualify. Because of the open test and tire testing, it didn't surprise me that people got up to speed quickly." While Luyendyk signed autographs for fans before practice, 1998 Bank One Rookie of the Year Steve Knapp walked up and asked Arie to autograph the front of his driver's suit. "At first I thought he was kidding, but he was serious," Arie said. "That is a first for me."

Off the track, a pair of drivers got last-minute rides. Jimmy Kite was named to the seat of the No. 30 Trans World Racing/McCormack Motorsports entry and Hideshi Matsuda got the nod in the No. 54 BMB Mini Juke/Beck Motorsports car.

The month of May was officially launched.

A compressed schedule had the teams concentrating on speed and most were ready. A total of 45 cars went through the technical inspection line and 37 ran on the track (the second-highest number in history for Opening Day since 1994 when 39 cars took to the track) during the first day of practice. The 1,553 laps turned were also the second-highest number of laps turned during an Opening Day (1,733 laps were completed on Opening Day in 1994).

One Indy tradition continued: throughout his career as a driver and owner, Dick Simon strived to be first on the track for the month of May. Now, back as a car owner with Stephan Gregoire in the cockpit, Simon's No. 7T Mexmil/Tokheim machine was the first to leave Gasoline Alley for pit road at 10:19 A.M. and first on the track when it opened at 11:02 A.M. "It starts out the month perfect," Simon said.

DAY-AT-A-GLANCE

Date: Saturday, May 15
Drivers on Track: 33
Cars on Track: 37

TOP FIVE DRIVERS OF THE DAY

Car	Driver	Speed (mph)
2T	Greg Ray	225.887
5	Arie Luyendyk	225.163
4T	Scott Goodyear	224.405
99	Sam Schmidt	224.394
14T	Kenny Brack	222.910

As practice intensified, Greg Ray set a blazing fast time for the second day in a row, but 1998 pole winner Billy Boat had a major setback.

Ray turned a lap at 225.124 miles per hour in his primary No. 2 Glidden/Menards entry, and produced a speed of 224.411 miles per hour in his backup for the first and third spots on the daily speed chart. Arie Luyendyk split Ray's speeds with a lap at 224.674 in the No. 5 Sprint PCS/Meijer machine. "Today, it was just windier," Ray said. "The air was thicker, more humid. We had to keep changing the setup to go quick."

For Boat, it was a quick trip to the Clarian Emergency Medical Center after he hit the Turn 1 wall in the No. 11 AJ Foyt Racing entry. The car sustained heavy left-side and left-rear damage. "We were trying a few things on the setup," Boat said. "I hadn't run this setup before and it just jumped out on me and got away. I think we were on a good combination. I'm just a little sore. It was an absolute-brand-new race car and that's what makes it difficult."

Meanwhile, after posting the seventh-fastest speed of the day (222.091 miles per hour), Tony Stewart talked about his plans for a double-duty adventure: running the Indianapolis 500 and a 600-mile stock car race at Lowe's Motor Speedway in Charlotte on the same day. Only John Andretti had done it previously. Stewart had his own team at Indy and was driving for Joe Gibbs at the Charlotte NASCAR race.

"[Joe] calls me every day and asks me how I did," Stewart said. "He knows how much of a dream Indy is for me and encourages me along the way. Larry [Curry] and I were trying to find a sponsor [for Indy]. We didn't want to just come here with nothing. Home Depot [his stock-car sponsor] stepped up at the last minute and helped us out.

"I felt like I was driving a slot car out there today. I pointed the car and it went where I wanted it. It's like this: If you take a tennis ball and a bowling ball together and someone asks you to change direction of one of them, you'll choose the tennis ball because it's lighter and easier to guide. That's what it's like to drive the Indy car compared to the stock car."

By the time the track closed on Day 2, a whopping 77 cars had seen the track during the two days of practice—the third-highest total since 1976. (There had been 90 cars on the track in 1994 and 78 in 1998.)

Rodger Ward, Indy 500 winner in 1959 and 1962, took a ceremonial lap around the track in the Leader Card Watson Roadster that he drove to victory in 1962. "You just can't explain what a wonderful feeling it was to get out there," Ward said. "It's was hard not to want to stand on it a little bit."

Off the track, the 19th Annual Save Arnold Barbecue was held to benefit the Special Olympics of Indiana, and nine drivers— Arie Luyendyk, Dr. Jack Miller, Stan Wattles, Scott Sharp, Donnie Beechler, Sam Schmidt, Mike Borkowski, Billy Roe, and Wim Eyckmans—took time out to participate in friendly competition with the Olympians. A $5,000 donation from General Motors pushed the 19-year contribution total to $1,000,456 for the Special Olympics program.

"We're thrilled to announce that $55,000 has been raised for Special Olympics of Indiana," said Speedway chairman Mari Hulman George. "I would personally like to thank GM and Jug's Catering. Jug has been a supporter for the last 20 years. He's the backbone of our program."

A trio of hot shoes share their thoughts on pit row: Two-time Indy 500 winner and 1999 polesitter Arie Luyendyk (right) confers with Team Foyt racers Billy Boat (left) and Kenny Brack (center).

DAY-AT-A-GLANCE

Date:	Sunday, May 16
Drivers on Track:	33
Cars on Track:	40

TOP FIVE DRIVERS OF THE DAY

Car	Driver	Speed (mph)
2	Greg Ray	225.124
5	Arie Luyendyk	224.674
2T	Greg Ray	224.411
4T	Scott Goodyear	222.750
8T	Scott Sharp	222.288

The crew of 1996 Indy 500 winner Buddy Lazier works on bended knee on pit row in search of the proper setup. With minimal track time between qualifying and the race, getting the most out of the car during each session is essential.

Greg Ray set the pace for the third consecutive day of practice, and some new names popped up near the top of the speed chart, raising some eyebrows. Ray circulated the 2.5-mile oval in the No. 2T Glidden/Menards entry at 224.843 miles per hour, more than 3 miles per hour faster than his nearest challenger.

"The setup was good but the track conditions were tricky," Ray said. "It was humid and the track temperature was about 103 degrees. The 40-mile-an-hour gusts were felt in Turn 4. Today's conditions were far from perfect, but I really thought we could do a 225 and I was really trying."

Ray's nearest challenger was rookie John Hollansworth Jr., who came from nowhere to grab the second spot on the speed chart with a lap at 221.669 in the No. 42 pcsave.com/Lycos Dallara. Reigning Pep Boys Indy Racing League champion Kenny Brack was next at 221.282 in the No. 14 AJ Foyt/Power Team Racing machine.

Meanwhile, Hollansworth sought counsel from 21-time Indy 500 starter Gary Bettenhausen to learn the wiles of the Speedway. "Gary has been a great help," Hollansworth said. "Really, I thought a lot of his help would be done as far as the driver instruction side of things, but he's jumped in and helped us with Mark Weida, our engineer. They've been working on car setup issues as well, so he's been a great addition to our team.

"For a rookie, it's a two-part sequence, or at least it is for me," he added. "You work a good part of your racing life, or all your racing life, to get here, but getting here doesn't mean you're here. You're here if you're here this time next week."

For Brack, the day was pleasant. "We're starting to pick up speed and there's more speed to find," he said. "We're confident we can dabble with the aero package. We've closed the gap. We're not there yet but we'll continue to keep working."

Billy Boat, Brack's teammate, had another rough day. After crashing on Day 2, he hit the outside wall in Turn 3, heavily damaging the right side of the No. 11 AJ Foyt Racing entry. "You can get behind here real fast," Boat said, "and now we have two bent race cars. I don't really know right now what happened. I knew early that I was in trouble. The car never attempted to turn."

Rookie Mike Borkowski brought out the caution for contact for the first time in the day when he hit the outside wall in Turn 2 in the No. 18 PDM Racing machine, heavily damaging the left side and rear of the car. Just before Boat's accident, veteran Scott Harrington

hit the walls in Turns 3 and 4 in the No. 66T Harrington Motorsports entry. Both were examined, released, and cleared to drive.

A.J. Watson, the legendary chief mechanic, was the honoree as part of the Speedway's Indy Racing Legends Week.

In all, 37 drivers took the track in 39 cars as practice continued at a feverish pace.

DAY-AT-A-GLANCE

Date: Monday, May 17
Drivers on Track: 37
Cars on Track: 39

TOP FIVE DRIVERS OF THE DAY

Car	Driver	Speed (mph)
2T	Greg Ray	224.843
42	John Hollansworth Jr.	221.669
14	Kenny Brack	221.282
5	Arie Luyendyk	221.119
4T	Scott Goodyear	220.848

As practice continued, some teams found speed, others lost speed, and some worked on Race Day setups, confident that the qualifying setup was solid on a rain-shortened day.

For the first time of the month, Greg Ray was bumped off the top rung of the speed ladder, dropping to fourth. Scott Goodyear was the fastest driver of the day with a lap at 223.842 miles per hour in the No. 4T Pennzoil Panther G Force, followed, surprising, by Stephan Gregoire at 223.647 in the No. 7 Mexmil/Tokheim G Force, and Kenny Brack at 223.447 in the AJ Foyt Power Team Racing entry. Ray was next with laps at 223.214 in his primary No. 2 Glidden/Menards entry and 223.209 in a No. 32 backup car. Teammates Dr. Jack Miller, in seventh with 222.519 in the No. 17 Dean's Milk Chug machine, and Tony Stewart, in ninth with 222.480 miles per hour in the No. 22 Home Depot entry, were also in the top 10.

"Everything went well," Goodyear said. "We're still trying to figure out the superspeedway configuration. We quit early to change an engine because it had about 600 miles on it. We're not focusing on the pole. We're just working on setting up the car with different conditions."

Gregoire's performance raised eyebrows of Speedway railbirds. "It was a great day because we went fast and because it's good for our guys," he said. "They've been working hard changing parts every day. We have a brand-new suspension configuration from G Force that nobody else wanted to try. The first time we tried it; it didn't work, I was not very optimistic. I'm glad [owner] Dick Simon wanted to stick with it because we made it work."

Meanwhile, Ray was running a Race Day setup. "We ran on full tanks and had exactly the same time in both cars," he said. "The rain slowed us up a bit and we had to start late today, but we're not really behind."

Miller got some help from Stewart and team manager Larry Curry before turning his fast lap. "The biggest thing here is having a good car, but it also takes confidence," Miller said. "Having Larry and Tony Stewart talking to me has really boosted my confidence. They took the time off the dash and said, 'Don't worry about it.' I didn't even know that I'd gone 222 and I still have training wheels on the car."

"With the short amount of time we had, it was very productive," said Stewart. "Tomorrow, if the weather is sensible, I think I can go out and get some work done and will be real fast. I wanted to spend some time getting [Miller] up to speed."

Three-time winner Johnny Rutherford was honored as part of the Speedway's Indy Racing Legends Week and drove ceremonial

laps in the 1952 Cummins Diesel put on the pole that year by the late Freddie Agabashian. "It felt great," Rutherford said. "That one was for Freddie. It's a great race car, and I now know how Freddie could have set a record in it."

Off the track, Donnie Beechler celebrated his 38th birthday. A present? "222 would be a nice birthday gift," Beechler said.

Three-time Indy 500 winner Johnny Rutherford sports a vintage helmet for a spin around the track in a Cummins-Kurtis roadster. The racing legend pilots the IRL pace car and serves as an adviser to up-and-coming drivers.

DAY-AT-A-GLANCE

Date: Tuesday, May 18
Drivers on Track: 37
Cars on Track: 39

TOP FIVE DRIVERS OF THE DAY

Car	Driver	Speed (mph)
4T	Scott Goodyear	223.842
7	Stephan Gregoire	223.647
14	Kenny Brack	223.447
2	Greg Ray	223.214
51T	Eddie Cheever Jr.	222.999

Never without an opinion or at a loss for words, three-time Indy 500 winner Bobby Unser checks the speed charts of son Robby Unser's car before making some suggestions.

As teams started gearing up for qualifying weekend, another new leader rose to the top of the speed chart, while others found the wall instead of speed. Tony Stewart climbed to the top of the list at 226.683 miles per hour in the No. 22 Home Depot entry, knocking Greg Ray off the perch. Ray was second at 226.085 miles per hour in the No. 32 Glidden/Menards machine but blew an engine during the sessions.

The midweek practice days usually present some surprises, and this day was no different. Arie Luyendyk was third on the speed chart at 225.096 in the No. 5 Sprint PCS/Meijer entry. The top 10 also included Kenny Brack in two different cars, Stephan Gregoire for a second straight day, and Robby Unser, as well as rookie Robby McGehee, Eliseo Salazar, and Roberto Guerrero, who all found new speed.

"Today was pretty good because I made $10 from Eddie Cheever for finishing ahead of him," Salazar joked.

"Indy is a great place to find out who you are," Unser said. "You have to find out what the track and the Speedway will give you each day and not ask for more."

"We haven't been running 'Happy Hour'," said McGehee. "We've wanted to do our work in the heat of the day. But we decided to [run Happy Hour] today to see where we stacked up." The so-called "Happy Hour" takes place from 5-6 P.M. when the front straight is shaded by the grandstand, resulting in more speed.

Unfortunately, Dave Steele, Tyce Carlson, and Mark Dismore all found the concrete barrier. Steele was the first at 11:33 A.M. in Turn 1, sending him to Methodist Hospital for examination and inflicting heavy left-side and rear damage to the No. 43 Pennzoil Panther G Force. The second occurrence took place at 12:23 P.M. when Ray's engine let go and Carlson spun in his oil, lightly tapping the wall between Turns 1 and 2 with the rear wing of the No. 20 Pennzoil/Damon's/Bluegreen entry. "Greg blew in front of us," said Carlson. "[Steve] Knapp and I got on the binders, but I hit Greg's oil."

Dismore's incident occurred at 4:25 P.M. when he hit the outside wall with the right side of his car in Turns 1 and 2, heavily damaging the No. 28 MCI Worldcom machine. "I don't know what happened," said Dismore. "I went into Turn 1 like I have 200 times this month. The car went right up into the gray and I just felt like a passenger."

An hour later—just 30 minutes before track closing—Stewart posted the fastest official practice lap of the month. "We stuck to our guns with our race setup," Stewart said. "We didn't anticipate that our race setup would run this fast." Ray went out after Stewart but couldn't match his lap. "I'd be lying to you if I said I didn't want to [beat his speed]," Ray said, "but it's hard to do with 35 gallons in the car and a heavy spec race engine and six gears in the car."

The gamesmanship had started, too.

DAY-AT-A-GLANCE

Date: Wednesday, May 19
Drivers on Track: 41
Cars on Track: 46

TOP FIVE DRIVERS OF THE DAY

Car	Driver	Speed (mph)
22	Tony Stewart	226.683
32	Greg Ray	226.085
5	Arie Luyendyk	225.096
14T	Kenny Brack	224.411
7	Stephan Gregoire	224.193

Greg Ray was back on top of the speed charts, Billy Boat was back in the top 10, Johnny Unser hit the wall, and Tony Stewart set his hopes back a notch as Pole Day drew nearer.

Ray cranked up the day's—and month's—fastest lap at 227.192 miles per hour in the No. 2T Glidden/Menards entry, topping Robby Unser's best of 225.079 in the No. 81 Petro Moly/Team Pelfrey machine. It was Ray's fourth trip to the top of the chart in six days. "It feels nice to be this consistently quick with this group," he said. "We regard our competitors very highly. We're not taking anything for granted by any means. Tomorrow, we'll try to go even faster because we'll need every bit of speed we can get. But more importantly, we'll need to keep it off the walls."

For Boat, ranking 10th fastest at 223.564 in the No. 11T AJ Foyt Racing entry was a welcome return after earlier accidents. "After you've had the kind of week we've had, you have to take small steps to get there," Boat said. "First, we had to get me comfortable. Now we have to get the car right. People just don't understand what it's like to drive into a corner at 235 [miles per hour] and hope it sticks. We're fine. Our only concern is what kind of weather gets thrown at us."

At 11:57 A.M., Johnny Unser brushed the wall in Turn 3, drifted down the track, then went up to hit the outside wall in Turn 4, causing heavy right-side damage to the No. 92 Tae-Bo/Hemelgarn Racing/Homier Tool/Delta Faucet car. "We don't really know what happened," Unser said. "The car was feeling good. I don't know if it was air. I was following another car by about 100 yards and it just pushed up into the wall. I don't think the wind was a factor."

Stewart's accident came at 5:10 P.M., when he hit the wall in Turns 3 and 4, lightly damaging the right side of the No. 22 Home Depot entry. "I'm just disgusted with myself for making a stupid mistake as a driver and creating a lot of extra work for my team that didn't deserve to have to work this hard," Stewart said. "They've done everything perfect up to this point."

As part of Indy Racing Legends Week at the Speedway, 1960 winner Jim Rathmann was honored. He was asked about the differences between racing today and racing in the 1950s and 1960s, and also what drivers impressed him today. "The difference between then and now was the cars were all even and there was really no money involved," Rathmann said. "Drivers like Tony Stewart and Jeff Gordon are guys who stand out today. Both of those guys are naturals."

Additionally, ABC Sports and the Speedway announced a five-year deal for ABC to continue televising the Indianapolis 500 and other Pep Boys Indy Racing League events. The announcement was made by Speedway President Tony George and ABC Sports President Howard Katz. "Our partnership with ABC Sports over the last 34 years is one of the great traditions of the Indianapolis 500," George said. "Special credit needs to be given to Howard Katz, who made

this agreement his personal priority. Without Howard's enthusiasm and commitment, we would not be here today making this announcement."

"Continuing the long relationship between the Indianapolis 500 and ABC Sports was one of my highest priorities when I took this job," Katz said, "and I'm proud to say we've accomplished that goal. Our relationship with the Speedway is one of the longest in sports television and we look forward to building upon this tradition into the new millennium."

One day remained to get up to speed for qualifying.

"On the hook" is not the way a racer wants to travel down pit row. Tony Stewart's car is carried back to the garage after a brush with the wall ended his run.

DAY-AT-A-GLANCE

Date:	Thursday, May 20
Drivers on Track:	40
Cars on Track:	50

TOP FIVE DRIVERS OF THE DAY

Car	Driver	Speed (mph)
2T	Greg Ray	227.192
81	Robby Unser	225.079
5	Arie Luyendyk	225.073
7	Stephan Gregoire	224.792
91	Buddy Lazier	224.361

It was the day before Pole Day, a day when everyone either shows what they have to offer, or hides it. On Friday, May 21, 1999, those who could, showed it.

Greg Ray was again fastest of the day, with a lap of 227.175 miles per hour in the No. 2 Glidden/Menards car, giving him bragging rights for five of the seven practice days, but narrowly missing his fastest speed of the month set a day earlier. Arie Luyendyk, the two-time winner winding down his Indy 500 career, was next at 226.131 in the No. 5 Sprint PCS/Meijer machine. His teammate Sam Schmidt was third in the No. 99 Unistar Auto Insurance entry at 225.468. Scott Sharp had the fourth and fifth spots in the No. 8T and No. 8 Delphi Automotive Systems cars, at 224.792 and 224.159 miles per hour, respectively.

Technology only goes so far, then it's time for some old-fashioned elbow grease. Serious wrenching in the garage helped Raul Boesel squeak into the field as the 33rd, and final, starter in the field.

While Sharp had two cars ready to go for Pole Day, Ray had three that he had used during the seven days of practice. "We made the change to the No. 2 primary car," Ray said. "All the cars are like people, different personalities, different compromises. This is the car I felt most comfortable with. Unless we change our minds tomorrow morning, it will be the No. 2 primary car. There is one car just a little quicker, but it's the No. 2 primary car we'll go with. We ran the cars before in windy, cloudy, and cool conditions. Today was sunny and windy. This is who we're going to dance with.

"The biggest factor tomorrow is the weather. You have to go four laps. You get one quick one, then the next ones begin to fade. I don't have a crystal ball. If I did, we'd get the pole and get out of here. This team is prepared. I don't get the jitters. We're prepared. I just go."

There was sadness and prayers off the track because Herb Porter, the legendary engine builder, had been critically injured in an auto accident the previous night. On the evening of Day 7, he was to be inducted, along with the late Eddie Sachs, into the Speedway Hall of Fame at the annual Hall of Fame/Old Timers gathering at the Adam's Mark Hotel.

On a brighter note, the Pep Boys Indy Racing League announced that year-end bonuses totaling $40,000 would be paid to the top finishers in the United States Auto Club's four national racing series. And Bank One, Indiana, announced that its annual Indy 500 Rookie of the Year award had increased from $10,000 to $25,000.

Two drivers suffered setbacks in their quest to make the 33-car starting field. Rookie Mike Borkowski spun and hit the outside wall in Turn 2 at 11:16 A.M. in the No. 18 PDM Racing machine, moderately damaging the left side of the car. "It's an unfortunate situation," Borkowski said. "I spun and hit the wall. Not much to say, really." And John Paul Jr., hit the outside wall in Turn 3 in the No. 10T Jonathan Byrd's Cafeteria/VisionAire machine, sending him to Methodist Hospital with a bruised back.

Lloyd Ruby was the driver honored during Indy Racing Legends Week. It was special for him. "It's like a homecoming to come back here," he said. "[In my day] everyone was running together. It was more of a family." He was asked his favorite driver of today. "Billy Boat," Ruby said. "He came up the hard way, through midgets, and I'm friends with his dad. I'd like to see him do good because he's driving for a mean, old man."

Arie Luyendyk, reflecting on his final Pole Day at Indy, talked about his challenge and its meaning. "The magic mark for the pole is in the 226 range," he said. "Tomorrow we have 80 cars entered. Indy is not just another race. Everything around Indy, the city, the history, it's just a special event. I think I can enjoy it just as much as a spectator as I will as a driver. I'm going to keep enjoying Indy, just in a different way."

Others prepared for their shot at the top qualifying spot. "The pole speed will be whatever Ray sets it at, probably 227," said rookie Robby McGehee. "Having picked the first draw to qualify, we can safely say we'll be on the pole for at least a time," said defending winner Eddie Cheever Jr. "Fifteen is a lucky number for me," said Billy Boat after drawing that number in the qualifying line. "I won a lot of races with that number." Because of his double-duty schedule with the Winston Cup race at Charlotte, Tony Stewart needed an early draw to qualify before heading to the airport. He drew second.

"We got the draw," said Stewart's team manager, Larry Curry. "Now it's up to Mother Nature."

DAY-AT-A-GLANCE

Date: Friday, May 21
Drivers on Track: 37
Cars on Track: 43

TOP FIVE DRIVERS OF THE DAY

Car	Driver	Speed (mph)
2	Greg Ray	227.175
5	Arie Luyendyk	226.131
99	Sam Schmidt	225.468
8T	Scott Sharp	224.792
14	Kenny Brack	224.087

The moment of truth had arrived. The teams would have to find out if the qualifying setups they developed in practice would work on Pole Day. Drama, excitement, and mystery are standard fare during Pole Day. In many years, fast practice speeds don't correlate into fast qualifying speeds. Conditions play a large part. If a team is prepared for warm, sunny weather and qualifies on a cool, cloudy day, the car requires a completely different setup. If the team hasn't run in similar track conditions, finding the right setup can be a guessing game.

On Pole Day 1999, the temperature at noon was 66 degrees with humidity at 84 percent and northwest winds at 15 miles per hour, which is a little windy, but not unusual. The weather would baffle some and benefit others as the qualifying line wound down.

Eddie Cheever Jr., the defending champion, was first to take to the track and the first defending winner since Emerson Fittipaldi in 1990 to be first in line the year after a victory. But he waved off after three laps in the 221 mile-per-hour range.

Next came Tony Stewart, who had drawn the second spot and just barely had time to qualify before he was whisked away to Charlotte for his "double duty" effort there in a Winston Cup car. He was forced by his schedule to accept a 220.653 four-lap average in the No. 22 Home Depot entry to become the month's first qualifier and immediately headed for the airport. Stewart was also the first to talk about the weather. "That's all the car had today," Stewart said. "The air is much thicker today. We had such a nice week, as far as temperature and humidity were concerned. We didn't get a chance to run in any conditions like today. With our setup on the car, it was good in the heat. I'm a little on the conservative side, but it was way too conservative for today."

Scott Sharp was next and drove the No. 8 Delphi Automotive Systems entry to a four-lap average of 222.771. "The air is more dense," Sharp said, echoing Stewart. "The wind is [blowing] a different way [than Friday] and you don't have much track time today. We didn't have the right gear. We took some wing out this morning. We didn't have the right rpm. Being Number 3 [in line], we just had to go."

Then came rookie Jaques Lazier, who fashioned a run of 219.165 in the No. 15 Tivoli Hotel G Force to qualify for his first 500. "It's something, really," the brother of the 1996 Indy winner said. "I can't even put into words how I feel right now. I'm still in awe. Looking back, it was kind of scary. While I was on my run, I just kept thinking I have to take it as smooth as I can. We had a meeting to talk about what we would stay with and decided on 219. We're real happy with the [speed] and feel it will stand."

It would be a long wait to see what the bump speed would be, but two veterans and a rookie were the next to make runs and raised the field to five. Lyn St. James averaged 218.970 in the No. 90 Garden Fresh Potatoes/Kroger machine, Hideshi Matsuda took the No. 54 BMB Mini Juke/Beck Motorsports Dallara to a 222.065 verdict, and rookie John Hollansworth Jr., put in four laps in the No. 42 pcsave.com/Lycos/Dallara at 221.698.

"I was flat out," said St. James. "It was the best four laps I put together. I hope it holds. It's all that's there. We got everything there was.

The track changed. I was fighting to get the balance I wanted."

"Now I can call my wife in Japan," said Matsuda, who has made a career out of joining a team at the last minute and putting a car in the show at Indy. "I want to share my feelings with everybody."

"It was a great feeling on the back straight and a great feeling to come out of Turn 4 and just have to keep it straight," said Hollansworth. "We're just happy to get four laps in. You just have to take what the day gives you."

After a waveoff by Dr. Jack Miller, Buddy Lazier took the No. 91 Delta Faucet/Coors Light/Tae-Bo/Hemelgarn Racing entry out and put it in the field at a four-lap average of 220.721. He, too, talked about the weather. "I ran it as hard as it would go," he said. "This is a strange day. You'd think it would be cool and fast but it wasn't. I'm baffled. [The weather] is changing by the minute. Usually, thick air is good for the engine."

Two of the next three drivers were victims. Billy Boat was the first on a warmup lap, hitting the Turn 2 wall. After Mike Groff waved off after two laps in the 218 bracket, Robbie Buhl also hit the wall on his warmup lap. "Just cold tires," Boat said. "It didn't hurt the car much. We're just going to fix it and try to come back." Buhl said, "You're trying to hustle the car in there and prepare for the next lap. Maybe the tires weren't completely warm and it just went around on me."

Next up was defending Pep Boys Indy Racing League champion Kenny Brack, who put together a steady run of 222.659 in the No. 14 AJ Foyt Power Team Racing entry. "They were kind-of different conditions," Brack said. "Two guys crashed in front of me and you kind-of wonder what's going on. We were talking about that. Be careful on the first lap with a new set of tires. [Foyt] was pretty cool about everything."

Rookie Wim Eyckmans became the day's ninth qualifier, getting 220.092 out of the No. 52 EGP/Beaulieu of America/Dallara/Oldsmobile/Goodyear car, a team entry to Cheever. "It's tough to get in four good laps," said Eyckmans. "Mentally, it's really hard."

During his last Indy 500, Arie Luyendyk, the two-time Indy 500 winner, put in a stellar qualifying effort. He roared through a four-lap qualifying run of 225.179 miles per hour, set a new lap record for a normally-aspirated car at 225.643 miles per hour, and won the pole position.

After Roberto Moreno waved off after a lap at 211-plus, Arie Luyendyk roared onto the oval for what was announced as his final qualifying run at Indy. The two-time Indy pole winner didn't disappoint, putting together a four-lap effort of 225.179, a record for a normally aspirated car at the Speedway, breaking Boat's mark of 223.503 from 1998. His second lap, at 225.643 also broke Boat's mark of 224.573 for the fastest single qualifying lap for a normally aspirated machine. For now, Luyendyk was on the pole.

He brought up a point that may have been lost on some. "I think with having two laps to get up to speed, instead of three, that might have caught somebody out like Robbie Buhl, who I think took the green and hit the wall in [Turn] 1. It was really important to me in the pits to get out and get up to speed really, really quickly to bring those pressures and temperatures up. The conditions were good. They were the same as this morning. The wind was going the same direction. It wasn't blowing any harder or less. The track temps were the same."

Davey Hamilton was next and the two-time Indy Racing League championship runner-up qualified the No. 9T Galles Racing Spinal Conquest backup at 221.866. "We couldn't find a good qualifying setup all week," said Hamilton. "I think we have a good race car for Race Day."

Others were starting to get Luyendyk's drift. Raul Boesel and Roberto Guerrero waved off, followed by Eliseo Salazar who completed a comeback cycle by qualifying the No. 6 FUBU Nienhouse Racing Special at 221.265. "We couldn't trim the car so late because it's a little risky," said Salazar, who was back at Indy after 1998 season-ending injuries at Dover. "We took the car exactly as we had it last night. It's very emotional to be back."

Stan Wattles put the No. 19 Metro Racing Systems/NCLD entry into the field at 220.833 and Tyce Carlson got the No. 20 Bluegreen/Damon's/Blueprint-Immke Racing Dallara in at 221.322. "This has been an up-and-down week," said Wattles. "We were prepared for today and actually, we did okay. This track is a real balancing act."

"I'm not as happy as I would be if I were on the front row," Carlson said, "but we're starting the race and that's all that matters."

Robby Gordon and rookie Jeret Schroeder waved off before Mark Dismore took the No. 28T MCI WorldCom entry off the line and put together a four-lap average of 222.963. "Just to be ahead of the others, that's fantastic," Dismore said. "I never had any expectations of doing 225. I thought the car could do 223. Starting in the first 11 rows, you can win it."

After Buzz Calkins waved off, Stephan Gregoire qualified the No. 7 Mexmil/Tokheim G Force at 219.423. "It was very strange," a disappointed Gregoire said. "It's a shame. A surprise for me, because Thursday night my car was very good. It's a little confusing, but we have a backup car just in case. It's unpredictable. We've run several laps at 224."

Scott Goodyear became the 17th qualifier on the day's 26th attempt with a run of 222.387 in the No. 4T Pennzoil Panther G Force. "We set the car for cool and overcast and then, on cue, the sun came out as I pulled out of the pit box," Goodyear said. "We expected to be a little quicker, but with the sun coming out, that hurt our average tremendously."

It was 2:29 P.M., and as the sun came out for the first time, Greg Ray, who had been fastest much of the week, was the third driver in line. Jeff Ward was next and recorded a run of 221.363 in the No. 21 Pagan Racing Dallara/Oldsmobile. "I feel frustrated to be down on horsepower," Ward said. "I wish it was a little quicker. We know we've got a good race car. I can do the same with full tanks."

After Scott Harrington waved off, it was up to Ray to unseat Luyendyk from the pole. He was in the hunt in the No. 2 Glidden/Menards entry, but his last lap of 224.439 brought down his average to 225.073. After four laps, the difference in time was only .075 of a second. He was second fastest and took the middle spot in the front row. "We are very, very close," Ray said of his car and Luyendyk's. "I drove all four laps exactly the same. My crew chief said on the last lap, 'We need a little more here.' I said, 'That's all there is.'"

Cheever, in his backup car, and rookie Nick Firestone waved off attempts around Sam Schmidt's 222.734 run in the No. 99 Unistar Auto Insurance G Force team car to Luyendyk. "I thought we could run 223-mile-an-hour laps but we didn't quite make it," Schmidt said. "I knew we didn't have enough to run for the pole, but the team did a great job and we're happy with it."

Just 16 minutes after Ray qualified, the Team Menard crew pushed his backup No. 2T car into the qualifying line, reminiscent of 1996, when the team withdrew a qualified second-row car and sent Scott Brayton out to unseat Luyendyk from the pole. After Jimmy Kite qualified the No. 30 McCormack Motorsports machine at 220.097, the Menard crew pulled the car back out of line.

For Kite, it was a smooth, welcome attempt. "I'm just happy because I still got the same tires and A-arms and everything else I started out with," said Kite, who had mechanical woes causing crashes leading up to his first Indy 500 starting berth. "I feel like there's been a big weight lifted off my shoulder. Everything has gone straight to plan."

Robby Unser became the 22nd qualifier on the 34th attempt, taking the No. 81 PetroMoly/Team Pelfrey machine into the field at 221.304. "Speeds were down on the straightaway," Unser said. "But it was a consistent run and we're there."

Rookie Robby McGehee rolled away next and took the No. 55 Energizer Advanced Formula Dallara to an average of 220.139. "The car actually felt good all the way around but I expected a better speed," McGehee said. "It would be nice to have a backup car and run the speeds we want to run."

Donnie Beechler waved off, followed by 1998 Bank One Rookie of the year Steve Knapp who joined his second Indy 500 field with a run of 221.502 in the No. 35 Thermo Tech/Prolong/ISM Racing G Force. "I just put my left foot over my right foot and did four laps," said Knapp. "I don't think it really matters where you start here. I'm just looking for another race like last year because our qualifying setup is pretty much our race setup."

Jeret Schroeder returned for a second attempt and, after pulling into the pits for a quick battery change, went out and posted a 220.747 run in the No. 96 Purity Farms/Cobb Racing/G Force/Infiniti/Firestone car, becoming the first New Jersey driver to make an Indy 500 field since Steve Krisiloff in 1983. "Earlier today, I waved off," he said. "We misjudged the wind. Later, we made a small wing change and picked another gear and we made it."

The line had been steady until Schroeder's run, but the track returned to practice mode for the first time since qualifying began. Three hours and 26 minutes had produced 38 attempts and 25 qualifiers and the rest searched for speed until Scott Harrington pushed into line at 4:20 P.M. He pulled to pit road after one warmup lap, but Cheever was back in line and registered a four-lap average of 221.315 in his backup No. 51T Team Cheever/The Children's Beverage Group Dallara.

"We're in the show," Cheever said. "I'm not at all worried about starting off in the middle of the pack. We won last year from 17th place."

Dr. Jack Miller's engine malfunctioned after one lap, so Roberto Guerrero stepped up and put the No. 50 Cobb Racing G Force/Infiniti into the field with a run of 220.479. "In the 15 years that I've been coming here, I've never had it where I wasn't fast enough," Guerrero said. "I'm glad it's over. I feel like a rookie."

It would be rapid-fire qualifying until the 6 P.M. gun closed the track for the day. Billy Boat came back to put together a run of 223.469 in the No. 11T AJ Foyt Racing Dallara. Robby Gordon, after problems with his original car, put the No. 32 Glidden/Menards backup entry for Ray in the field at 223.066, then Donnie Beechler returned to post an average of 221.228 in the No. 98T Cahill Racing/Firestone/Oldsmobile/Dallara.

"It's been a tough week, not just a tough day," said Boat, relieved to be in the field after practice mishaps and the earlier accident. "It takes a little bit to get back, but the guys did a great job of putting the car back this morning. We knew we had speed. We just had to put it all together."

"We lost a motor this morning," said Gordon. "Greg Ray obviously did a good job in setting up the car and I could get in and just flat-foot it. I think I did a total of seven flying laps in that car and that includes qualifying."

"We came out this morning and thought we had everything covered," said Beechler, who made his second Indy 500 field. "I did 218 and I was flat-out. We pulled out all the stops and stiffened everything up. We even went to an option tire from Firestone, a harder compound for speed in the turns."

After rookie Nick Firestone waved off his second attempt, Moreno became the 31st qualifier with a run at 220.705 in the No. 33 Truscelli Team Racing/Warner Brothers G Force and Buzz Calkins got the No. 12 Bradley Food Marts/Sav-O-Mat G Force into the show at 220.297.

"We had trouble this morning," Moreno said. "We were running at 211. I think we made the cut by going back to basics."

"This week has been very frustrating," Calkins said. "It shouldn't have been, but we did what we had to do. The difficulty is with the little things. That's where you can get caught."

Light rain started to fall as Mike Groff waved off his second unsuccessful attempt, but Harrington went back out at 5:57 P.M. for the final run of the day and averaged 219.702 in the No. 66 CertainTeed Building Products entry to become the 33rd qualifier. "I just can't figure out what's up with our luck here at Indy," Harrington said. "Our first lap out [last] Saturday, we blew an

engine. And we crashed on Monday. I'm not sure how well that time is going to hold up."

The field was full. Forty-nine attempts had been made. Luyendyk, Ray, and Boat would be on the front row. For Ray and Boat, it was their second straight year on the front row. For Luyendyk, in his final Indianapolis 500, it was his third pole, matching his efforts in 1993 and 1997.

"It all comes down to people," Luyendyk said. "The whole package of guys—there's a great chemistry. They really made me look good today."

Others would have to wait for a final try to bump their way into the field.

DAY-AT-A-GLANCE

Date: Saturday, May 22
Qualification Attempts: 49
Qualifiers: 33

POLE DAY QUALIFIERS

Car	Driver	Speed (mph)
5	Arie Luyendyk	225.179
2	Greg Ray	225.073
11	Billy Boat	223.469
32	Robby Gordon	223.066
28	Mark Dismore	222.963
8	Scott Sharp	222.771
99	Sam Schmidt	222.734
14	Kenny Brack	222.659
4	Scott Goodyear	222.387
54	Hideshi Matsuda	222.065
9	Davey Hamilton	221.866
42	John Hollansworth Jr.	221.698
35	Steve Knapp	221.502
21	Jeff Ward	221.363
20	Tyce Carlson	221.322
51	Eddie Cheever Jr.	221.315
81	Robby Unser	221.304
6	Eliseo Salazar	221.265
98	Donnie Beechler	221.228
19	Stan Wattles	220.833
96	Jeret Schroeder	220.747
91	Buddy Lazier	220.721
33	Roberto Moreno	220.705
22	Tony Stewart	220.653
50	Roberto Guerrero	220.479
12	Buzz Calkins	220.297
55	Robby McGehee	220.139
30	Jimmy Kite	220.097
52	Wim Eyckmans	220.092
66	Scott Harrington	219.702
7	Stephan Gregoire	219.423
15	Jaques Lazier	219.165
90	Lyn St. James	218.970

With the field full at 33 starters, teams trying to get into the show began their frantic search for speed, and those high on the bump list tried to backstop themselves.

Just 55 minutes into practice, one of the plans went awry. Lyn St. James, first on the bump list at 218.970, took the backup No. 90T into Turn 1, it started smoking, and she spun into the wall moderately damaging the right side of the machine. "The engine blew," the 1992 top rookie said. "There's nothing you can do. It's hugely disappointing. I wrecked the car that I was going to use if I got bumped. Ultimately, I did what no driver wants to do and that's crash."

When practice concluded, Raul Boesel was third fastest with a lap at 222.662 miles per hour and Robbie Buhl was fourth at 221.653, both looking to bump their way into the field when time trials opened at noon. Boesel was first up and sent St. James to the sidelines with a run of 220.101 in the No. 3T Brant Racing Riley & Scott. "Yesterday, I prayed the weather would hold up and we'd have a chance to qualify," Boesel said. "Today my praying has changed. Now that I got in, I hope it rains. Soon."

Johnny Unser was next, and recorded a run of 221.197 in the No. 92 Tae-Bo/Hemelgarn Racing/Homier Tool/Delta Faucet car to bump Jaques Lazier. "It's definitely been [my] toughest 500 so far," Unser said. "Some things we can account for, some things we can't. But it's been the best car we've had all week. And right now, I wish thunderstorms would come. Last year, I was on the bubble, and this year, it's going to be close."

Next came Buhl, for the month's 52nd qualifying attempt. But on Lap 1, smoke poured from the No. 44T Dreyer & Reinbold Racing/Purex/Dallara/Infiniti creation and he pulled to the pits. Buhl's plight was one of several in the garage area. Fifteen minutes after his attempt, the Sinden Racing Services team was working feverishly to install a new engine. But, a half-hour after that, A.J. Foyt's team, including driver Billy Boat, was putting together a car to help Buhl.

Meanwhile, rookie Mike Borkowski was being fitted into the No. 22T backup car to Tony Stewart. And Hemelgarn Racing pushed a car across the garage to Team Pelfrey for St. James.

Dr. Jack Miller was next to go at 1:12 P.M., and registered a run of 220.276 in the No. 17 Dean's Milk Chug entry to bump Stephan Gregoire. "It's a shame to run 222 on the second lap and 216 on the last lap," Miller said. "Right now, we'll take it."

Andy Michner was next, but spun on a warmup lap without making contact.

At 1:34 P.M., Buhl got on the track in the No. 14T from the Foyt stable. The number was taped on the sides of the car with black electrical tape.

At 1:48 P.M., Mike Groff went out for a third and final try with the No. 46 Linc Capital/Mi-Jack Dallara and posted a run of 220.066 to knock Scott Harrington from the show. But Groff was in the field for only 10 minutes.

Michner tried again five minutes later with rain clouds threatening, but waved off after two laps in the 218 bracket.

Buhl took the track in the Foyt machine with light sprinkles falling at 1:58 P.M. He finished his run at 220.115 to bump Groff by .036 of a second over the four laps as the sprinkles turned into a downpour that ended qualifications for 1999. "They buckled me into the car back there [in Gasoline Alley]," Buhl said. "I thought they were just fitting me. We went to the line, talked for a minute, shook hands and said, 'Let's do what we can here.' Today, what I had to do was look in A.J.'s eyes and he looked in mine. I didn't have much choice, but he had confidence in me. Never again do I want to come out at 10 to 6 and qualify. I don't want to do that, and the next 10 years, to make a living."

A.J. Foyt said, "They [speedway officials] said the rain was about 10 or 15 minutes away and I said to Robbie, 'Are you comfortable?' And he said, 'Yeah, let's go for it.' It's like old times. It's like open-wheel racing used to be. Money doesn't call the shots here. You can have money or not have money here. When Billy Boat got hurt, Robbie helped us out. If they help you out, you turn around and help them out."

As the rain finally closed the track at 4:30 P.M., the field was set. Luyendyk, at 45 and the oldest driver in the field, was on the pole. The last time the oldest driver in a Indy 500 field was on the pole was in 1981 when 47-year-old Bobby Unser started first. For others, it was "next year."

"It happens to a lot of people," said Groff. "It was just difficult and we just didn't make it."

"I just really appreciate the huge effort that three teams put [in] to get us in the field," said St. James.

"We were extremely disappointed, but we were ready to go again," Harrington said. "I can't believe this but no one can control the rain."

Dr. Jack Miller (17) leaves pit row on Carburetion Day for his final practice laps prior to race day. Once the red flag flies on Thursday, it's a waiting game until race day.

DAY-AT-A-GLANCE

Date:	Sunday, May 23
Qualification Attempts:	7
Qualifiers:	5
Bumped:	4

BUBBLE DAY QUALIFIERS

Car	Driver	Speed (mph)
92	Johnny Unser	221.197
17	Dr. Jack Miller	220.276
84	Robbie Buhl	220.115

Coors Carburetion Day is the final shakedown before Race Day and a strong indication of who will run up front. It retains its name from the days when carburetors were used. Today, it offers a two-hour window of practice for teams to scuff tires, run on full tanks for race setup, and make a final check on systems before the cars and drivers embark on the ultimate 500-mile test.

From 11 A.M., when Davey Hamilton was the first driver on the track, to 1 P.M., when the track closed until Race Day, all 33 cars and 32 drivers were on the 2.5-mile oval. Greg Ray shook down the car qualified by new teammate Robby Gordon, who was at another race in St. Louis.

Indianapolis Mayor Steve Goldsmith had proclaimed the day "Arie Luyendyk Day" in honor of the two-time winner's final Indy 500. Luyendyk was fourth fastest of the session with a lap at 221.380 miles per hour in the No. 5 Sprint PCS/Meijer machine as others emerged on the speed chart. Sam Schmidt, his Treadway Racing teammate, took the top spot at 222.458 in the No. 99 Unistar Auto Insurance entry. Ray was next at 221.822 in his own No. 2 Glidden/Menards car and 221.790 in Gordon's No. 32 Glidden/Menards team car.

Fifth place and sixth place on the speed chart were a different story. Hideshi Matsuda, who has made an Indy 500 career of going fast with little practice time, checked in fifth at 221.185 in the No. 54 Mini Juke/Beck Motorsports car. Tyce Carlson, who had hovered around the top 10 in practice leading up to qualifying, was next at 221.114 in the No. 20 Pennzoil/Damon's/Bluegreen entry.

"The engine had much more power than qualifying day," said the affable Matsuda. "Qualifying day, I thought the car was perfect, but today, oooooh, the car is good! It's my dream to win the 500. I can't wait for Sunday."

When speed chart surprises happen on Carburetion Day, however, no one is really sure what it means. "We purposely didn't run for any times today," said Dr. Jack Miller. "Someone asked me if I had any superstitions and I said 'No.' But that's not true today, because for Carburetion Day, the least amount you run, the better. I've been here too many times and seen too many things happen."

Miller's teammate, Tony Stewart, echoed his thoughts. "We didn't hit anything and the car is in one piece," he said. "We did everything we needed to do today."

"Every lap we do here is a lap we take away from the car in the race," said defending champion Eddie Cheever Jr.

"We're ready to go and it's starting to hit me that I am going to drive in the greatest race in the world," said rookie Robby McGehee.

For Schmidt, who led practice for the first time ever at the Speedway, it was also a systematic drill. "We wanted to scuff the tires," he said, "and we wanted to check the electrical systems. We wanted to make sure the motor installation went in correctly. We accomplished them all. We just went through our checklist and we kept it off the wall. We might have gotten a little tow on the 222 lap but the car is really solid.

"I think everybody's objective is the same. You have your checklists. Some may be a little more conservative than most. But

the thing that's at the top of the list I think with everybody out there is 'Do not crash the car.' It would be hard to walk in the garage if you crashed the car today."

After practice, Galles Racing, with crew chief Darren Russell and driver Davey Hamilton, took the top prize of $37,500 in the Coors Indy Pit Stop Challenge on pit road. In the final, Galles defeated the No. 14 AJ Foyt entry of Kenny Brack, by posting a time of 12.680 seconds for a four-tire change and simulated fuel hose connection to the Foyt group's 14.560 seconds.

It's something the Galles team has always taken seriously. The win was the sixth for Galles, tying Team Penske for the most wins in the 23-year-old contest. Galles also won in 1989, 1990, 1993, 1996, and 1997. "I'm just so proud of my guys," Russell said. "We've worked so hard."

"I hope this race comes down to the last pit stop because they'll win it for me," Hamilton said.

Race Day awaited.

Eddie Cheever Jr. leaves a trail of smoke and rubber as he pulls across the finish line of the annual pit stop contest on Carburetion Day.

DAY-AT-A-GLANCE

Date: Thursday, May 27
Drivers on Track: 32
Cars on Track: 33

TOP FIVE DRIVERS OF THE DAY

Car	Driver	Speed (mph)
99	Sam Schmidt	222.458
2	Greg Ray	221.822
5	Arie Luyendyk	221.380
54	Hideshi Matsuda	221.185
20	Tyce Carlson	221.114

Indianapolis 500 Retrospective

Dean Martin and Jerry Lewis were among the celebrities who visited the track during practice, seen here with 1950 Indianapolis 500 winner Johnnie Parsons (above Jerry's head, pointing) and Speedway owner Tony Hulman.

The front row qualifiers for the 1954 Indianapolis 500-mile race, Jack McGrath, Jimmy Daywalt, and Jimmy Bryan, pose in the pace car, a 1954 Dodge Royal.

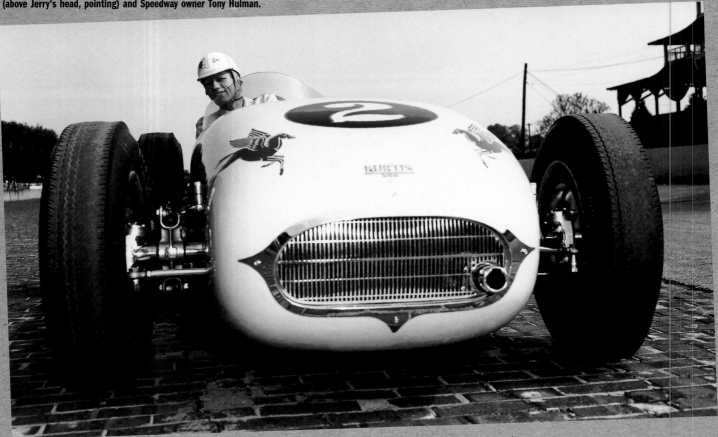

Polewinner Jack McGrath was the first driver to officially lap in excess of 140 miles per hour, and he set the blistering pace on all four of his qualifying laps, recording 141.287 miles per hour on one of them. The body of Jack's Kurtis-Kraft "roadster" is offset to the left in an attempt to improve handling through the 800 left-hand turns encountered during the 200-lap event.

This truly dramatic post-race study shows a thoroughly battered and fatigued Bill Vukovich contemplating his winning drive while perched on top of a work bench, soaked in perspiration and splattered with oil.

Bill Vukovich comes up to lap Jimmy Bryan in the closing stages of the race. Bryan hung on for second place in spite of a rough riding car that had a broken shock absorber. He collapsed in the garage shortly after the race ended.

A change of drivers during a pit stop used to be quite a common occurrence on a hot day. This is Bob Scott replacing a fatigued Andy Linden in 1954. The extreme example of driver changes took place during this same event when Art Cross, whose car eventually finished 11th, was relieved by Johnnie Parsons, Sam Hanks, Andy Linden, and Jim Davies.

Jack McGrath leads the field into Turn 1 with his Offenhauser-powered Hinkle.

The seven former winners in the 1984 starting field pose with the Borg-Warner trophy at the Drivers' meeting: (left to right) Johnny Rutherford, Mario Andretti, Tom Sneva, Rick Mears, Al Unser Sr., A.J. Foyt, and Gordon Johncock.

Rick Mears (8), driving a Penske March-Cosworth, jumps ahead of polesitter Tom Sneva (1) and Michael Andretti (99) to lead the opening lap of the race.

Dicing for position: Chris Kneifel and Kevin Cogan are side by side racing for position, with Danny Ongais and Josele Garza in hot pursuit.

Roger Penske elected to use the March chassis over his own Penske chassis. The decision paid off for Rick Mears, but his victory was far from assured. Tom Sneva applied pressure to Mears all race long. When Sneva was taken out of the race by a broken CV joint on the Lap 168 restart, Mears went unchallenged to the checkered flag.

Tom Sneva accepts the accolades after being the first to qualify at over 210 miles per hour. Sneva was more than 2 miles per hour faster than second place qualifier and teammate Howdy Holmes.

Scott Brayton leads this pack of cars down the front straight as the pursuing cars look for a way around the cars in front.

During an eventful run, standout "rookie" Roberto Guerrero spun once, rode up over another car's wheel during a caution period and stalled on two of his pitstops, yet he still finished in second position. He split the Rookie of the Year balloting with Michael Andretti, who placed fifth.

Rick Mears celebrates a well-deserved second victory with a sip of the ceremonial milk. Mears, who won the race in 1979, would go on to score two more Indy 500 victories in 1988 and 1991 before retiring from the cockpit in 1993.

HOW SWEDE IT IS!

Kenny Brack and A.J. Foyt Win the Indy 500

by Jonathan Ingram

Inset: It was time to celebrate for Kenny Brack and A.J. Foyt. Their only win of the season was at the biggest and most prestigious race of all—the Indy 500.

The 83rd Indianpolis 500 lived up to the long tradition of open-wheel speed and suspense at the Indianapolis Motor Speedway. After 199 laps had been completed, the greatest prize in motor racing came down to one singular moment. With just over a lap to go until the checkered flag, who will forget seeing the orange, yellow, and blue Team Menard entry driven by Robby Gordon, leading by 1.5 seconds, cough and sputter helplessly while exiting Turn 4, then roll into the pit entrance, out of fuel?

Immediately, it was apparent that an entry from the legendary AJ Foyt Racing team was on its way to victory lane. Buoyed by an ample supply of methanol and the relief that Gordon had—as anticipated with excruciating suspense—finally run out of fuel at the beginning of the last lap, driver Kenny Brack needed just one more circuit to complete a flawless 500-mile performance.

As much a part of Indy tradition as the yard of bricks at the start-finish line, Foyt returned to victory lane with his team for the first time in 22 years. Typical of the old-fashioned racer who relied

Kenny Brack and A.J. Foyt certainly did their homework and it paid off bigtime. Brack reviewed many past Indy 500s on video tape and specifically developed a training regimen for the race. Using a carefully designed race strategy, Brack took over the lead of the race when it counted the most—on the final lap.

Green Flag: Polesitter and two-time winner Arie Luyendyk (5) sweeps wide as he leads Greg Ray (2) into the first turn of the race—the final race of Luyendyk's career.

on his own head, his gut feelings, and the seat of his pants to win the Indy 500 four times from the cockpit, the Texan said he used "the computer in my head" to calculate his Swedish driver's fuel mileage during the crucial stretch run.

The old-fashioned method worked, but just barely. Had one more yellow flag flown on a day that saw veterans and recent arrivals find the wall often enough to illuminate the caution lights eight times, John Menard and Gordon might have been toasting their savvy and daring with a bottle of milk in victory lane. If the final yellow period had lasted one or two more laps, star-crossed Gordon might have also had enough methanol to go the distance. As it was, Menard, the home building supply magnate from Wisconsin who first began participating at Indy in 1979, came up empty—again.

It was a race that was as much about endurance and strategy as it was about speed, executed under enormous pressure before a crowd of 375,000 with millions more watching the worldwide broadcast by ABC Sports. The seven drivers who started ahead of Brack (Arie Luyendyk, Greg Ray, Billy Boat, Gordon, Mark Dismore, Scott Sharp, and Sam Schmidt) failed to slip their heads under the elusive winner's wreath due to miscalculations, driver error, or mechanical malfunctions. Looking at the day, each of these men had comprised a telling tale of how the Borg-Warner Trophy was lost.

As if to underline the beguiling mystique at Indy, retiring Arie Luyendyk—who won his third pole in his final appearance at the Brickyard in Treadway Racing's G Force-Aurora—crashed while leading with 83 laps to go after misjudging a lapped car during an overtaking maneuver. Having set the single-lap record for outright speed

chassis carried him into the wall with 31 laps to go, setting up the decisive final yellow period.

Dismore's Kelley Racing teammate Scott Sharp started sixth in a Delphi Automotive Dallara-Aurora, but fell prey to an engine problem. He pitted before the start and then retired after transmission trouble. Sam Schmidt, Luyendyk's teammate at Treadway Racing, started on the inside of the third row next to Brack, but crashed in Turn 1, just 26 laps after taking his first lead in the Indy 500.

It was that kind of a day for the participants in the Pep Boys Indy Racing League, whose formula of universally available chassis and V-8 engines forced teams and drivers to squeeze every last horsepower out of their cars. As usual, new heroes emerged. Jeff Ward demonstrated remarkable acumen for four-wheeled racing

Hard-charging Jeff Ward always seems to run well at Indianapolis. He qualified 14th, but made his usual run to the front and ended up as the runner-up.

with a mark of 237.498 miles per hour in 1996, two-time race winner Luyendyk stood testimony to a day when 18 lead changes took place among seven drivers, each anxiously checking his mirrors and then trying to find better lap times.

As the driver who started next to the Dutchman on the front row, Greg Ray, in the Glidden Dallara-Aurora, might have fared better had he looked in his mirrors while exiting the pits three laps after Luyendyk's accident. With track position at a premium among so many contenders, Ray's Menard entry collided with Mark Dismore, who was making a hasty exit from his pit stall in an attempt to hold the lead handed him by Luyendyk's miscalculation.

Having crashed three times in practice, Foyt's entry driven by Billy Boat came home third—the place in which he started. His oft-rebuilt Compaq Dallara-Aurora left its consistency, if not speed, somewhere in the wake of his three meetings with the wall. Dismore, who started fifth next to Gordon on the second row in the MCI WorldCom Dallara-Aurora, fought back from a lap deficit caused by handling problems at the outset. But the same pushing Dallara

For many laps it looked like two-time winner Arie Luyendyk would close out his career with another Indy 500 win. Here he leads Greg Ray (2), Robby Gordon (32), and Scott Goodyear (4) through Turn 2.

Sam Schmidt (99) came into the race with high hopes—and even led for four laps—but his aspirations were shattered when a Turn 1 crash ended his day after just 62 laps.

once again. Starting 14th, the Pagan Racing's Dallara-Aurora driver finished as the runner-up to Brack, who passed the hard-pedaling former motocross champion 12 laps from the finish. Ward put himself into the championship lead by adding his second-place finish at Indy to a third place at Disney and a second place at Phoenix.

Remarkable Rookie of the Year Robbie McGehee finished 5th after starting 27th in the Energizer Advanced Formula Dallara-Aurora. He came home behind Gordon despite the fact that the day's lone major injury occurred in his pits. A collision involving Jimmy Kite and Jeret Schroeder during the first round of pit stops sent McGehee's Chief Mechanic Steve Fried to Methodist Hospital after he was flipped onto his head by errant traffic.

Then there was Tony Stewart, who soldiered to a ninth-place finish in an oversteering Home Depot Dallara-Aurora with his own new Tri Star Motorsports team before jetting to Charlotte, North Carolina, for 600 miles of Winston Cup racing.

Capping the Foyt team's incredible day, Robbie Buhl took a late third entry from the Texan, which was crewed by Sinden Racing Service, to sixth place. Seven days previous to the race, during the qualifying weekend, Buhl switched from a crashed Sinden-prepared entry to one of the Foyt Racing machines. He then became the last driver to make the field before rain ended the second day of qualifying. By a scant 0.036 seconds after four laps, he bumped Mike Groff out of the field.

The two-day qualifying format, introduced in 1998, created palpable tension symbolized by veteran Buhl's struggle. During his first qualification attempt on Saturday's pole day, he crashed during the warm-up lap in an Infiniti-powered Dallara sponsored by Dreyer &

Another year, another disappointment at Indianapolis for veteran Scott Goodyear. His Pennzoil Panther/G Force completed just 101 laps before engine trouble ended his day.

One of the pivotal moments of the race involved Tyce Carlson. On Lap 166, Arie Luyendyk tried to pass Carlson in Turn 3. Carlson took the low line and pinched off Luyendyk. Luyendyk jumped on the brakes, lost traction, and slid into the outside wall, ending his chances of winning his final Indy 500.

Front row starter Greg Ray (2) led four times for 32 laps in the Glidden-Menards Dallara/Aurora/Firestone, but a pit row collision with Mark Dismore put Ray out of the race on Lap 120.

Scott Sharp (8) is the first to pull out of the busy pits as most of the field makes a stop under yellow. A failed transmission ended Sharp's day after just 83 laps.

Follow the leader: Greg Ray (2) leads the pack through Turn 2. Those who were hot on his heels include: Robby Gordon (32), Scott Goodyear (4), and Eddie Cheever Jr. (51).

Reinbold. Then, in his first attempt on Sunday, the engine blew in his back-up car shortly after noon.

Buhl and Foyt quickly made a deal that put the Indianapolis resident behind the wheel of a back-up Dallara-Aurora built from the spares of the entries for Boat and Brack. "I made a mistake in Turn 1 yesterday and wound up in the fence," said Buhl. "Today, what I had to do was look in A.J.'s eyes, and he looked in mine. I didn't have much choice."

Johnny Unser, Dr. Jack Miller, and Raul Boesel also qualified on "Bubble Day"—a testimony to the feverish atmosphere. Getting bumped were Lyn St. James, Buddy Lazier, Stephan Gregoire, and Scott Harrington; a testimony to the number of quality drivers and chassis on hand. Luyendyk's pole of 225.179 miles per hour was just over 4 seconds, or 1 second per lap, ahead of the slowest car driven by Boesel. Thus, it was a qualifying weekend that set the table for the 3 hours, 15 minutes, and 51 seconds of wall-to-wall racing in the 83rd Indy 500.

Billy Boat (11) screams past the stands between Turns 3 and 4 en route to an outstanding finish. He started third and finished third, earning over $400,000.

Defending Indy 500 Champion Eddie Cheever Jr. piloted the only Infiniti-powered car in the field. He ran strong and led once for four laps, but his day ended prematurely as engine failure sent him back to the garage for good after 139 laps.

Once race day rolled around, Luyendyk counted on his 13 years of experience on the 2.5-mile Indy oval. There would be no getting around his Sprint PCS machine at the start, which commenced under perfect conditions of 85 degrees Fahrenheit and azure skies. After the field swarmed past the yard of bricks at the start-finish in three-wide and four-wide abandon, the Dutchman led the 31 cars (minus the ailing cars of Sharp and Miller) as they funneled into Turn 1.

The pattern of the race was established early. While Luyendyk and Ray pushed the pace at the front, Brack chose to go easy on his Goodyear tires under orders from Foyt, who wanted to be certain to avoid any blisters. But four laps after an early yellow for the crash of Eliseo Salazar in Turn 2 and the re-start, Brack had his red, white, and gold Power Team entry up to third place behind the two front runners. Recalling, perhaps, the fact that Brack had run out of fuel and lost two laps in 1998, Foyt had the Swede and Boat

Robby McGehee (55) moved up 22 positions—starting 27th and finishing 5th—earning a quarter-million dollar payday, some of the greatest thrills of his young racing career, and Rookie-of-the-Year honors for the race.

outlines of the possible fuel mileage under the IRL's mandate for 1999 of 10,300 rpm were drawn. Then, as if in a foreshadowing of the finish, Hideshi Matsuda and Roberto Guerrero both ran out of fuel on course two laps later, bringing out the second yellow and demonstrating the vagaries of fuel mileage calculation. Even more significant, Gordon re-entered the pits due to a vibration in one of his wheels, resulting in the loss of a lap on the track after the re-start, and putting him in the position of needing to gamble at race's end.

Following the second re-start, the race settled into a pattern of dashes between pit stops under yellow. On Lap 63, Schmidt ran afoul of traffic in Turn 1 and slid into the dust and cast off tire bits outside the groove, skating into the wall. This, too, was a forecast of sorts as Luyendyk would later run afoul of traffic. "Everyone checked up while lapping traffic," said Schmidt. "Arie was in front of me and I didn't want to hit him. I got up into the gray stuff."

For the next 60 laps, the lead would alternate between Luyendyk, Ray, and Brack, according to pit stops and re-starts after yellows. In the meantime, two drivers who traditionally come on strong in the second half of the race began to show their hand.

On a re-start with 99 of 200 laps complete, Scott Goodyear's Pennzoil Panther Racing G Force-Aurora and the Infiniti-powered Dallara of defending Indy 500 champion Eddie Cheever rode in fourth and fifth, respectively. Goodyear, unfortunately, barely made it past halfway when his engine expired on the 101st lap. Engine reliability was a concern for Cheever, too. The development program established between his team and Infiniti had produced the necessary oomph, but a 500-mile test had not been run since the emphasis had been placed on finding horsepower.

Big dogs running together: Eventual winner Kenny Brack (14) led runner-up Jeff Ward (21), Buddy Lazier (91), and third-place-finisher Billy Boat (11) through the first turn.

brought down pit road the earliest among the leaders despite seven laps having been run under yellow for the crash of the Chilean. Ward, who vaulted from 14th to 7th in the Pagan Racing Dallara, and Gordon, who slipped from 4th to 11th, came in on the 32nd lap.

At this point in the race, Gordon was already showing the effects of not running on "Coors Carburetion Day" the previous Thursday. (He instead practiced his entry in CART's Motorola 300 in Madison, Illinois.) "The one mistake we made was not putting a bigger wicker [on the trailing edge of the rear wing]," said Gordon, who lacked downforce at the back. "I was holding on to my butt for the first stint."

At the 33-lap mark, leaders Luyendyk and Ray rolled down the long pit road at the mandated speed of 80 miles per hour. Thus, the

The gamble that didn't pay off. After 199 laps Robby Gordon (32) made a final pit stop, similar to this one, so he could get a splash of fuel and finish the race—a race he was leading on Lap 199.

The yellow that flew on Lap 162 for the stalled car of Jimmy Kite set up Team Menard's fateful decision. With 36 laps remaining, Gordon trundled into the pits, running seventh and last on the lead lap. He rejoined the line and took the re-start two laps later behind the other cars on the lead lap, which had not pitted. Brack, meanwhile, maintained his lead over Ward by forcing a slow re-start to prevent the second-placed car from jumping him which allowed Brack to conserve his Goodyears.

Having worked his way back up to fourth place from a lap down, Dismore then hit the wall at Turn 2, losing a right, front wheel. With 31 laps to go, all the cars on the lead lap were well within their final window for fuel. Brack, Ward, Boat, McGehee, and Buhl all entered the pits for fuel and tires. Meanwhile, Gordon and his Menard team elected to stay out, thus taking the lead and setting up the final, fateful run to the checkers. "We could have come into the pits and put a splash of fuel in," said Menard. "But our calculations showed we had enough fuel." When the green flew, Gordon had run six laps of yellow and two laps of green after re-fueling and 26 laps of potential green flag racing remained. The team had enough confidence that on the re-start, Gordon shot away in fifth gear from Ward, who was busy passing Brack when the green flew.

Brack later dispatched Ward after the latter was balked in Turn 4 by a backmarker. Brack dove inside at the start-finish and carried the pass through Turn 1 with 12 laps to go. But the Swede was still in the fuel-saving sixth gear. "I didn't drive the car real hard until the last 10 laps," said Brack, who got the message from Foyt to go to

Winner Kenny Brack rolls his AJ Foyt PowerTeam Racing Dallara/Aurora/Goodyear into the winner's circle. The car carried Foyt's famous No. 14—a number A.J. took to victory lane four times.

One and five: First-time winner Kenny Brack waves to cheering fans while team owner and four-time Indy 500 winner A.J. Foyt basks in the glory of his first win as an owner.

The race's first major change of course occurred on the 116th lap when Luyendyk, worried about increasing his lead to provide a little extra cushion on pit stops, nearly hit Tyce Carlson's Dallara in Turn 3. "I should have known better than to race traffic that hard," he said of his final appearance at Indy. "I went underneath Tyce. I thought he would give me room, but he came down on me. I had to slam on the brakes, and when I touched the brakes the car became unstable." Luyendyk led four times for 63 laps. "I was driving with confidence and maybe that confidence bit me," said the driver whose straight talk and cool demeanor will be missed.

Three laps later, Ray joined the Dutchman on the sidelines after swinging wide while leaving his pit stall and breaking the front suspension of his Dallara when it collided with Dismore's Dallara as the latter pitted. "It just breaks your heart to have it end this way," said Ray, who led four times for 32 laps.

Ray's demise put an Infiniti powered car into the lead of the Indy 500 for the first time and gave the Japanese company only its second race leader since joining the IRL in 1997. Alas, Cheever, who was passed on the re-start by Brack, led only under yellow and within 15 laps of green, his Infiniti V-8 had expired. "I'm glad we made the switch to Infiniti," he said, "but I wish we had done it earlier. We tried to cram six months work into two months."

Brack, who had been running conservatively, held the lead without challenge in the absence of his four previous adversaries. But two new ones emerged, one in the form of Ward, just a half second behind. Then after those two pitted, Gordon's new-found pace, after some chassis adjustments, put him on the tail-end of the lead lap.

fifth gear with five laps remaining. "We were only able to go 28 laps or 29 [under green]. I thought he was going to have to go into the pits. We were thinking it was impossible [for Gordon to finish], but the last laps we had to pick it up."

Driving with his left wheels well below the white line and with his right wheels nearly clipping the wall at the corner exits, Brack cut the lead to 3.757 seconds with nine laps remaining. But Gordon said he wasn't worried about getting caught from behind. "Kenny didn't have any chance," said the ever-confident Gordon. "I had a lead of 4.5 seconds and put it up to sixth gear. When he cut into the lead, I popped it back into fifth and the lead went to four seconds again. After that, I put it in sixth gear."

With five laps remaining, Brack got the word from Foyt to drop into fifth gear while trailing by 3.5 seconds. He steadily cut the lead by a second a lap for two circuits, then lost 3/10ths of a second and trailed Gordon by 1.5 seconds after the 198th circuit. "I told Kenny I didn't want second," said Foyt. Whether Brack could have passed Gordon once he caught him on that final lap, the racing world will never know. Gordon steered into the pits, reminiscent of ol' A.J.'s first victory in 1961 when Eddie Sachs elected to pit for tires while leading, giving the victory to Foyt. "We were one lap short," said Gordon. "It makes me sick."

For his part, winner Brack declared himself happy for his legendary team owner. "But I think I'm more happy for me," he said. "A.J. has won it four times already."

OFFICIAL BOX SCORE
PEP BOYS INDY RACING LEAGUE
Indianapolis 500 at Indianapolis Motor Speedway
Sunday, May 30, 1999

FP	SP	Car	Driver	Car Name	C/E/T	Laps Comp.	Running/ Reason Out	IRL Pts.	Total IRL Pts.	IRL Standings	IRL Awards	Designated Awards	Total Awards
1	8	14	Kenny Brack	A.J. Foyt PowerTeam Racing	D/A/G	200	Running	52	66	7	$985,560	$479,630	$1,465,190
2	14	21	Jeff Ward	Yahoo-MerchantOnline-Dallara-Olds	D/A/G	200	Running	40	115	1	531,670	51,480	583,150
3	3	11	Billy Boat	A.J. Foyt Racing	D/A/G	200	Running	36	90	3	386,670	48,530	435,200
4	4	32	Robby Gordon	Glidden/Menards	D/A/F	200	Running	32	32	22	215,670	37,600	253,270
5	27	55 R	Robby McGehee	Energizer Advanced Formula	D/A/F	199	Running	30	30	23	202,670	45,080	247,750
6	32	84	Robbie Buhl	A.J. Foyt Racing	D/A/G	199	Running	28	73	5	198,670	58,830	257,500
7	22	91	Buddy Lazier	Delta Faucet/Coors Light/Tae-Bo/Hemelgarn Racing	D/A/G	198	Running	26	58	10	259,670	25,430	285,100
8	17	81	Robby Unser	PetroMoly/Team Pelfrey	D/A/F	197	Running	24	45	12	176,670	18,830	195,500
9	24	22	Tony Stewart	The Home Depot	D/A/G	196	Running	22	22	28	169,670	17,000	186,670
10	10	54	Hideshi Matsuda	Mini Juke-Beck Motorsports	D/A/F	196	Running	20	20	29	164,670	21,330	186,000
11	11	9	Davey Hamilton	Galles Racing Spinal Conquest	D/A/G	196	Running	19	46	11	161,670	58,830	220,500
12	33	3	Raul Boesel	Brant Racing R&S MKV	R/A/G	195	Running	18	60	9	232,670	15,930	248,600
13	12	42 R	John Hollansworth Jr.	Pcsave.com/Lycos/Dallara	D/A/F	192	Running	17	43	12	229,670	35,730	265,400
14	15	20	Tyce Carlson	Pennzoil-Damon's-Bluegreen	D/A/F	190	Running	16	41	14	225,670	21,330	247,000
15	21	96 R	Jeret Schroeder	Purity Farms/Cobb Racing/G Force/Infiniti/Firestone	G/I/F	175	Engine	15	15	33	147,670	28,580	176,250
16	5	28	Mark Dismore	MCI WorldCom	D/A/G	168	Accident	14	20	6	219,670	15,630	235,300
17	20	19	Stan Wattles	Metro Racing Systems/NCLD	D/A/G	147	Running	13	19	30	142,670	15,330	158,000
18	16	51	Eddie Cheever Jr.	Team Cheever/The Children's Beverage Group/Dallara	D/I/G	139	Engine	12	75	4	214,670	32,130	246,800
19	26	12	Buzz Calkins	Bradley Food Marts/Sav-O-Mat	G/A/F	133	Running	11	40	15	212,670	15,330	228,000
20	23	33	Roberto Moreno	Truscelli Team Racing/Warner Bros.	G/A/G	122	Transmission	10	38	16	210,670	15,000	225,670
21	2	2	Greg Ray	Glidden/Menards	D/A/F	120	Accident Pits	11	34	20	132,670	72,230	204,900
22	1	5	Arie Luyendyk	Sprint PCS/Meijer	D/A/F	117	Accident T3	11	11	34	130,670	251,680	382,350
23	29	52 R	Wim Eyckmans	EGP/Beaulieu of America/Dallara/Oldsmobile/Goodyear	D/A/G	113	Timing Chain	7	7	36	129,670	15,580	145,250
24	28	30	Jimmy Kite	Alfa Laval-Team Losi-Fastrod-McCormack-Haas CNC	G/A/F	110	Engine	6	6	38	202,670	25,330	228,000
25	25	50	Roberto Guerrero	Cobb Racing/G Force/Infiniti	G/I/F	105	Engine	5	36	17	201,670	15,330	217,000
26	13	35	Steve Knapp	Delco Remy-ThermoTech Microphonics-Prolong-G Force	G/A/G	104	Handling	4	35	18	200,670	15,330	216,000
27	9	4	Scott Goodyear	Pennzoil Panther/G Force	G/A/G	101	Engine	3	96	2	198,670	18,830	217,500
28	6	8	Scott Sharp	Delphi Automotive Systems	D/A/G	83	Transmission	2	63	8	197,670	28,830	221,500
29	19	98	Donnie Beechler	Cahill Racing-Big Daddy's BBQ	D/A/F	74	Engine	1	24	27	122,670	20,330	143,000
30	7	99	Sam Schmidt	Unistar Auto Insurance	G/A/F	62	Accident T1	1	26	26	196,670	17,130	213,800
31	31	17	Jack Miller	Dean's Milk Chug	D/A/G	29	Clutch	1	1	41	130,670	15,330	146,000
32	30	92	Johnny Unser	Tae-Bo/Hemelgarn Racing/Homier Tool/Delta Faucet	D/A/G	10	Brakes	1	1	41	145,670	15,330	161,000
33	18	6	Eliseo Salazar	FUBU Nienhouse Racing Special	G/A/F	7	Accident T2	1	11	34	120,670	20,330	141,000
										Total	7,400,000	1,647,150	9,047,150

Time of Race:3:15:51.182   Average Speed: 153.176 mph   Margin of Victory: 6.562 seconds   Fastest Lap: #2 Greg Ray Lap 101-218.882 mph
Fastest Leading Lap: #5 Arie Luyendyk Lap 108-218.224   PPG Pole Winner: #5 Arie Luyendyk (225.179 mph)   PPG Team Pole Award: #5 Sprint PCS/Meijer   MBNA America Lap Leader: #14 Kenny Brack
MCI Long Distance Award: #84 Robbie Buhl   Firestone First AI 99 Award: #5 Arie Luyendyk   Delphi "Leader At Halfway" Award: #5 Arie Luyendyk   Coors Light Pit stop Contest: #9 Davey Hamilton
Chassis Legend: D-Dallara(22); G-G Force(10); R-Riley&Scott(1)   Engine Legend:A-Oldsmobile Aurora(30); I-Infiniti Indy (3) Tire Legend: F-Firestone(15); G-Goodyear(18)

Lap Leaders
Laps	Car	Driver				
1-32	#5	Arie Luyendyk	60-64	#14	Kenny Brack	
33	#2	Greg Ray	65-69	#5	Arie Luyendyk	
34-37	#99	Sam Schmidt	70-82	#14	Kenny Brack	
38-44	#5	Arie Luyendyk	83-95	#2	Greg Ray	
45-59	#2	Greg Ray	96-98	#14	Kenny Brack	
			99-117	#5	Arie Luyendyk	
			118-120	#2	Greg Ray	

121-124	#51	Eddie Cheever Jr.
125-150	#5	Kenny Brack
151-153	#21	Jeff Ward
154-170	#14	Kenny Brack
171-198	#32	Robby Gordon
199-200	#14	Kenny Brack

Caution Flags:
Laps	Reason/Incident
9-14	#6 Salazar, accident Turn 2
35-39	#54 Matsuda stalled
63-68	#99 Schmidt, accident Turn 1
93-98	#35 Knapp, spin Turn 2
102-105	#4 Goodyear, engine
118-124	#5 Luyendyk, accident Turn 3
	#2 Ray abd #28 Dismore accident Pits
162-164	#30 Kite stalled
169-173	#28 Dismore accident Turn 2

Total: 8 caution flags, 42 laps

Once again, Goodyear Eagles
sweep Indy 500.
First place, second place, third place.

Kenny Brack wins fifth Indy 500 title for A.J. Foyt.

For the second year in a row, Goodyear swept the competition with a stunning one, two, three finish at the Indianapolis 500. Goodyear Racing Eagles also took four-time Indy winner A.J. Foyt back to the winner's circle. This time as team owner. Foyt entered three cars in this year's 33-car field. And all three of A.J.'s entries finished in the top six. Kenny Brack took the checkered flag, winning his first Indy 500. Billy Boat finished third. And Robbie Buhl finished sixth. And all of A.J.'s Dallara/Oldsmobile Auroras took to the Brickyard on Goodyear Eagle racing radials. Congratulations to Kenny Brack, Billy Boat, Robbie Buhl and to second place finisher Jeff Ward in his Pagan Racing Dallara/Oldsmobile Aurora. To A.J. Foyt we offer special congratulations. It's good to have you back home again in Indianapolis. Back home in the winner's circle.

MORE VICTORIES. MORE PLACES. MORE OFTEN.

GOOD YEAR
#1 in Racing. #1 in Tires.

KENNY BRACK

DALLARA/OLDSMOBILE AURORA/GOODYEAR

Kenny Brack is a methodical analytical, calculating racer with a hard work ethic. And most importantly, he has the talent to run on the absolute edge when it is necessary. That is how he won the greatest race of the all—the Indianapolis 500.

After last year's Indy 500, Brack realized he had to be better prepared than his competitors. He collected and digested all the information he could from previous Indy 500s. He analyzed various Indy 500 races on video tape, taking notes on important factors that would allow him to win the race. He developed a physical and mental training regimen to prepare himself for all the demands of the race. He knew that during the race he would have to make clean passes and quick pit stops, adopt a sound fuel strategy, and anticipate his competitors' strategies.

Throughout the week leading up to time trials, Brack was consistently in the top eight and turned a lap at 222.151 miles per hour in the morning practice before qualifications, third fastest of his group. He earned the eighth starting position for the 500 with a four-lap run of 222.659 miles per hour.

In the race, Arie Luyendyk, starting from the pole position, was the dominant driver; cutting fast laps and easily leading the race. For the first 50 laps, Team Menard's Greg Ray shadowed Luyendyk waiting for an opportunity. Mistakes and accidents eliminated Luyendyk and Ray and blew the race wide open for the other racers.

Brack took his first lead on Lap 60 and returned to the front five more times as the remainder of the race unfolded. On Lap 188, he passed Jeff Ward for second, moving 4.048 seconds behind leader Robby Gordon. He chipped away at Gordon's lead, knocking it down to 1.563 seconds with two laps to go. Gordon pitted on Lap 199 for a splash of fuel. Had the final caution period lasted another two laps, Gordon may have won the race, but luck is one essential element necessary for winning the Indy 500. Brack took over the lead for the final lap and won his first Indianapolis 500 by 6.56 seconds over Ward. He became the first defending series champion to win the succeeding Indy 500 since Bobby Unser in 1975.

"I didn't run the car real hard until the last 10 laps," Brack said. "Then we enriched it. I was running really hard just to catch Robby because I knew if he didn't pit, I'd have to try to pass him. It is very hard to win this race. You don't know what is going to happen."

Success after a bitter failure can taste sweeter than the best steak. The flying Swede scored revenge for the heartbreak the team suffered last year. Kenny Brack added the Indy 500 title to his 1998 series championship, and firmly etched himself in the record books.

The 33-year-old Brack grew up in Karlstad, Sweden, the son of an electrician. During his younger years, Brack raced mopeds around his parents' property, and at the age of 12 bought a Saab to run on the frozen lakes during the winter. Brack's boyhood hero was Swedish Formula 1 driver Ronnie Peterson who had several successful years with Lotus.

Brack's ambition was to follow his hero into Formula 1, and he worked his way up the European ladder system to achieve that goal. In 1986, he won his first title: the Swedish Junior Formula Ford Championship. In 1988, Brack graduated to the Swedish Formula 3 Championship and came away with one win and four podium finishes. The following year, Brack ran the British and Swedish Formula 3 championship and proved he was coming of age by winning three races. In 1990, he moved on to the Formula Opel Lotus team in Europe, but the team struggled and they only came up with one podium finish.

Brack decided he would not race with equipment that wasn't capable of winning. It didn't matter whether it was a national series that didn't have the same profile as an international series, Brack was going to compete where he could win. Moving back to Sweden in 1992, he secured adequate financial backing and won the Renault Clio Scandinavian Championship with nine victories and a second-place finish. For 1993, Brack raced in Europe and the United States. He won two of four Renault Clio Eurocup races and won the U.S. Xerex Barber Saab series with six victories. That dominating performance got him recognized by the Formula 1 community. He tested a Williams Renault Formula 1 car, a car Alain Prost used to win the World Championship.

1999 INDY 500 PERFORMANCE PROFILE

Starting Position:	8
Qualifying Average:	222.659 mph
Qualifying Speed Rank:	8
Best Practice Speed:	224.411 mph (5/19)
Total Practice Laps:	293
Number of Practice Days:	10
Finishing Position:	1
Laps Completed:	200
Highest Position 1999 Race:	1
Fastest Race Lap:	6 (215.043 mph)
1999 Prize Money:	$1,465,190
Indy 500 Career Earnings:	$1,978,190
Career Indy 500 Starts:	3
Career Best Finish:	1st 1999

The test was conducted in the rain at Paul Ricard circuit in France. Brack's quick lap times and smooth car control won him more kudos. And more importantly, it attracted sponsors to fund a full-season of racing in Formula 3000.

Moving up to the stepping stone series to Formula 1 was a big break for Brack. He signed with the Madgwick International Formula 3000 team and his rookie effort produced an 11th-place finish. He returned with Madgwick the following year and scored one victory and three pole positions, which was good enough for third in the series. The 1996 season was bitter and sweet. He moved to Super-Nova Racing and dominated in true style, capturing three victories, two seconds, and two thirds. In the final race of the season at Hockenheim, Germany, Brack made a controversial pass on championship rival Jorg Muller and went on to win the race and the championship. However, the FIA, the series governing body, deemed the pass overly aggressive and stripped Brack of the title and awarded it to Muller. During that year, he tested an Arrows Formula 1 car and looked to graduate to F1. But Arrows didn't have the financial resources and the technical infrastructure to run a winning campaign, so Brack headed to the United States for employment.

Galles Racing recognized Brack's talent and offered Brack a ride to replace the injured Davy Jones. In his debut race at the Phoenix 200, he led 24 laps before hitting the wall on Lap 146, finishing 11th. The remainder of the 1997 season proved to be a learning year for Brack. However, he produced some respectable results by finishing fifth at Charlotte and New Hampshire International Raceway.

A meeting with A.J. Foyt in Las Vegas was another pivotal moment in Brack's career. He signed with AJ Foyt PowerTeam for the 1998 season and all the ingredients for success started to come together. Under the guidance of one of racing's living legends, Brack's competitiveness took a giant leap forward. In only his second

Indy 500, Brack qualified third and led the race when a fuel miscalculation cost him two laps. It knocked him out of contention, but he eventually finished sixth.

By mid-season Brack and the team started to gel, and they learned from many of the costly mistakes. He finished third in the True Value 500 at Texas Motor Speedway. At Charlotte, Brack dominated the race but made a critical error and missed his pit box. He had to complete another lap and pit again. The mistake moved him to the back of the lead lap with 20 laps to go and 10 cars ahead of him. He passed them all and won the race. At the next race at Pikes Peak, Brack was the fastest as well as the most economical on fuel. A deft fuel management strategy engineered by Foyt in the pits allowed him to take the win. In the fourth turn of the final lap, the car ran out of fuel. The crowd came to their feet and cheered as Brack triumphantly coasted over the finish line to claim a thrilling win. The next race at Atlanta, Brack lost a lap at mid-race distance, but smooth, quick driving allowed him to get that back and charge to the win.

Brack had won three consecutive races in dramatically different fashions. In the process, he had shown his versatility, patience, speed, and ultimate talent. With the championship points lead firmly in the AJ Foyt PowerTeam's grasp, Kenny Brack forged ahead with the goal of winning the championship. In the Lone Star 500 at Texas Motor Speedway, the penultimate race of the season, an extra pit stop for a cut tire sacrificed victory but collected vital points with a fifth finishing position. At the season finale held at Las Vegas Motor Speedway, Brack and the team battled with mechanical maladies. The No. 14 machine never ran strong that day, but he soldiered on to finished 10th and won the championship.

As soon as the final race of the 1998 season ended, Brack set his sights on winning the 1999 Indianapolis 500. And all his preparations paid off.

JEFF WARD

DALLARA/OLDSMOBILE AURORA/GOODYEAR

Former motocross champion Jeff Ward showed he can go fast on four wheels. In the 1997 Indy 500 race, the rookie led from Lap 137 until Lap 192 but was outpaced by Scott Goodyear and Arie Luyendyk in the last few laps. Ward took a fine third place. For the 1999 edition of the Indy 500, Ward came to the Speedway with a new team, Pagan Racing, and put in another impressive performance, finishing second.

Early in the week, Ward was steadily among the top 10 in practice, but as Pole Day approached, he wasn't in the hunt. He made the 27th qualifying attempt on Pole Day and registered a four-lap run of 221.363 miles an hour. "Everything went pretty well, exactly as we expected it to be," Ward said. "The car was consistent. I was flat out. I feel frustrated to be down on horsepower. I wish it was a little quicker. We know we've got a good race car. I can do the same with full tanks."

He saved the best for Race Day. After starting 14th, he moved to 6th by the end of the first lap. Ward hovered in the second half of the top 10, then moved to the lead on Lap 151. He stayed in the top three, battling Robby Gordon and Kenny Brack through the remainder of the race before finishing second, 6.562 seconds behind Brack. "I would rather be where Kenny is right now," Ward said. "I was strong all day. The car went loose. We went one lap down but got that back. It was exciting for me. I wanted to win this one and once I got loose, I couldn't get around [Brack]."

1999 INDY 500 PERFORMANCE PROFILE

Starting Position:	14
Qualifying Average:	221.363 mph
Qualifying Speed Rank:	14
Best Practice Speed:	223.164 mph (5/20)
Total Practice Laps:	223
Number of Practice Days:	10
Finishing Position:	2
Laps Completed:	200
Highest Position 1999 Race:	1
Fastest Race Lap:	192 (214.041 mph)
1999 Prize Money:	$583,150
Indy 500 Career Earnings:	$1,239,450
Career Indy 500 Starts:	3
Career Best Finish:	2nd 1999

#11 AJ Foyt Racing
Entrant: AJ Foyt Enterprises Crew Chief: Craig Baranouski

BILLY BOAT

DALLARA/OLDSMOBILE AURORA/GOODYEAR

Billy Boat, the polesitter for the 1998 Indy 500, had a tremendously frustrating experience during practice and qualifying for the 1999 race. On Day 2, he hit the wall in Turn 1. On Day 3, he hit the Turn 3 barrier. On Pole Day morning, he posted a lap at 223.059 miles per hour for fifth fastest in morning practice. But on his warmup lap while preparing to make the ninth qualifying attempt of the day, he hit the Turn 2 wall in his backup machine, setting back his hopes. Later, with the car repaired, he returned to post the day's 42nd attempt and qualified at 223.469 miles per hour to take the outside spot on the front row.

"I knew we had the speed," Boat said. "The start of the run, the car was a little bit loose, so I was trying to stay on top of the car. [During] Laps 2 and 3, the car was perfect. Right there at the end, we had sort of a push. It takes a little bit to get back, but the guys did a great job of putting the car back together this morning. This is a tough place. I haven't appreciated this place more than I do now. I don't think you can appreciate this place until you struggle."

On Race Day, Boat stayed in third behind Arie Luyendyk and Greg Ray at the start, dropped back to the end of the top 10, then surged back to finish third on the lead lap, 24.826 seconds behind his winning teammate, Kenny Brack. "Overall, it's obviously a great day for AJ Foyt Racing," Boat said. "First and third. We just never really had the race car to run up front. Kenny Brack drove a tremendous race and I'm very happy for him."

1999 INDY 500 PERFORMANCE PROFILE

Starting Position:	3
Qualifying Average:	223.469 mph
Qualifying Speed Rank:	3
Best Practice Speed:	223.847 mph (5/21)
Total Practice Laps:	278
Number of Practice Days:	9
Finishing Position:	3
Laps Completed:	200
Highest Position 1999 Race:	3
Fastest Race Lap:	5 (214.163 mph)
1999 Prize Money:	$435,200
Indy 500 Career Earnings:	$1,069,100
Career Indy 500 Starts:	3
Career Best Finish:	3rd 1999

#32 Glidden/Menards
Entrant: Team Menard, Inc. Crew Chief: Dave Forbes

ROBBY GORDON

DALLARA/OLDSMOBILE AURORA/FIRESTONE

Robby Gordon was chasing a childhood dream—an Indy 500 victory. In the waning stages of the race, Gordon and Team Menard gambled on fuel strategy. When the yellow flag was brought out on Lap 169, Gordon stayed out on the track to maintain his position on the track rather than pit for fuel. He stayed with the front runners and took the lead from reigning series champ Kenny Brack on Lap 171. Eventually, he built up a lead of 4.064 seconds with seven laps remaining. But on Lap 199, disaster struck. His car sputtered out of fuel. He relinquished the lead and victory over to Brack and settled for fourth place.

"We should have come in [earlier] and gotten a splash of fuel," Gordon said. "The car said we had two gallons and all we needed was one. We knew what it takes to win and we let it slip away. It's very unfortunate. We were one lap away from winning the Indy 500. We stayed on the same pace as the leaders, kept working on our car, then we got lapped. We got the lap back. I thought all the stars were aligned."

After a two-year absence, Gordon started his fifth Indy 500 after an extensive pre-May testing program at the Speedway. He didn't reach the top 10 in practice on any day leading up to time trials and waved off his first attempt, the 21st of the day. By late in the day, he had not returned, but Team Menard pushed the No. 2T originally assigned as Greg Ray's backup in line for him, running as No. 32. He responded with a four-lap average of 223.066 miles per hour, good for the fourth starting spot.

"We lost a motor this morning," Gordon said. "It put us behind the eight-ball pretty severely. We're very fortunate to be associated with Team Menard and John Menard. Greg Ray obviously did a good job in setting up the car and I could get in and just flat-foot it. I think I did a total of seven flying laps in that car and that includes qualifying."

1999 INDY 500 PERFORMANCE PROFILE

Starting Position:	4
Qualifying Average:	223.066 mph
Qualifying Speed Rank:	4
Best Practice Speed:	222.794 mph (5/21)
Total Practice Laps:	178
Number of Practice Days:	6
Finishing Position:	4
Laps Completed:	200
Highest Position 1999 Race:	1
Fastest Race Lap:	72 (215.043 mph)
1999 Prize Money:	$253,270
Indy 500 Career Earnings:	$1,023,703
Career Indy 500 Starts:	5
Career Best Finish:	4th 1999

#55 Energizer Advanced Formula
Entrant: Conti Racing Crew Chief: Steve Fried

ROBBY McGEHEE

DALLARA/OLDSMOBILE AURORA/FIRESTONE

Robby McGehee entered the 1999 Indy 500 as a virtual unknown, but emerged from the race with Rookie of the Year honors and recognition as a genuine talent. After the first day of practice, he was on a high from the experience. "I consider it a great first day," he said. "I love being here. This is such an awesome place to race. But now we've got to go to work."

McGehee cracked into the top 10 on Day 5 with a lap at 224.025 miles an hour. On Pole Day, he became the 23rd qualifier on the 35th attempt with a four-lap average of 220.139. "It feels pretty good but I'm not too happy," McGehee said. "It wasn't as good as we wanted it to be. The crew decided we should go out and I did. The car was a little loose in [Turns] 1 and 2 because the track is a little greasy. This place kind of confuses me. It's pretty tough. You always learn something new here. The car actually felt good all the way around, but I expected a better speed."

On Race Day, McGehee started 27th, but a pit-road accident on Lap 12 seriously injured his crew chief, Steve Fried, who was changing his right front tire. Fried was to recover after a hospital stay, but the accident left McGehee without his team leader.

After the accident, McGehee went on the move. By Lap 36, he had moved up 24 spots to 3rd. He remained in the top eight the rest of the way and finished 5th (the highest finishing rookie). "The only thing that could be better would be winning the race," McGehee said. "It's a dream come true. We've worked so hard to get here. Overall, the result was fantastic." Fried's injury was on his mind. "It made it harder for me to drive," he said. But he added that the best news he received during his race to the front was that Fried was awake in the hospital and had given a thumbs-up.

1999 INDY 500 PERFORMANCE PROFILE

Starting Position:	27
Qualifying Average:	220.139 mph
Qualifying Speed Rank:	29
Best Practice Speed:	224.025 mph (5/19)
Total Practice Laps:	286
Number of Practice Days:	8
Finishing Position:	5
Laps Completed:	199
Highest Position 1999 Race:	3
Fastest Race Lap:	74 (212.857 mph)
1999 Prize Money:	$247,750
Indy 500 Career Earnings:	$247,750
Career Indy 500 Starts:	1
Career Best Finish:	5th 1999

#84 AJ Foyt Racing
Entrant: AJ Foyt Enterprises Crew Chief: Rod Behlke

ROBBIE BUHL

DALLARA/OLDSMOBILE AURORA/FIRESTONE

Robbie Buhl had a month of May that was more adventurous than he would've liked. He came to the Speedway with a car prepared by Sinden Racing Service, a veteran team, but didn't get on the track until Day 4. He was in the hunt on Day 6 with a lap at 223.253 miles per hour. When qualifying came, the real adventure started.

On a warmup lap, he hit the Turn 1 wall, damaging his primary machine. At 12:10 P.M. the next day, he took the green for an attempt, but pulled to the pits with his backup car smoking and rain threatening. Shortly after that, it was reported that the team, headed by four-time 500 winner A.J. Foyt, was putting together a car for Buhl to make a run, just as the Sinden crew started to change engines.

At 1:58 P.M., with rain starting to fall in light sprinkles, Buhl qualified the Foyt car at a four-lap average of 220.115. At 2:03 P.M., Buhl finished the run and rain closed the track for the day. It put him in the 32nd starting spot. "We kind of scattered around to see what other people had," Buhl said. "Somebody went to A.J., so I went to see him and it was a pretty casual conversation. A.J. was kind enough to say, 'Hey, I've got two cars. See which one works best for you.' Our two teams pulled together and made a couple calls that were right. I think we timed it just right."

On Race Day, Buhl steadily drove to as high as fifth place on Lap 198 and wound up sixth, giving the Foyt team a sixth-place finish. "We didn't quite have the balance we needed," Buhl said. "But other than that, the car really didn't miss a beat. When you start in the back and finish sixth, it's not too bad."

1999 INDY 500 PERFORMANCE PROFILE

Starting Position:	32
Qualifying Average:	220.115 mph
Qualifying Speed Rank:	30
Best Practice Speed:	223.253 mph (5/20)
Total Practice Laps:	148
Number of Practice Days:	6
Finishing Position:	6
Laps Completed:	199
Highest Position 1999 Race:	5
Fastest Race Lap:	139 (211.015 mph)
1999 Prize Money:	$257,500
Indy 500 Career Earnings:	$910,403
Career Indy 500 Starts:	4
Career Best Finish:	6th 1999

#91 Delta Faucet/Coors Light/Tae-Bo/Hemelgarn Racing
Entrant: Hemelgarn Racing, Inc. Crew Chief: Dennis LaCava

BUDDY LAZIER

DALLARA/OLDSMOBILE AURORA/GOODYEAR

Buddy Lazier was looking to extend his streak of having the best Indy 500 record over the previous three years—a win in 1996, a fourth place in 1997, and a second in 1998. His success at Indianapolis is no mystery. He is one of the most experienced racers in the Indy 500 field, having first run at Indy in 1989. However, Lazier has never been known for spectacular qualifying efforts. Instead, he has consistently been a threat on race day.

Under the Hemelgarn Racing banner, Lazier took his Dallara/Aurora/Goodyear machine as high as fifth on the speed chart on Day 6 of practice leading up to Pole Day. He then made the ninth qualification attempt of the day and recorded a four-lap run of 220.721 mph, putting him 22nd on the grid—his lowest starting position of the four-year period. "It was wide open," Lazier said. "I'm disappointed for my guys because they've been working so hard. I ran it as hard as it would go. It's a strange day. You'd think it would be cool and fast but it wasn't. I'm baffled. It (the weather) is changing by the minute. The air is real thick."

In the race, Lazier, who had been so competitive in previous 500s, struggled to find the pace he needed to run with the leaders. However, he gained four spots on the first lap. He lost a lap by taking an early pit stop, and by the 30th lap he was running in 28th place. With solid, consistent driving, he methodically picked his way through the field and eventually got back on the lead lap. After the halfway point, he started gaining spots.

He was holding down ninth position on Lap 150 and moved up to seventh, the position he held for the final 26 laps. "I'm a little tired. A little disappointed, too," Lazier said. "We were basically fighting it all day. That first yellow, I hit a piece of debris and it was kind of an omen for the day. My guys gave me great pit stops. We'll have to come back and get 'em next time."

But the seventh place finish continued his streak and the 1996 champion has the best Indy 500 record over the past four seasons.

1999 INDY 500 PERFORMANCE PROFILE

Starting Position:	22
Qualifying Average:	220.721 mph
Qualifying Speed Rank:	23
Best Practice Speed:	224.361 mph (5/20)
Total Practice Laps:	340
Number of Practice Days:	10
Finishing Position:	7
Laps Completed:	198
Highest Position 1999 Race:	7
Fastest Race Lap:	176 (213.467 mph)
1999 Prize Money:	$285,100
Indy 500 Career Earnings:	$2,888,280
Career Indy 500 Starts:	7
Career Best Finish:	1st 1996

#81 PetroMoly/Team Pelfrey
Entrant: Team Pelfrey Crew Chief: John King

ROBBY
UNSER

DALLARA/OLDSMOBILE AURORA/FIRESTONE

Last year, Robby Unser made his Indy Racing League debut with Team Cheever at the Indy 500. Team boss Eddie Cheever Jr., drove a fantastic race and took the victory while Unser held more than his own by taking fifth. Only one other rookie bettered him; Steve Knapp finishing in third position. Unser's sterling performance in the Indy 500 wasn't the only high note of the season. He drove to a strong second place in the Lone Star 500 at Texas Motor Speedway, which helped him take the series Rookie-of-the-Year title. Like many members of his fast family, Robby made a name for himself at the Pikes Peak hillclimb by winning multiple championships in various classes before coming to Indy.

With a switch from Team Cheever to Team Pelfrey, Robby Unser looked at bettering last year's finish and adding another Unser name to the Borg-Warner trophy. At the wheel of Dallara/Aurora/Firestone machine, the son of three-time winner Bobby Unser cracked into the top-10 on Day 5 with a lap at 224.042 miles-per-hour, and was second on Day 6 at 225.079 miles-per-hour. He made the 34th attempt of qualifying and checked in at 221.304 miles-per-hour, good for the 17th starting spot. "Speeds were down on the straightaway, but it was a consistent run and we're there," Unser said. "These last four laps were probably the hardest of the year. Indianapolis is a special place and the fans are real special."

On Race Day, he drove a steady and consistent race. On the first lap, he charged ahead four positions and continued to work his way forward. By Lap 70, he was running in 21st place. Unser kept passing cars ahead of him and found himself in eighth place at the finish. This gives the young hot shoe two top-10s in the last two years at Indy 500. "The car was great on the track," Unser said. "(We had) hard times in the pits where we stalled the car a couple of times. The first time was my fault. The second time, it was the clutch. We just didn't get her through the pits well."

1999 INDY 500 PERFORMANCE PROFILE

Starting Position:	17
Qualifying Average:	221.304 mph
Qualifying Speed Rank:	17
Best Practice Speed:	225.079 mph (5/20)
Total Practice Laps:	290
Number of Practice Days:	9
Finishing Position:	8
Laps Completed:	197
Highest Position 1999 Race:	8
Fastest Race Lap:	19 (212.319 mph)
1999 Prize Money:	$195,500
Indy 500 Career Earnings:	$404,900
Career Indy 500 Starts:	2
Career Best Finish:	5th 1998

#22 The Home Depot
Entrant: Tri Star Motorsports, Inc. Crew Chief: Rob Grossman

TONY STEWART

DALLARA/OLDSMOBILE AURORA/GOODYEAR

Tony Stewart did double duty on Sunday May 30th: he ran both the Indianapolis 500 and the Coca-Cola 600 Winston Cup race at Charlotte. It was also his first year as a car owner at Indy, fielding entries for himself and Dr. Jack Miller.

The 1,100 miles of racing required 5,208 nautical miles of air travel on 14 trips between Indianapolis and Charlotte during the month of May. Three planes, two helicopters, eight golf carts, four cars, and a Navigator Transporter, plus 51 logistics people were all needed to complete the complicated schedule.

At Indy, Stewart hit the top rung on the speed chart on Day 5 with a lap at 226.683 miles per hour. However, the next day, he hit the wall in Turns 3 and 4, setting back his program. For qualifying—with a trip to Charlotte immediately to follow—he drew the second spot in line and qualified at 220.653. "We wanted to go quicker, obviously," Stewart said on the way to the airport. "But we were flat out the whole way around. That's all the car we had today. The air is much thicker today. We had such a nice week as far as temperature and humidity were concerned. We didn't get a chance to run in any conditions like today."

On Race Day, he started 24th, but by Lap 36 he was 2nd, his best position of the day. He stayed in the top 10 throughout before finishing 9th, four laps down. "I stuck to my game plan," Stewart said. "I didn't really worry about getting to the front in a hurry, but we struggled out there today. We never did any long runs and I think that cost us a bit. We didn't really know what was going to happen."

From there, he went to Charlotte and finished fourth. "I don't think it's anything you're going to see me do in the next year or two," Stewart reflected, "because the last 25 laps [at Charlotte] were really draining. The experience? It was more than I hoped it would be. The support of the fans made it all worthwhile. If I ever do it again, it would be for the fans."

1999 INDY 500 PERFORMANCE PROFILE

Starting Position:	24
Qualifying Average:	220.653 mph
Qualifying Speed Rank:	24
Best Practice Speed:	226.683 mph (5/19)
Total Practice Laps:	124
Number of Practice Days:	8
Finishing Position:	9
Laps Completed:	196
Highest Position 1999 Race:	2
Fastest Race Lap:	76 (213.457 mph)
1999 Prize Money:	$186,670
Indy 500 Career Earnings:	$974,023
Career Indy 500 Starts:	4
Career Best Finish:	5th 1997

#54 Mini Juke/Beck Motorsports
Entrant: Beck Motorsports Crew Chief: Tom Bose

HIDESHI MATSUDA

DALLARA/OLDSMOBILE AURORA/FIRESTONE

Hideshi Matsuda continued his Indy 500 career of posting impressive qualifying efforts with minimal practice. In 1995, he qualified 7th with a year old car, but a conservative approach only netted a 15th place finish. However, Matsuda showed that he had the speed to run up near the front and the potential for a much stronger finish was evident. In the following year's race, he qualified a 1994 Lola/Cosworth/Firestone machine in 30th position. This time the race day setup and strategy was right. He picked his way through the pack and finished the day in eighth position.

For the 1999 edition of the 500, he got in little practice during the week and reached 220.881 miles per hour the day before qualifying began. Then, as the sixth driver to attempt qualification for the month, he reeled off a four-lap average of 222.065 miles per hour in his Dallara/Aurora/Firestone machine. He was more than a mile-per-hour faster than he'd practiced—good for the 10th starting spot.

His longtime union with Greg Beck of Beck Motorsports had worked its magic again. "I'm very happy," Matsuda said. "My crew does a very good job every time. I hope to win. This is my dream, to win. I've always been thinking about this race since five years ago. It's a very special day. Now I can call my wife in Japan. I want to share my feelings with everybody."

In the race, his car was one of six which turned a lap in less than 42 seconds, his best being a 41.922 second, 214.684 mph effort on Lap 74. He quickly moved up six positions to 4th place by Lap 32, but he ran into problems that dropped him down to 29th place. Matsuda patiently worked his way back up the order, picking up a position or two about every 10 laps. He finished where he started, in 10th, four laps down.

1999 INDY 500 PERFORMANCE PROFILE

Starting Position:	10
Qualifying Average:	222.065 mph
Qualifying Speed Rank:	10
Best Practice Speed:	221.185 mph (5/27)
Total Practice Laps:	200
Number of Practice Days:	6
Finishing Position:	10
Laps Completed:	196
Highest Position 1999 Race:	4
Fastest Race Lap:	74 (214.684 mph)
1999 Prize Money:	$186,000
Indy 500 Career Earnings:	$770,818
Career Indy 500 Starts:	4
Career Best Finish:	8th 1996

#9 Galles Racing Spinal Conquest
Entrant: Galles Racing Crew Chief: Darren Russell

DAVEY
HAMILTON

DALLARA/OLDSMOBILE AURORA/GOODYEAR

Davey Hamilton has been a model of consistency in the IRL since its inception. Hamilton finished in the top 10 in all the IRL races last year and finished the season in the runnerup position in points. Hamilton and his Galles Racing crew were looking to add more speed to the consistency they had achieved. Hamilton came to Indy with top-six finishes in the two previous 500s, and this year he was looking for a win.

Hamilton had a fastest lap in practice of 222.222 miles per hour on Day 6, the first day he practiced in his backup machine. He then became the 11th qualifier on Pole Day with a four-lap run of 221.866 in the backup, only his third day in the car. "It was a consistent run all the way around," Hamilton said. "It was difficult because we didn't test here. We're happy with the speed. It's been trouble-free, so to speak."

The run put him in the 11th starting spot. Hamilton steadily worked his way forward during race day moving from 11th to 5th by Lap 64. He hovered around the top 10 through much of the route before finishing 11th, four laps off the pace.

Although Hamilton has been in the hunt for numerous IRL race victories, he has yet to score a race win. The Galles crew and Hamilton were looking to improve upon last year's fourth-place finish, but the team encountered unexpected setup problems during their run. "We thought we had a great race car, but we missed a few things," said Hamilton. "Our balance just wasn't there but we gave it all we had."

1999 INDY 500 PERFORMANCE PROFILE

Starting Position:	11
Qualifying Average:	221.866 mph
Qualifying Speed Rank:	11
Best Practice Speed:	222.222 mph (5/20)
Total Practice Laps:	352
Number of Practice Days:	10
Finishing Position:	11
Laps Completed:	196
Highest Position 1999 Race:	5
Fastest Race Lap:	23 (211.705 mph)
1999 Prize Money:	$220,500
Indy 500 Career Earnings:	$970,153
Career Indy 500 Starts:	4
Career Best Finish:	4th 1998

#3 Brant Racing R&S MKV
Entrant: Brant Racing   Crew Chief: Tony Kenter

RAUL BOESEL

RILEY & SCOTT/OLDSMOBILE AURORA/GOODYEAR

Raul Boesel joined a new team, Brant Racing, to bid for his 11th start in the Indianapolis 500. During the 1994 Indy 500, Boesel showed phenomenal speed, carving his way to the front after suffering several setbacks. With a new team behind him, Boesel looked to recapture that same form for this year's race.

Boesel reached a top practice speed of 223.253 miles per hour on Day 6 of practice, barely missing the top 10 on the speed chart. When his qualifying turn came on Pole Day, he waved off after two laps in the 217 bracket. The next morning, prior to final time trials, he was third fastest in practice with a lap at 222.662 miles per hour. He was the first qualifier of the second day at 220.101. Although Boesel had posted some fast times in practice, his qualifying speed was much slower and he was on the bubble and in danger of losing his position in the field.

"I'm relieved in one way, but I'm still worried," Boesel said. "Yesterday I prayed the weather would hold up and we'd have a chance to qualify. Today my praying has changed, now that I got in, I hope it rains soon! Your objective is different when you're trying to get into the field than when you're making a run for the pole."

After starting 33rd, he moved all the way to 7th by Lap 41, but technical problems and a few tactical miscues stunted the fine run. He eventually slipped back to finish 12th, five laps down. "I just ran all day, trying to stay out of trouble," Boesel said. "In the beginning, we made a good pit stop, which got us to the front. But then we left a set of tires on the car too long so I had to back off. We ended up chasing [a] loose condition the whole race. But we stayed out of trouble, and given everything else, I'm happy we finished where we did."

1999 INDY 500 PERFORMANCE PROFILE

Starting Position:	33
Qualifying Average:	220.101 mph
Qualifying Speed Rank:	31
Best Practice Speed:	223.253 mph (5/20)
Total Practice Laps:	285
Number of Practice Days:	10
Finishing Position:	12
Laps Completed:	195
Highest Position 1999 Race:	7
Fastest Race Lap:	34 (206.588 mph)
1999 Prize Money:	$248,600
Indy 500 Career Earnings:	$2,060,634
Career Indy 500 Starts:	11
Career Best Finish:	3rd 1989

JOHN HOLLANSWORTH JR.

DALLARA/OLDSMOBILE AURORA/FIRESTONE

The Indianapolis Motor Speedway's 2.5-mile oval didn't prove to be too excessively daunting for John Hollansworth Jr. He was ninth fastest on the first day of practice and second fastest to Greg Ray on Day 3. On Pole Day morning, he was fourth fastest of his group at 221.658 miles per hour. When his turn came in qualifying, he increased his speed on each of his four laps to register a run of 221.698. "It was intense with a capital 'I', and I was relieved with a capital 'R' when it was done," Hollansworth said. "It seemed a bit surreal. It was a great feeling on the back straight and it was a great feeling to come out of Turn 4 and just have to keep it straight. We're just really excited."

He followed in the footsteps of his father, who drove Indy-type cars but did not make a 500 field. "I think he's on his way to the moon right now," Hollansworth said.

The 221.698-mile-an-hour run put him on the outside of the fourth row in the 12th starting spot. On Lap 31 he advanced to 10th, but dropped to 26th on Lap 60. However, he soldiered his way back to 13th at the end despite being faced with an adverse racing situation. "I'm glad to finish a 500-miler," Hollansworth said. "It's pretty rewarding. We lost every gear but fourth at about the 80-mile point. I got high two times, touched the wall and knocked out my [steering], which made it difficult. I also had two wrecks right in front of me."

1999 INDY 500 PERFORMANCE PROFILE

Starting Position:	12
Qualifying Average:	221.698 mph
Qualifying Speed Rank:	12
Best Practice Speed:	222.783 mph (5/20)
Total Practice Laps:	292
Number of Practice Days:	10
Finishing Position:	13
Laps Completed:	192
Highest Position 1999 Race:	10
Fastest Race Lap:	22 (212.399 mph)
1999 Prize Money:	$265,400
Indy 500 Career Earnings:	$265,400
Career Indy 500 Starts:	1
Career Best Finish:	13th 1999

TYCE CARLSON

DALLARA/OLDSMOBILE AURORA/FIRESTONE

Tyce Carlson came to the Indianapolis Motor Speedway looking for his second Indy 500 start teamed with Blueprint-Immke Racing. Although he wasn't high on the charts during the week, he recorded a lap at 223.137 miles per hour on the day before qualifications to claim the 10th-fastest speed of the day. Then, in the Pole Day morning practice, he reeled off a lap at 224.933, second-fastest of the session behind Arie Luyendyk.

Carlson went out for the 20th qualification attempt of Pole Day and put together a four-lap run of 221.322 as the track slowed, good for the 15th starting spot. "I'm not as happy as I would be if I were on the front row," he said. "But we're starting the race and that's all that matters. We're in the Indy 500."

On Race Day, Carlson maintained his position through the first 30 laps before pitting. On Lap 118, Luyendyk, while leading, tried overtaking him in Turn 3. Luyendyk was forced down to the bottom of the track, backed off the throttle, lost traction, and spun into the wall. Carlson continued to the finish to wind up 14th. "We started off having trouble with both the dash and my radio," Carlson said. "I could only hear occasionally. The car changed at every pit stop and we ran out of gas as I was getting ready to pit mid-race. We finally got the right setup toward the end."

Carlson commented on the incident with Luyendyk, "I really don't know what happened [with Luyendyk]. I saw him on the inside and tried to stay as high as possible. I even went off throttle. There was no contact. Arie's a great guy and I never would've gotten in his way."

1999 INDY 500 PERFORMANCE PROFILE

Starting Position:	15
Qualifying Average:	221.322 mph
Qualifying Speed Rank:	15
Best Practice Speed:	224.933 mph (5/22)
Total Practice Laps:	117
Number of Practice Days:	8
Finishing Position:	14
Laps Completed:	190
Highest Position 1999 Race:	13
Fastest Race Lap:	43 (213.447 mph)
1999 Prize Money:	$247,000
Indy 500 Career Earnings:	$420,250
Career Indy 500 Starts:	2
Career Best Finish:	14th 1999

15

#96 Purity Farms/Cobb Racing/G Force/Infiniti/Firestone
Entrant: Cobb Racing Crew Chief: Dave Meehan

JERET SCHROEDER

G FORCE/INFINITI INDY/FIRESTONE

Jeret Schroeder has shown considerable potential in other series by winning the Formula Ford national championship in 1995 with four wins and 10 events. He entered the month of May bidding to become the first New Jersey native to make a 500 field since Steve Krisiloff in 1983. On the first day of practice in a Cobb Racing Infiniti-powered G Force, he posted a lap at 218.648. "I'm having as much fun with the fans as I am out on the track," he said. "These fans are incredible. We have a full week ahead of us to get the car even better."

On Pole Day, he waved off a run after three laps at a 219-plus average. He went out later, returned to the pits for a battery change, and registered a run at 220.747 mph. It was a very respectable qualifying effort for a rookie using an Infiniti engine. "I'm really ecstatic that I did make it," Schroeder said. "We misjudged the wind (on the first run). Later, we made a small wing change and picked another gear and we made it. The headwind down the back straightaway slowed us down quite a bit."

On Race Day, Schroeder collided with Jimmy Kite in the pits on Lap 12. By Lap 154, he was in fourth place and was running seventh at Lap 170. But engine failure sidelined him after 175 laps and he finished 15th. Even though he finished 15th, he piloted the highest finishing Infiniti powered car in the field. Teammate Roberto Guerrero's car required a 36-lap pitstop to fix a problem and he eventually finished 25th. Eddie Cheever Jr., briefly led the race before his engine expired and he finished 18th. "I was just buying time, picking off cars one at a time," Schroeder said. "I was just trying to stay out of trouble."

1999 INDY 500 PERFORMANCE PROFILE

Starting Position:	21
Qualifying Average:	220.747 mph
Qualifying Speed Rank:	22
Best Practice Speed:	221.043 mph (5/21)
Total Practice Laps:	206
Number of Practice Days:	9
Finishing Position:	15
Laps Completed:	175
Highest Position 1999 Race:	4
Fastest Race Lap:	60 (213.548 mph)
1999 Prize Money:	$176,250
Indy 500 Career Earnings:	$176,250
Career Indy 500 Starts:	1
Career Best Finish:	15th 1999

MARK DISMORE

DALLARA/OLDSMOBILE AURORA/GOODYEAR

Mark Dismore sneaked up on competitors bidding for starting spots in the Indianapolis 500. He didn't crack the top 10 in practice on any day leading up to time trials. With qualifying looming, he turned a lap at 222.651 miles per hour in his backup Kelley Racing entry on Pole Day morning, good for fourth in his group. Suddenly he became a factor.

Dismore was back in the qualifying line and made the 23rd attempt of the day with Arie Luyendyk already leading the way. Dismore recorded a four-lap run of 222.963, good for the front row at the time. Greg Ray, Billy Boat, and Robby Gordon followed, sending him back to fifth. "Starting in the front three rows, I'll be happy," Dismore said after the run. "Just to be ahead of the others, that's fantastic. I never had any expectations of doing 225 [miles per hour]. I thought the car could do 223. I have the right horse under me. We just have to put our heads together now. This place requires patience."

In the race, he hung with the leaders and moved to fourth on Lap 28. On his sixth lap, he turned a lap at 215.471, the third fastest lap in the field. In contention for the win, he entered the pits in sixth place on the lead lap, but collided with the exiting Greg Ray, damaging the nose cone. He continued after repairs, but hit the Turn 2 wall on Lap 169, ending his day. "I was trying to win the race and trying to get around [Billy] Boat," Dismore said. "I got in his air and it just pushed up into the wall."

1999 INDY 500 PERFORMANCE PROFILE

Starting Position:	5
Qualifying Average:	222.963 mph
Qualifying Speed Rank:	5
Best Practice Speed:	222.651 mph (5/22)
Total Practice Laps:	343
Number of Practice Days:	9
Finishing Position:	16
Laps Completed:	168
Highest Position 1999 Race:	4
Fastest Race Lap:	6 (215.471 mph)
1999 Prize Money:	$235,300
Indy 500 Career Earnings:	$764,853
Career Indy 500 Starts:	4
Career Best Finish:	16th 1999

#19 Metro Racing Systems/NCLD
Entrant: Metro Racing Systems, Inc. Crew Chief: John West

STAN
WATTLES

DALLARA/OLDSMOBILE AURORA/GOODYEAR

Stan Wattles came to the Indianapolis Motor Speedway for the second time as a driver/owner, this time with a Dallara chassis to go along with his all-American Riley & Scott effort. As the month developed, he ran a lap of 221.381 miles per hour with the Dallara on Day 6, his best of practice. When he rolled out to make Pole Day's 19th qualifying attempt he posted a four-lap average of 220.833 in the Dallara, which was good for the 20th starting spot.

"This has been an up-and-down week," Wattles said. "We were prepared for today, and actually, we did okay. The track conditions were good but it was pretty windy and the air was a little dense, so we made a change before I went out. The first lap was awesome, then I had a little understeer in [Turn] 2. The car got a little worse with each lap because of the understeer but I feel very good about the run."

On Race Day, Wattles dropped back early but soldiered to 17th place despite problems. "That was an extremely difficult run," Wattles said. "We had very little warm-weather running this month, which caused us to be a little off on our setup. The first 50 laps were so frustrating, but the guys took the car back to the garage and made some adjustments that allowed me to get back into the hunt."

1999 INDY 500 PERFORMANCE PROFILE

Starting Position:	20
Qualifying Average:	220.833 mph
Qualifying Speed Rank:	21
Best Practice Speed:	222.381 mph (5/20)
Total Practice Laps:	155
Number of Practice Days:	9
Finishing Position:	17
Laps Completed:	147
Highest Position 1999 Race:	17
Fastest Race Lap:	30 (201.604 mph)
1999 Prize Money:	$158,000
Indy 500 Career Earnings:	$296,550
Career Indy 500 Starts:	2
Career Best Finish:	17th 1999

EDDIE
CHEEVER JR.

DALLARA/INFINITI INDY/GOODYEAR

Eddie Cheever Jr. returned to the Indianapolis Motor Speedway with the honor, challenge, and popularity of the defending champion. He came with a new program in his role of driver/owner, shepherding the fortunes of rookie Wim Eyckmans as a teammate, and taking on the development role of the Infiniti engine. During practice, he hovered in the top 10 on the speed chart early in the week before dropping off.

On Pole Day, Cheever became the first defending winner to be first in line for qualification since Emerson Fittipaldi in 1990, but waved off after three laps at a 221+ average. Later, he waved off after two laps in the same range with his backup car. Then, on the 39th attempt of the day, he took his backup car to the line and registered a 221.315 average for a four-lap run, eventually good for the 16th spot in the starting lineup. "The car was loose," Cheever said. "We're in the show. We've been working hard with the Infiniti and we're getting there. I'm not at all worried about starting in the middle of the pack. We won last year from 17th place. It was a very difficult day. We were like a dog chasing its tail. The smoke came from the engine and I knew we were close to a failure. But it held on."

On Race Day, Cheever moved quickly. He gained five spots on the first lap and was in the top 10 by Lap 4. Despite falling back, he took the lead on Lap 121. At Lap 130, he was second, 3.373 seconds behind leader Kenny Brack. But on Lap 140, he pulled to a stop on the backstretch with an engine problem and was done for the day. "We got a good start," he said. "We got a lap down and then we caught up. The engine started vibrating and that was it. Nobody can touch us in traffic. The Infiniti is definitely capable of winning races."

1999 INDY 500 PERFORMANCE PROFILE

Starting Position:	16
Qualifying Average:	221.315 mph
Qualifying Speed Rank:	16
Best Practice Speed:	224.193 mph (5/20)
Total Practice Laps:	274
Number of Practice Days:	8
Finishing Position:	18
Laps Completed:	139
Highest Position 1999 Race:	1
Fastest Race Lap:	74 (213.853 mph)
1999 Prize Money:	$246,800
Indy 500 Career Earnings:	$3,198,452
Career Indy 500 Starts:	10
Career Best Finish:	1st 1998

#2 Glidden/Menards
Entrant: Team Menard, Inc. Crew Chief: John O'Gara

GREG RAY

DALLARA/OLDSMOBILE AURORA/FIRESTONE

Greg Ray came out of the gate fast in his new Team Menard ride, setting the pace at the top of the speed charts for the first three practice days. On Day 4, he was fourth and fifth in two different cars. When the bar was pushed to 226 miles per hour on Day 5, he was second fastest to Tony Stewart. On Day 6, Ray became the first to reach 227. And he repeated it the following day as qualifications awaited.

As time trial day arrived, Ray had been only third fastest in his morning practice group and others seemed to move into contention with ever-changing conditions. He got his chance as the 29th driver to attempt qualification and he was shooting to beat Arie Luyendyk's run of 225.179 miles per hour for the pole.

Ray's four-lap run of 225.073 miles per hour missed the pole by just .075 of a second, good for the middle spot of the front row for the second straight year. "The sun came out for us," Ray said. "Our first car didn't make tech so we had to pull it off the line. I drove all four laps exactly the same. We were close. My crew chief said on the last lap: 'We need a little more here.' I said: 'That's all there is.' "

During the race, Ray was in the thick of the action from the drop of the green flag, leading four times for 32 laps. He had the fastest lap of the race on the 101st circuit at 218.882 miles per hour. But after leading on Lap 120 and pitting, Ray collided with Mark Dismore, who was entering pit road, damaging the suspension on Ray's machine and sending him to the sidelines. "I have no idea what happened," Ray said. "I was told to go and another car came up and hit me. We hurt the front suspension pretty bad. The car is not in any shape to go back out there and race. The championship is about points and finishing position but the Indianapolis 500 is all about winning. I just want to cry."

1999 INDY 500 PERFORMANCE PROFILE

Starting Position:	2
Qualifying Average:	225.073 mph
Qualifying Speed Rank:	2
Best Practice Speed:	227.192 mph (5/20)
Total Practice Laps:	383
Number of Practice Days:	10
Finishing Position:	21
Laps Completed:	120
Highest Position 1999 Race:	1
Fastest Race Lap:	101 (218.882 mph)
1999 Prize Money:	$204,900
Indy 500 Career Earnings:	$551,550
Career Indy 500 Starts:	3
Career Best Finish:	18th 1998

#5 Sprint PCS/Meijer
Entrant: Treadway Racing LLC Crew Chief: Skip Faul

ARIE LUYENDYK

G FORCE/OLDSMOBILE AURORA/FIRESTONE

Arie Luyendyk made the most of what was announced as "Arie's Final 500." The holder of most Indy 500 speed records, it was hard for Luyendyk to hold a focus with all the autographs to sign and well-wishers to greet. On the first day, 1998 Rookie of the Year Steve Knapp asked Luyendyk to sign his uniform. "At first, I thought he was kidding," Luyendyk said, "but he was serious. This was a first for me. I want to make every run productive. The car is running good but it could be better. I realize it's my last race, but right now I'm just thinking about qualifying."

He came out fast, trailing only Greg Ray the first two days. He hovered in the top three throughout the week and led Pole Day morning practice with a lap at 226.683 miles per hour. As the 14th qualifier, he recorded a four-lap run of 225.179, the fastest qualifying average for a normally-aspirated car at the Speedway. After withstanding a final assault from Greg Ray, Luyendyk had his third 500 pole, joining Johnny Rutherford, Mario Andretti, and Tom Sneva as three-time pole winners.

"Having two laps to get up to speed instead of three, I think that might have caught somebody out," Luyendyk said. "It was really important to get out and get up to speed really, really quickly to bring those pressures and temperatures up. The conditions were good. They were the same as this morning. The wind was going the same direction. The track temps were the same."

In the race, Luyendyk dominated the front of the pack through the first two thirds, leading the first 32 laps and pacing the field a total of four times for 63 circuits. He had the second-fastest lap of the race at 218.224 on Lap 108 while in command. But on Lap 118, he hit the wall in Turn 3 to end his day.

"I had so much fun driving today. It was, like, really cool. I want to thank everybody for what they've done for me. In thinking back, when I got out of the car, the crowd was going nuts. I was trying to take it all in. It's been great throughout the years. I had the best car here today that I've ever had."

1999 INDY 500 PERFORMANCE PROFILE

Starting Position:	1
Qualifying Average:	225.179 mph
Qualifying Speed Rank:	1
Best Practice Speed:	226.683 mph (5/22)
Total Practice Laps:	279
Number of Practice Days:	8
Finishing Position:	22
Laps Completed:	117
Highest Position 1999 Race:	1
Fastest Race Lap:	108 (218.224 mph)
1999 Prize Money:	$382,350
Indy 500 Career Earnings:	$5,589,771
Career Indy 500 Starts:	15
Career Best Finish:	1st 1990, 1997

#52 EGP/Beaulieu of America/Dallara/Oldsmobile/Goodyear
Entrant: Team Cheever Crew Chief: Dane Harte

WIM EYCKMANS

DALLARA/OLDSMOBILE AURORA/GOODYEAR

Wim Eyckmans sat in the grandstand to watch the 1998 Indianapolis 500, but returned in 1999 with his helmet and uniform to team up with Eddie Cheever Jr. and Team Cheever to bid for his first 500 start.

In practice, Eyckmans reached 222.327 miles per hour on Day 5 as he built up to speed. He became the ninth qualifier on Pole Day, posting a four-lap average of 220.092. "It's tough to get in four good laps," Eyckmans said. "Mentally, it's really hard. It's a great feeling to have qualified. Eddie's experience helped me quite a lot. He told me to drive like I always do and do what you have to, to qualify."

As the second qualifying day evolved, Eyckmans was watching the weather. But after Robbie Buhl bumped Mike Groff from the field, leaving Eyckmans on the bubble, rain fell to close qualifications. His qualifying time was only 3.695 seconds slower than Arie Luyendyk's pole time, providing the closest field in Indy 500 history.

On Race Day, after starting 29th, he moved to 13th on Lap 111. But two laps later, a timing chain failed, ending his day. "I think we were having problems with the engine from early on," Eyckmans said after the race. "It seemed as though we lost more power after every pit stop. It's very disappointing. This is a very powerful race, but even tougher when you have problems."

1999 INDY 500 PERFORMANCE PROFILE

Starting Position:	29
Qualifying Average:	220.092 mph
Qualifying Speed Rank:	33
Best Practice Speed:	222.327 mph (5/19)
Total Practice Laps:	313
Number of Practice Days:	10
Finishing Position:	23
Laps Completed:	113
Highest Position 1999 Race:	13
Fastest Race Lap:	108 (208.933 mph)
1999 Prize Money:	$145,250
Indy 500 Career Earnings:	$145,250
Career Indy 500 Starts:	1
Career Best Finish:	23rd 1999

#30 Alfa Laval/Team Losi/Fast Rod/McCormack/Haas CNC
Entrant: McCormack Motorsports Crew Chief: Brad McCanless

JIMMY KITE

G FORCE/OLDSMOBILE AURORA/FIRESTONE

The former dirt track champion has had many ups and downs in the Indy Racing League. Last year's Indy 500 experience was a trying one for the Stockbridge, Georgia, native. He crashed three times during practice and qualifying and started 26th. In the race he made significant progress, clawing his way up the field to an 11th place finish. During his Indy Racing League career, Kite has shown flashes of brilliance as he led the 1997 VisionAire 500 at Charlotte before the car got away from him and he crashed.

Kite got a seat to bid for his second Indy 500 starting berth in a driver shuffle that put him in the McCormack Motorsports ride. He reached a top practice speed of 221.571 miles per hour on Day 6 with his G Force/Aurora/Firestone machine. He became the 21st qualifier on Pole Day with a four-lap average of 220.097 miles per hour that was good enough for the 28th starting position.

He remembered a frustrating month of May in 1998 that was dotted with accidents as he made his way into the field. "The first lap was good," Kite said. "On the second lap, I scared myself a little bit. The wind came in and that freaked me out because that's what happened last year. I can breathe again. I'm tickled to death that this is over. Now I can go up in the stands tomorrow and get me a seat and sit back and watch everybody else go through what I went through last year."

After starting 28th, he was involved in a pit-road collision with Jeret Schroeder which caused his car to stall on Lap 12. Although dropping to the back of the pack, he struggled to find the pace needed to run up front. He ran between 33rd and 28th for much of the day until he began to move up the field. His engine expired on lap 111 and left him in 22nd place when the results were finalized.

1999 INDY 500 PERFORMANCE PROFILE

Starting Position:	28
Qualifying Average:	220.097 mph
Qualifying Speed Rank:	32
Best Practice Speed:	221.571 mph (5/20)
Total Practice Laps:	127
Number of Practice Days:	7
Finishing Position:	24
Laps Completed:	111
Highest Position 1999 Race:	22
Fastest Race Lap:	42 (209.800 mph)
1999 Prize Money:	$228,000
Indy 500 Career Earnings:	$515,300
Career Indy 500 Starts:	2
Career Best Finish:	11th 1998

#50 Cobb Racing/G Force/Infiniti
Entrant: Cobb Racing/Price Cobb Crew Chief: Phil Spano

ROBERTO GUERRERO

G FORCE/INFINITI INDY/FIRESTONE

Roberto Guerrero came to the Indianapolis Motor Speedway with a new team, Cobb Racing, tied with Arie Luyendyk atop the veterans' list with 14 previous Indy 500 starts. The former track record holder reached the top 10 on Day 5 with a lap at 223.380 miles per hour and was fifth in his group on Pole Day morning with a lap at 221.419 as the track slowed. After waving off on his first attempt, he came back on the 41st qualifying effort of the day to register a four-lap average of 220.479, good for the 25th starting spot.

"I'm glad it's over," Guerrero said. "I feel like a rookie. Each year, you have to do something a little different, but to go through this is not good. In the 15 years that I've been coming here, I've never had it where I wasn't fast enough. We made a couple mistakes on the setup this morning. It's been a little bit of a roller coaster. The race will be a different story. Our strategy will be to bring it home."

On Race Day, he gained three spots in the first two laps and moved to second place on Lap 35 during pit stops. But his team was forced to push the car to Gasoline Alley for lengthy service on Lap 102, causing a loss of 36 laps. After his return, an engine problem ended his day. "The engine started smoking really bad and I just turned it off," Guerrero said. "I don't really know what happened. I think we had been running really well, too. It's too bad we didn't get a break. It's still disappointing. Maybe we'll get a break next year."

1999 INDY 500 PERFORMANCE PROFILE

Starting Position:	25
Qualifying Average:	220.479 mph
Qualifying Speed Rank:	26
Best Practice Speed:	223.380 mph (5/19)
Total Practice Laps:	172
Number of Practice Days:	7
Finishing Position:	25
Laps Completed:	105
Highest Position 1999 Race:	2
Fastest Race Lap:	90 (214.250 mph)
1999 Prize Money:	$217,000
Indy 500 Career Earnings:	$2,721,063
Career Indy 500 Starts:	15
Career Best Finish:	2nd 1984, 1987

#35 Delco Remy/Thermo Tech/Microphonics/Prolong/G Force
Entrant: ISM Racing Corp. Crew Chief: Chuck Buckman Jr.

STEVE KNAPP

G FORCE/OLDSMOBILE AURORA/GOODYEAR

Steve Knapp was one of the revelations of the 1998 Indy 500. In the first 20 laps, the former U.S. F2000 champion and Toyota Atlantic racer blitzed the field, moving up 10 positions in 20 laps; by Lap 30, he was in 7th. Knapp ran as high as second, but ended up finishing third. The reigning Rookie-of-the-Year returned with ISM Racing for the 1999 race. Knapp scored in an impressive run at the the Indy 200 held at Walt Disney World Speedway in Lake Buena Vista, Florida, taking seventh position. Last year, *USA Today* had Knapp as a 1,000-to-1 odds to win the race. Knapp had become a definite threat for the 1999 title. Driving a G Force/Aurora/Goodyear machine, he reached a top lap of 222.982 mph on Day 6. When Pole Day arrived, he went out to make the 37th attempt of the session and registered a four-lap run of 221.502 mph, good for the 13th starting spot.

With Arie Luyendyk retiring, he asked the two-time Indy 500 winner to auto-graph his driver's suit early in practice. "It must have helped me because I've never run through Turn 1 flat out," Knapp said. "I just put my left foot over my right foot and did four laps. We were pretty consistent. It gets us solid in the race. I'm just looking for another race like last year because our qualifying setup is pretty much our race setup."

On Race Day, Knapp struggled with an ill-handling car. Although he moved to ninth on Lap 33, he ended his day just past the halfway point with a spin in Turn 2. "The car had a big push on full tanks," Knapp said. "It started getting better after the last stop. I went down into (Turn) 1 and it went sideways on me. I had a lot of steering wheel cranked in it and it straightened out in the short chute. Then it just got away from me. I feel bad for the team."

1999 INDY 500 PERFORMANCE PROFILE

Starting Position:	13
Qualifying Average:	221.502 mph
Qualifying Speed Rank:	13
Best Practice Speed:	222.982 mph (5/20)
Total Practice Laps:	281
Number of Practice Days:	9
Finishing Position:	26
Laps Completed:	104
Highest Position 1999 Race:	9
Fastest Race Lap:	86 (207.795 mph)
1999 Prize Money:	$216,000
Indy 500 Career Earnings:	$554,750
Career Indy 500 Starts:	2
Career Best Finish:	3rd 1998

#4 Pennzoil Panther/G Force
Entrant: Panther Racing Crew Chief: Kevin Blanch

SCOTT GOODYEAR

G FORCE/OLDSMOBILE AURORA/GOODYEAR

Scott Goodyear came to the Speedway with Panther Racing to bid for his ninth start in the Indianapolis 500 and hoped for a chance at victory after an extensive testing program. He was in the top five in practice for the first three days before commanding the No. 1 spot on Day 4 with a lap at 223.842 miles per hour. On Pole Day, he put together a run of 222.387 on the 26th qualifying attempt, good for ninth spot in the starting lineup.

"We had the car set for cool and overcast and then, on cue, the sun came out as I pulled out of the pit box," Goodyear said. "The run was consistent until the last lap and then I got a big understeer in Turn 1. Actually, I'm very pleased. We wanted to have a shot at the pole but we had a soft spot in the middle of the week. We expected to be a little quicker, but with the sun coming out, that hurt our average tremendously."

On Race Day, after the field sorted out, Goodyear moved steadily to fourth place, a position he held for 32 laps. But he slowed on the front straightaway just past the halfway point, out with an engine problem. "We lost something in the motor," Goodyear said. "It started to seize up and tighten up. We had to deal with some tire issues and handling issues. I thought we were in good shape. I think we had a reasonable race car. But I'm not sure if we had as much speed as Arie [Luyendyk]."

1999 INDY 500 PERFORMANCE PROFILE

Starting Position:	9
Qualifying Average:	222.387 mph
Qualifying Speed Rank:	9
Best Practice Speed:	224.416 mph (5/15)
Total Practice Laps:	428
Number of Practice Days:	10
Finishing Position:	27
Laps Completed:	101
Highest Position 1999 Race:	4
Fastest Race Lap:	19 (213.270 mph)
1999 Prize Money:	$217,500
Indy 500 Career Earnings:	$2,508,865
Career Indy 500 Starts:	9
Career Best Finish:	2nd 1992, 1997

#8 Delphi Automotive Systems
Entrant: Kelley Racing Crew Chief: Mike Horvath

SCOTT
SHARP

DALLARA/OLDSMOBILE AURORA/GOODYEAR

Scott Sharp hoped for a better month of May at the Speedway. He hovered in the top 10 in practice during the week, then put both his primary and backup in the top five the day before qualifications were to begin, with a best lap of 224.792 miles per hour in his backup for fourth place. His turn came early, making the third qualifying attempt of Pole Day and registering a four-lap run of 222.771, which held up for the pole position until Arie Luyendyk checked in at 225.179 on the 14th attempt.

"My car was sliding this morning," Sharp said. "The guys made the car safe for me. I prayed to God and held the throttle down. We're happy, considering everything. We threw in the dice and made a few adjustments."

The run was still good for the sixth starting spot. But on the second parade lap, he pulled to the pits with reports of spray and to fix a radio problem. As the green fell, Sharp pulled off pit road, but he was 32nd after one lap. However, he charged back to 12th spot on Lap 64 and was returning to the hunt. On Lap 82, he returned to the pits, smoking. He was out after completing 83 circuits with a transmission problem. "Obviously, we had a great car," Sharp said. "We almost caught the leaders."

1999 INDY 500 PERFORMANCE PROFILE

Starting Position:	6
Qualifying Average:	222.771 mph
Qualifying Speed Rank:	6
Best Practice Speed:	224.792 mph (5/21)
Total Practice Laps:	410
Number of Practice Days:	9
Finishing Position:	28
Laps Completed:	83
Highest Position 1999 Race:	12
Fastest Race Lap:	42 (213.280 mph)
1999 Prize Money:	$221,500
Indy 500 Career Earnings:	$978,019
Career Indy 500 Starts:	5
Career Best Finish:	10th 1996

29 #98 Cahill Racing/Big Daddy's BBQ
Entrant: Cahill Racing, Inc. Crew Chief: Gilbert Lage

DONNIE BEECHLER

DALLARA/OLDSMOBILE AURORA/FIRESTONE

Donnie Beechler is one of the many drivers to come out of the grass roots dirt track ranks to take on the greatest race of them all. This veteran dirt tracker made eight USAC Silver Crown starts with one win, won three USAC midget races, and competed in seven IRL races in 1998. Beechler and the Cahill team teamed up for their first assault on the Indy 500 in 1998. Beechler qualified 24th and was running a great race, taking 18th position by Lap 30, but his day ended early when his engine let go on Lap 34.

This year, the team sneaked up on speed during the week of practice. "We're not pushing it today," Beechler said on Day 2. "If we ran 225 today, I don't know what we'd do the rest of the week."

He didn't crack the top-10, but did reach a top lap of 221.402 miles per hour on Day 5 with his Dallara/Aurora/Firestone machine. His turn came in qualifying for the 36th attempt, but the team waved off after three laps in the 218 bracket. He came back to the line with 33 minutes left on Pole Day to record a four-lap run of 221.228 miles per hour. Saving his best for last, he made a final lap of 221.948 miles per hour, which was his fastest of the month.

"We came out this morning and thought we had everything covered," Beechler said. "I did 218 and I was flat-out. We needed to free the car up."

The run put him 19th in the starting lineup. When "The Greatest Spectacle in Racing" commenced, he had moved up to 14th by the 31st lap, but an engine failure sent him to the sidelines after 74 circuits. "It's broke," Beechler said. "We lost all our oil pressure."

1999 INDY 500 PERFORMANCE PROFILE

Starting Position:	19
Qualifying Average:	221.228 mph
Qualifying Speed Rank:	19
Best Practice Speed:	221.402 mph (5/19)
Total Practice Laps:	285
Number of Practice Days:	9
Finishing Position:	29
Laps Completed:	74
Highest Position 1999 Race:	14
Fastest Race Lap:	22 (212.475 mph)
1999 Prize Money:	$143,000
Indy 500 Career Earnings:	$275,300
Career Indy 500 Starts:	2
Career Best Finish:	29th 1999

SAM
SCHMIDT

G FORCE/OLDSMOBILE AURORA/FIRESTONE

Sam Schmidt made the most of his new ride with Treadway Racing and being a teammate of Arie Luyendyk for the two-time winner's final Indy 500. Schmidt stayed in the top 10 throughout most of practice before turning a lap at 225.468 miles per hour the day before qualifications began, good for third on the speed chart. He was also the third fastest on Pole Day morning at 224.540.

On Pole Day, Schmidt waited his turn, and on the 31st attempt he recorded a four-lap run of 222.734, good for the seventh starting spot. "We ran flat-out for four laps and I thought we could run 223 mile per hour laps, but we didn't quite make it," Schmidt said. "Overall, I thought it was pretty solid and consistent. I knew we didn't have enough to run for the pole, but the team did a great job and we're happy with it. The good thing is that what I qualified with is darn close to what I'm going to race with."

In the race, Schmidt moved to the front quickly, taking the lead on Lap 34. He stalked Arie Luyendyk and Greg Ray from third place until a Turn 1 accident sent him to the sidelines on Lap 63. "I was just trying to be conservative," Schmidt said. "But everyone in front of me checked up while lapping traffic. Arie was in front of me and I couldn't check up fast enough. I didn't want to hit Arie. I got up in the gray stuff. I just lost it. It's too bad. The car was hooked up."

1999 INDY 500 PERFORMANCE PROFILE

Starting Position:	7
Qualifying Average:	222.734 mph
Qualifying Speed Rank:	7
Best Practice Speed:	225.468 mph (5/21)
Total Practice Laps:	323
Number of Practice Days:	9
Finishing Position:	30
Laps Completed:	62
Highest Position 1999 Race:	1
Fastest Race Lap:	44 (214.255 mph)
1999 Prize Money:	$213,800
Indy 500 Career Earnings:	$579,350
Career Indy 500 Starts:	3
Career Best Finish:	26th 1998

DR. JACK
MILLER

DALLARA/OLDSMOBILE AURORA/GOODYEAR

The racing dentist Dr. Jack Miller made a run at his third Indianapolis 500 starting field as a teammate to Tony Stewart. With Larry Curry serving as team manager, the former Indy Lights veteran responded to the new seat with a lap at 222.519 miles per hour on Day 4, seventh fastest on the speed chart, and a best of 223.480 miles per hour on Day 6.

Driving a Dallara/Aurora/Goodyear car, he waved off on his first qualifying bid on Pole Day, then had an engine malfunction on his second try later in the day. On Sunday he couldn't match his previous practice speeds, but he posted a run of 220.276 miles per hour to bump Stephan Gregoire from the field and nail down the 31st starting spot, despite a 216-plus final circuit.

"I came out of Turn 2 and the car was loose," Miller said, "so I had to get off the throttle. It knocked down my straightaway speed going into Turn 3. It's a shame to run 222 on the second lap and 216 on the last lap. Right now, we'll take it."

His race started with frustration as his car stalled on the grid, then his crew pushed him back to the pits. The field took the green, but Miller didn't pull off pit road until Lap 7. After several stops for repairs, he finally called it quits after 29 laps with clutch problems.

"You can get the car in gear, but when you get off the throttle, it comes out," Miller said. "It's a shame because the car has been running great."

1999 INDY 500 PERFORMANCE PROFILE

Starting Position:	31
Qualifying Average:	220.276 mph
Qualifying Speed Rank:	28
Best Practice Speed:	223.480 mph (5/20)
Total Practice Laps:	171
Number of Practice Days:	10
Finishing Position:	31
Laps Completed:	29
Highest Position 1999 Race:	30
Fastest Race Lap:	9 (199.822 mph)
1999 Prize Money:	$146,000
Indy 500 Career Earnings:	$477,050
Career Indy 500 Starts:	3
Career Best Finish:	20th 1997

32 #92 Tae-Bo/Hemelgarn Racing/ Homier Tool/Delta Faucet
Entrant: Hemelgarn Racing, Inc. Crew Chief: Scott Marks

JOHNNY UNSER

DALLARA/OLDSMOBILE AURORA/GOODYEAR

Another member of the hard-charging Unser clan, Johnny, son of late Indianapolis 500 driver Jerry Unser, cut his racing teeth competing at the Pikes Peak Hillclimb. He gained a lot of racing experience competing in endurace racing. He has driven in the 24 Hours of LeMans, 24 Hours of Daytona, and co-drove to victory in the GTU at the 1989 12 Hours of Sebring. Unser, along with Hemelgarn Racing, was searching for Indy glory and he had a full program from the opening day of practice for the first time.

Last year in his first qualifying attempt, he ran out of fuel. He qualified 25th at an average of 216.316 miles per hour with only 90 practice laps. In the race, Unser showed he had the speed and car control to run with the other Indy Racing League regulars. After starting 25th, he climbed his way up to 12th after 50 laps. Unfortunately for Unser, engine problems sidelined him before Lap 100.

At the wheel of a Dallara/Aurora, he had a top practice lap of 221.773 miles per hour on Day 6, but made heavy contact with the outside wall in Turn 4 to severely damage his machine. The team made repairs and Unser posted a four-lap run of 221.197 miles per hour as the second qualifier of the second day to bump Jaques Lazier from the field. "I'm real happy," Unser said. "We've been struggling and early this week, we went in the fence. This morning, we made some changes and Hemelgarn Racing just did an incredible job. And it (speed) was there. It's definitely been the toughest Indy 500 so far. Some things we can account for, some things we can't."

On race day, his race ended before it ever began. He started 30th, but his brakes were terminal from almost the beginning. Just after 10 laps, he pulled out of the race and ended his day in 32nd position.

"It's very strange," Unser said as his crew tried to make repairs. "I'm going crazy here. It appears we have a problem with our seals."

1999 INDY 500 PERFORMANCE PROFILE

Starting Position:	30
Qualifying Average:	221.197 mph
Qualifying Speed Rank:	20
Best Practice Speed:	221.773 mph (5/20)
Total Practice Laps:	253
Number of Practice Days:	9
Finishing Position:	32
Laps Completed:	10
Highest Position 1999 Race:	30
Fastest Race Lap:	5 (200.374 mph)
1999 Prize Money:	$161,000
Indy 500 Career Earnings:	$599,253
Career Indy 500 Starts:	4
Career Best Finish:	18th 1997

#6 FUBU Nienhouse Racing Special
Entrant: Nienhouse Motorsports Crew Chief: Don Basala

ELISEO SALAZAR

G FORCE/OLDSMOBILE AURORA/FIRESTONE

The Chilean had a less than spectacular month of May last year. During Pole Day, he crashed his Riley & Scott Aurora machine trying to qualify. He came back on Bubble Day and qualified at the back of the starting order. In the final minutes of the session, he got nudged out of the field by Billy Roe.

The 44-year-old Salazar has had a distinguished racing career. He has raced in Formula 1, competed in numerous 24 Hour of LeMans races, and won three IMSA World Sportscar races for Momo Ferrari in 1994. During the 1995 Indy 500, in his rookie start, he charged from 24th all the way up to finish 3rd. However, Christian Fittipaldi, another rookie, also had a phenomenal race and finished second to take rookie honors. In Salazar's second Indy 500 start in 1996, he qualified third. On the final lap in Turn 4, he was involved in an accident with Roberto Guerrero and Alessandro Zampedri. He was classified as finishing in sixth place.

For 1999, he looked for a much more successful effort and a much better result. After missing six races recuperating from multiple fractures sustained in a practice crash at Dover Downs last year, he reached 223.724 miles per hour on Day 5 of practice in his comeback bid.

"Today was pretty good because I made $10 from Eddie Cheever for finishing (on the speed chart) ahead of him," Salazar said. "Every day we improve a little more."

He then became the 12th qualifier with the G Force/Aurora/Firestone machine, posting a four-lap run of 221.265 miles per hour on Pole Day. "Obviously, I would like to be quicker," Salazar said. "I missed the last year after the accident (at Dover). The four laps weren't that tough, but a little bit mentally. The air is very dense. We couldn't trim the car so late because it's a little risky. It's very emotional to be back."

After starting 18th, Salazar progressed forward two positions and appeared to have a competitive race setup. But he was struggling with a push or understeer in his car. After seven laps, his car met the wall in Turn 2 and his race was over.

"It pushed," Salazar said. "I tried to compensate. I got loose. I went into the wall. It was my mistake."

1999 INDY 500 PERFORMANCE PROFILE

Starting Position:	18
Qualifying Average:	221.265 mph
Qualifying Speed Rank:	18
Best Practice Speed:	223.714 mph (5/19)
Total Practice Laps:	328
Number of Practice Days:	10
Finishing Position:	33
Laps Completed:	7
Highest Position 1999 Race:	15
Fastest Race Lap:	5 (208.623 mph)
1999 Prize Money:	$141,000
Indy 500 Career Earnings:	$844,070
Career Indy 500 Starts:	4
Career Best Finish:	4th 1995

MAXIMUM OVERDRIVE

IRL Chassis and Engine Development

by Jonathan Ingram

After three years under the series' unique engine and chassis formulas, the 1999 Pep Boys Indy Racing League proved to be a highly competitive arena for the various manufacturers. Chassis constructors Dallara and G Force fought throughout the season for both the honor of carrying the points championship winner as well as for individual race victories. And although the Aurora Indy V-8 continued its dominance in the engine category (winning every race and pole), the Indy Infiniti V-8 made significant strides through a new development program with Team Cheever.

In 1999, the chassis manufacturers entered their final season with the cars first introduced in 1997. The IRL rulebook requires chassis tubs to remain fundamentally unchanged for three years, which means factories can only pursue development through update kits—an effort to both hold down costs and allow for technical improvements.

The Chassis Battle Heats Up

The chassis battle hinged on the decision by the British G Force firm to use its update kit—which included sidepods, undertrays, and engine covers—to decrease drag at the rear of the car. G Force's update kit also gave teams the option of reducing the track width of the rear tires, which also decreases drag. The new design proved effective at a majority of the tracks on the Pep Boys IRL schedule, specifically at the Indianapolis Motor Speedway and the 1.5-mile high-banked ovals.

"I felt like the G Force was slightly inferior to the Dallara in 1998," said John Biddlecomb, director of G Force. "It showed up at Indy more than anywhere else." For the 1999 season, Biddlecomb brought additional personnel on board to help design and implement new developments. Nigel Bennett, formerly the designer of Penske Racing's chassis for the CART series, became a consultant to the team. And Tim Wardrop, formerly an engineer with Treadway Racing, was hired by the company to help teams adapt to new technical developments.

The G Force update kit was most recognizable by the reduction in size of the engine air intake, which helped to reduce drag while still retaining the trademark triangular opening. The idea of reducing the size of the air intake was taken directly from the Dallara's 1998 update kit, which featured a smaller, albeit round, intake very similar to those used by Formula 1 constructors.

The key elements to the G Force update kit could be seen on the sidepods and at the rear of the engine cover. The exit ducts and the "tire kickers" (winglets at the trailing edge of the sidepods) were altered to help give the chassis a narrower waist behind the engine at the gearbox. That configuration reduced the area at the rear of the engine cover and decreased drag as well without losing any of the previous performance.

More difficult to see was the narrower undertray developed by G Force to accommodate the changes in the sidepods and engine cover at the back. It also gave the teams an additional option: If they ran narrower exit tunnels in the undertray at the rear of the car, they could run a narrower rear track width and pull the rear tires inward, out of the slipstream.

If imitation is the sincerest form of flattery, then the G Force was regarded as the best car for the high-banked 1.5-mile ovals. By July, defending series champion team owner A.J. Foyt decided to build his own narrow rear track for the Dallara of defending champion Kenny Brack. The swift Swede had already won the Indy 500 in a Dallara, but Foyt had his mind on repeating the championship of 1998 and a number of 1.5-mile banked tracks remained on the schedule.

Without the complete conceptual approach and the absence of a reduction in tunnel width at the rear on the Dallara, Foyt's gambit, introduced at the Atlanta Motor Speedway, failed to produce results for Brack's Dallara. So the team scuttled the plan after qualifying—and then switched to a G Force chassis for the final two races of the season on the 1.5-mile high-banked tracks at the Las Vegas Motor Speedway and the Texas Motor Speedway.

Other evidence of the G Force's potency were the victories by Scott Goodyear and the Pennzoil Panther Racing team on the mile oval at Phoenix and in the season's first race at the Texas Motor Speedway. The Las Vegas Motor Speedway event was decided by a duel between two G Force cars in the hands of Treadway Racing's Sam Schmidt (who eventually prevailed) and Brack.

At Indy, Arie Luyendyk won the pole in a Treadway Racing G Force at a record speed (225.179 miles per hour) for the current formula, and was the race leader when a collision with a backmarker took him out. At the Brickyard, Wardrop began his transition from Luyendyk's engineer at Treadway Racing to his role as advisor to G

Force teams by using a G Force mono-shock front suspension during the Indy 500 on Luyendyk's car. It's an available option that teams have not used. G Force believes the suspension will work better than the standard twin-shock configuration, but teams need to learn how to use it through consultant Wardrop.

"Arie was the class of the field at Indy," said Biddlecomb, who planned to make the front of all cars mono-shock for the 2000 season. Indy not only is the most important track on the Pep Boys circuit, it also is the only track that demands both outstanding downforce for the high-speed corners and low drag for the long straights. Since teams are free to adjust rear wing angles (which are mandated at a minimum six degrees for the 1.5-mile ovals), Indy allows the widest variety of choices for teams. That combined with numerous practice days meant that both G Force and Dallara were competitive.

"I agree that in 1998, we probably had a slight advantage in lower drag at Indy," said Sam Garrett, director of Dallara's American operation. "In 1999, the advantage went in the other direction in the favor of G Force. But we're talking about very small increments."

In the absence of Luyendyk, when the laps wound down at the Indy 500, Brack took the win from another Dallara driver, Robby Gordon. Greg Ray, the teammate of Gordon and full-time driver for the Pep Boys IRL effort of Team Menard, was also among the leaders at Indy before his pit road accident.

Ray later scored victories with the Dallara at Dover Downs International Raceway's mile oval and at both Pikes Peak International Raceway rounds on the Colorado mile. Dallara driver Eddie Cheever Jr., was the winner on the mile oval at the Walt Disney World Speedway. At these shorter tracks, mechanical grip becomes more of an issue, which means a wider rear tire track is the desired option. Also, low drag is not as important due to the slower speeds.

Ironically, G Force had a better update kit in 1999 because the company was no longer consumed with building its land speed record car. Prior to the 1999 season, Dallara was heavily focused on introducing a new Formula 3 chassis and on building a new Formula 1 chassis for Honda, a project eventually dropped by the Japanese car maker. This meant the Italian concern lost some of its edge versus G Force due to relatively few changes to its update kit.

"They did some things over the winter and made some big improvements and we didn't," said Garrett. But Dallara continued to enjoy an advantage in numbers, usually getting 18 of the 26 entries with eight belonging to G Force. The third chassis manufacturer, Riley & Scott, soldiered through the season with a lone entry from Brant Racing. Due to a merger with Reynard Cars that took place during the 1999 season, Riley & Scott placed its focus on building the new generation car for the 2000 season in conjunction with British manufacturer Reynard, a regular competitor in the CART and Formula 1 series.

New for all chassis manufacturers during the 1999 season was the Suspension & Wheel Energy Management System (SWEMS). All three constructors helped introduce the system designed to reduce the possibility of wheel assemblies becoming detached during high-speed accidents. The SWEMS principle utilized multiple restraints attached at various points to a car's chassis and suspension with Federation Internationale de l'Automobile—approved Zylon. The high-tensile cable of wound construction has a breaking strength of 5 tons.

Engines That Power Champions

The IRL's change in engine rules for the 1999 season heavily influenced G Force's decisions concerning its update kits. The sanctioning body elected to reduce the maximum rpm from 10,500 rpm to 10,300 rpm for the 4.0-liter, dual overhead cam V-8s used in the series. The move was designed to reduce speeds on the longer tracks. The speeds had already been slowed as much as was practical by aerodynamic rules, which require a six-degree wing angle on the 1.5-mile banked tracks and a mandated Speedway wing at Indy.

The result of the rpm reduction meant speed would need to be found primarily through a reduction in drag. The rpm maximum was further reduced to 10,000 after the Indy 500, putting an even greater premium on reduced drag. All drivers could qualify at the 1.5-mile tracks, for example, without lifting from the accelerator. So in addition to gearing, reduction in drag was crucial.

For engine builders, the lower rpm meant increased reliability and different cam profiles to keep the power curve just under the rev limiter. After both reductions, horsepower was reduced by 35 to 40 horsepower from the standard of 730 horsepower.

The IRL Aurora V-8 once again dominated the chase for victories over the Infiniti Indy V-8. With 12 different engine builders supplying almost all of the entries in each race, Aurora powered the vast majority of podium finishers as well as all of the pole winners and race winners.

GM Motorsport focused on maintaining supply lines to meet the demand from its engine builders. "We recognize under the IRL rules, all of the engines competing in the series will eventually arrive at the same performance level," said Joe Negri, manager of the IRL

The Oldsmobile Aurora 4.0-liter V-8 won 10 races, 10 poles, and the Indy Racing League's engine manufacturer championship. This methanol-burning mill features a 32-valve head design, dual overhead camshafts, and churns out about 700 horsepower at 10,000 rpm.

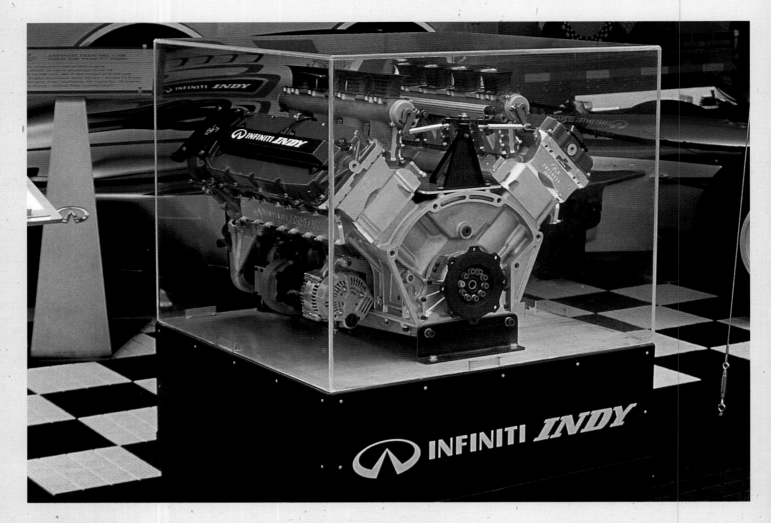

INFINITI *INDY*

program. "We are focusing on customer support as well as hardware."

After a slow start, the Infiniti V-8 did indeed arrive at the performance level of the Aurora during the 1999 season. Nissan's program reached Oldsmobile's playing field with the introduction of the Phase 2.5 engine at Indy in May of 1998. The engine produced an increase of 83 horsepower and a reduction in weight of 55 pounds over the original Infiniti. Since then, the same block has been used in all of the Infiniti development engines produced by Nissan. The Phase 2.5 powered a race leader (Eddie Cheever Jr.) for the first time in September of 1998 as Roberto Guerrero led twice for 22 laps in the G Force of CBR Cobb Racing at the Texas Motor Speedway.

"The development curve for the engine has leveled off," said Frank Honsowetz, manager for Infiniti Motorsports. "We are on equal ground with the competition in terms of horsepower and weight. We are focusing on incremental changes to give us the competitive edge."

The prescribed formula for the IRL engines has been criticized at times for not allowing enough technology development. While some opportunities may have been limited by restricting the valve train to 10,000 rpm, areas outside of air flow or engine speed have been crucial to catching Aurora, said Honsowetz. "Air flow is always important," he said. "But we've found the biggest gains by eliminating parasitic losses and with friction reduction."

In order to sustain reliability, one has to take into consideration the incredible turnover of the reciprocating parts in an IRL race engine. Even at 10,300 rpm, each piston travels up and down rough-

ly 172 times per second. Each spark plug fires 86 times per second and the 32 valves get a similar workout. Forged aluminum pistons weigh less than a pound, but the inertia generated while completing a cycle renders the piston weight the equivalent of 10.5 tons.

Once up to speed with reliability, the Infiniti program faced a problem with the numbers game. Absent the 12 different engine builders that were producing a variety of independent developments with the Aurora V-8, Nissan had only a small cadre of teams using its Infiniti V-8 in 1999. The majority of engines were built at Ed Pink Racing Engines, Nissan's own development shop.

"The numbers thing is the most frustrating for us," said Honsowetz. It became apparent at Round 2 on the Phoenix Mile that the Infiniti had drawn even with the Aurora in power and reliability and was down to the minimum weight limit. But teams continued with programs already established through Aurora engine builders.

In that Phoenix race, Robbie Buhl finished third and gave Infiniti its first podium finish since 1997 while driving Sinden Racing's Dallara. "Robbie had that Nissan running very well," said Billy Boat, the driver of the AJ Foyt Enterprises Dallara-Aurora that finished fourth at Phoenix. "It made it hard to catch him. We definitely have two motors on this track now."

But without the cachet of a victory, Honsowetz knew that teams would not have any incentive to switch from what other competitors had. So prior to Round 3 in Indianapolis, Honsowetz signed Eddie Cheever's team to a testing and development contract. In return for helping to develop the engine—and proving its potency on the track—Cheever would receive the latest development engines from Nissan as well as a fee for testing.

Cheever proved to be an excellent development driver with the necessary sensitivity to engine characteristics and excellent recall following stints on the track. But the new partners still faced the problem of having to beat all the Aurora engine builders as well as the bulk of the field. With a strategy of producing an engine that clearly had an edge on the competition, Nissan also was forced to constantly use untested parts and configurations in races due to time constraints. The engine configuration Cheever drove at Indy, where he led four laps before transmission problems developed during pit stops, had not been tested for 500 miles.

But that didn't bother the 1998 Indy 500 winner. "The guys at Infiniti are doing a great job," said Cheever after his initial stint with the Infiniti Indy V-8 program. "The biggest plus for us is that we've gotten competitive with people who show off what we're doing," said Honsowetz. "We're working with people who can give us feedback."

Cheever eventually led 13 laps at the Texas Motor Speedway in June after starting fifth, but failed to finish due to running out of fuel and an electrical problem. Cheever led 32 laps at the Las Vegas Motor Speedway in September before internal conditions led to the failure of a connecting rod bearing.

Unfortunately, two of the teams that ran the Infiniti Indy at the beginning of the year did not continue the season, leaving Cheever as the lone driver powered regularly by the Infiniti V-8. Sinden Racing and CBR Cobb Racing both withdrew after the Indy 500. Scott Harrington, who finished fifth under Infiniti power at Phoenix, alternated use of the Infiniti with the Aurora V-8.

The degree of difficulty involved in beating so many other engine builders was illustrated by the success of Team Menard. Menard driver Greg Ray led the league in poles and victories. At the Pikes Peak

International Raceway, he swept both the wins from the pole. When asked why his team does so well at the Colorado track, where Tony Stewart landed his first career IRL victory in 1997, John Menard credited his in-house engine builder, Butch Meyer. "I think he's got a real good formula worked out for running at higher elevations,'" said Menard.

With so many engine builders putting together "cookbooks" on each of the tracks with the Aurora V-8, Honsowetz and his development team had their work cut out for them all year.

"What we do is make and acquire all the parts," said Honsowetz. "An engine builder is like a chef. We give them all the ingredients and the recipe—meaning parts and a manual— with all the dimensions, clearances, and assembly procedures. They do the rest of the work. Like chefs, they start with the same ingredients, but depending on how they prepare the seasonings and how long they cook the food and at what temperature, the final result may vary. The ultimate goal is to make them fast and reliable."

While the Dallara chassis had a technical advantage over the G Force chassis during the 1998 season, G Force made significant strides in 1999. The winglets on the side pods and narrow cowling area around the engine produced an aerodynamic gain that made the G Force the chassis to have on the 1.5 mile high-banked ovals.

The Dallara chassis was very competitive on the various tracks the IRL visits. Although G Force may have had a more aerodynamically efficient update package for 1999, the Dallara chassis took Greg Ray, Eddie Cheever Jr., Mark Dismore, and Kenny Brack to victory lane over the course of the season. Ray won the driver's championship with the Dallara.

Scott Goodyear Out Guns Rivals in Texas

Inset: The win at Texas gave Scott Goodyear's team its second trip to Victory Lane in three races. Goodyear held off Team Menard's Greg Ray and Treadway Racing's Sam Schmidt to earn the victory and take the points lead.

Panther Racing Takes Win No.2

by Tim Tuttle

JUNE 12, 1999

Scott Goodyear outgunned Greg Ray and Sam Schmidt in spirited wheel-to-wheel duels that carried him to victory in the Longhorn 500 at Texas Motor Speedway. Goodyear's typical mistake-free blend of patient and aggressive driving was built upon a dialed-in Panther Racing G Force-Aurora, which played a critical role in the team's second Pep Boys Indy Racing League victory of the season.

The racing team always plays an important part in the success or failure of a driver, but Panther's ability to provide Goodyear with a chassis that didn't excessively wear on the right-rear Goodyear tires was of paramount importance. The majority of the cars using Goodyear rubber experienced blistering on the right rear, forcing them into unscheduled pit stops and a slower pace.

Scott Goodyear, of course, still had to beat Ray, Schmidt, and the rest of the Firestone runners, who didn't have to cope with the tire-blistering problem. Goodyear and Panther fought a war on two fronts, winning both of them and putting this victory into a remarkable category.

Panther Racing came up with a setup for Scott Goodyear's car which wouldn't excessively wear out his Goodyear tires. Goodyear went out on the track to beat Greg Ray, Sam Schmidt, and the rest of the IRL field.

Sam Schmidt held the lead until the eventual winner, Scott Goodyear, took over on Lap 166 of 208. Schmidt, who qualified sixth, ran strong to the end to take third.

Greg Ray posed for pre-race photos with the track mascot, but things were not as jovial on the track. Ray dueled for several laps with Scott Goodyear and finished less than a second behind the winner.

The win also allowed Goodyear and the Panther Racing team to regain the momentum they lost at the Indianapolis 500, where Goodyear fell out with a blown engine just past halfway while in the fourth position and poised for a charge to the checkered flag. "I was in disbelief after Indy," Goodyear said. "I was depressed for about a week. We came into this season with two goals. One was to win races and chase the championship, and the other was to win Indianapolis. Indy is gone, and there's nothing we can do about it. We need wins to go for the championship. We're delighted, especially after Indy, to have won [at Texas]. This is, obviously, nice."

Goodyear qualified eighth in his Pennzoil G Force-Aurora and never fell out of the top 10. By Lap 101 of the 208-lap race, Goodyear was second behind Ray. Ray, in Team Menard's Glidden Dallara-Aurora, staved off Goodyear for the next 35 laps, never more than a couple of car lengths in front.

Goodyear broke off the battle to pit on Lap 136 and Ray came in for service two laps later. Cahill Racing's Donnie Beechler, on a different pit strategy, was elevated into the lead. Goodyear emerged one position in front of Ray following the stop. Ray passed Goodyear on Lap 149, but Goodyear moved around Ray in Turn 4 on Lap 153.

Low on fuel, Beechler and Robby Unser were forced to make green flag stops (Beechler on Lap 148 and Unser on Lap 153), putting Schmidt's Treadway Racing G Force-Aurora into the lead, followed by Simon Racing's Stephan Gregoire (also on a different pit strategy), Goodyear, and Ray.

Then, on Lap 156, a caution intervened. Exiting the pits, the left-rear wheel on Unser's Team Pelfrey Dallara rolled off the car. That allowed the four cars on the lead lap—Schmidt, Gregoire, Goodyear, and Ray—to make their final stops. They emerged in the same order.

Goodyear made quick work of passing Gregoire and began challenging Schmidt. The Panther driver looked for a way around

The Texas sun and heat took a toll on drivers, teams, and equipment. Even though the race was run in the evening, the sun—and temperatures—were still high at the start.

Schmidt as they went down the back straight on Lap 165. The two leaders were in heavy traffic entering Turn 3. "I went to go low and he [Schmidt] went low, so I went to the high side and kept my foot in the throttle in [Turns] 3 and 4 on the high side." Goodyear weaved through the lapped cars and carried greater momentum into Turn 1, where he was able to overtake Schmidt for the lead on the outside on Lap 166.

"There were a bunch of lappers and I chose the low line," Schmidt said. "I chose wrong." Ray, also using the traffic, passed Schmidt on the back straight for second position.

Goodyear led the final 43 laps, finishing .888 second in front of Ray with Schmidt .951 second behind in third. Ray's runner-up finish was bittersweet. Nothing would have felt better for the 32-year-old from nearby Plano, Texas, than winning his first IRL race before the hometown folks. But second place provided Ray and the Menard operation with much-needed relief from what had been an agonizing campaign. Ray had been competitive in the previous races, but had only three 21st-place finishes to show for it.

Owner John Menard had revamped his operation following the 1998 season, hiring team manager and engineer Thomas Knapp in addition to Ray. "We had winning cars at [canceled] Charlotte and Indianapolis, and we were very competitive in the other races," Knapp said. "There are lots of ways to lose a motor race and we've done all of them. We had a loss of horsepower and [chassis] balance that cost us this one, but it beats the hell out of 21st [place]."

Ray's Aurora powerplant had a cylinder head crack on Lap 158. The chassis also had a slight understeer in the segment of the race following Ray's final pit stop. The race's final caution, from Lap 179 to Lap 189, left Goodyear with a clear track for the final 19 laps and left Ray without the traffic he needed to make an attempt at regaining the lead.

"I couldn't pass anybody without the draft after the cylinder head cracked and I couldn't use top gear," Ray explained. "We were still quick in the corners, but once Goodyear got me in traffic, he walked away. At the end, I needed lapped traffic to have a shot at him and didn't get any."

Schmidt went into Texas with only one goal: to have his G Force-Aurora running at the checkered flag. His season had been similar to Ray's. Schmidt had joined the strong Treadway Racing team over the winter, the replacement for Arie Luyendyk, and had crashed out of two events.

Kelley Racing's Mark Dismore and Scott Sharp qualified on the front row. The pole was the first in the IRL for Dismore, who was forced into his backup Dallara-Aurora after banging the wall in practice. Dismore averaged 215.272 miles per hour (24.332 seconds), far off the track record of 225.979 miles per hour (23.896 seconds) set by Billy Boat in September of 1998.

Buddy Lazier continued to qualify poorly: He started 24th in the 25-car field. However, he moved up to finish 14th—despite rear-ending Robby Unser during a caution period.

On Lap 47 Sharp fell behind Ray and Cheever and he pitted on the next lap with another blistered right rear tire. Beechler made his initial pit stop on Lap 50 and Cheever, with the lone Nissan Infiniti engine in the field, took the lead.

Boat, several laps down because of his tire woes, had an engine failure on Lap 51, bringing out another caution. It put Sharp out of contention, two laps down. Rookie Robby McGehee had charged from 21st on the grid to 3rd, behind Cheever and Ray, by then. The leaders took advantage of the caution to pit, resuming in the same order. The race restarted on Lap 58, and Ray went inside Cheever in Turn 3 on Lap 66 to take the lead.

Racing with an on-board camera mounted above his cockpit to give television viewers a good feel for the action, Stephan Gregoire worked his way up to 4th place after starting 16th.

There were two factors contributing to Dismore's slower speed. Prior to the 1999 season, the IRL reduced the maximum engine revs from 10,500 to 10,300 rpms. But they decided that wasn't enough and cut 300 rpms more for the rest of the season, starting with Texas. The IRL also remeasured the Texas track, shortening the official distance from 1.5 to 1.455 miles. That had the effect of reducing speed, too. Outright speed and records are sidecourses to the main meal, and the pole was a feast for Dismore. "It has not been an easy day," he said. "In fact, it has been a bit of a downer, actually, but this [pole] sure makes up for it. We almost won a couple of poles last year, but missed it by a few 10ths [of a second]. This feels great."

It was a situation that put a premium on a good-handling car in traffic, allowing it to use the draft exiting the corners, for the race. Originally scheduled for a night race, the starting time was moved up to 6:30 P.M. for television. It meant that the majority of the 208 laps would be run in daylight, although the front straight was draped in a big shadow from the beginning.

Sharp passed Dismore on the outside of Turn 1 on the start and led the opening 28 laps. The first sign of trouble for the Goodyear-tired cars was when Boat, in A.J. Foyt's Dallara-Aurora, pitted with a blistered right rear on Lap 18. Kenny Brack, Davey Hamilton, and Buddy Lazier also suffered from blistered tires. The IRL ordered a caution one lap later to check for debris. Leader Sharp and the next seven cars pitted. Sharp, Dismore, and Eddie Cheever (another Goodyear runner) all reported blistered right rears.

Robby Unser, who had qualified 12th, stayed out in Team Pelfrey's Dallara-Aurora and took the lead. Buddy Lazier was right behind Unser. Under yellow, Lazier tapped Unser and spun, extending the caution to Lap 33. "I saw Robby accelerate and I accelerated behind him," Lazier said. "Then, he slowed down. I braked, but on the cold tires the car didn't stop and I hit him."

Beechler, who also didn't pit under the first caution, passed Unser on the restart. Sharp was third, chased by Cheever and Ray.

Ray extended his advantage to 2.8 seconds over Cheever by Lap 78. Cheever, inexplicably, ran out of fuel on Lap 80. He managed to coast into the pits in his Dallara, but went down a lap. McGehee pitted on the same lap, but missed his pit box. The Conti Racing team had to push the Dallara-Aurora (on Firestones) back to the pit box, and then they had trouble refiring the engine. McGehee went several laps down.

Still under green, Goodyear, in fourth, had to come in for fuel on Lap 82, and he was followed a lap later by Ray. Schmidt took the lead for two laps before he stopped for service. That elevated rookie Jacques Lazier, driving for Truscelli Racing in his first IRL race, into the lead. Lazier was on a different pit sequence, but once in the front, he stayed there.

Lazier, in a G Force-Aurora (on Goodyears) finally came in for fuel and tires on Lap 94. Lazier had been having trouble with his clutch and while exiting the pit lane it suddenly fully engaged. Lazier darted to the left and clipped the inside wall, damaging his G Force and knocking him out of the race.

Jeff Ward had qualified seventh in Pagan Racing's Dallara (on Goodyears) and had stayed in the hunt. He took over the lead when Jacques Lazier pitted, then pitted when Lazier brought out the yellow for the pit lane incident. Ray and Goodyear, needing less fuel than Ward, had gone longer without a pit stop, and moved into the lead after pitting under caution on Lap 100. Ward was third, Robby Unser fourth, and Beechler fifth.

On the restart, Cheever and Ronnie Johncox, driving for Tri Star Motorsports in his first IRL race, made contact in Turn 4. Cheever kept going, but Johncox spun and went airborne exiting the racing surface onto the grass. Johncox landed safely, on all four wheels, and later rejoined the race.

The caution flag flew again. Gregoire and Schmidt, the final two cars on the lead lap in seventh and eighth places, respectively, pitted under the caution. They had nothing to lose.

Goodyear made a scheduled pit stop on Lap 136 and Ray did the same on Lap 138. Goodyear emerged in front, but the new leader was Beechler.

Beechler stopped under green on Lap 149. Meanwhile, Ray had passed Goodyear on Lap 149, and Goodyear had repassed the Team Menard driver on Lap 154. Unser was forced to pit on Lap 153, elevating Schmidt into the lead. Exiting the pits, Unser's left-rear wheel came off in Turn 1, bringing out the race's next-to-last caution. Unser was the victim of a faulty airgun.

Schmidt, Gregoire, Goodyear, and Ray, the four cars on the lead lap, pitted and rejoined in that order. There were 11 lapped cars in front of Schmidt. Goodyear, making use of the traffic, passed Schmidt for the lead on Lap 166.

There was one caution remaining. Tyce Carlson cut a tire and hit the wall exiting Turn 2 on Lap 189. Beechler was in fifth, a lap down (the result of pitting just prior to Unser losing his wheel). Beechler was

Eddie Cheever Jr. (right) described for Buzz Calkins (left) his collision with Ronnie Johncox. The incident sent Johncox's car airborne, yet Johncox finished 11th while Cheever came home 16th.

Ray maintained the lead on the Lap 107 restart. Ward was third until he slowed in Turn 1 on Lap 113. Ward's Dallara had a wheel bearing fail, forcing him into the pits for a lengthy stop and eliminating him from contention. Ray held off Goodyear for 24 laps, with Beechler in third, Unser fourth, and Schmidt fifth.

The pre-race fine-tuning in Scott Goodyear's garage paid off as he had the power and handling to go flat out at the end and hold off Greg Ray for the victory.

low on the track in Turn 2 when the pace car, driven by Johnny Rutherford, came out for Carlson's crash, on the transition road on the inside.

Beechler was forced to move quickly to the left to avoid Eddie Cheever's car, which had veered left to miss some debris. The pace car ran over the left front of Beechler's Dallara, ruining what would have been his best IRL finish.

Goodyear led easily on the final restart on Lap 190 and wasn't threatened by Ray to the checkered flag. Gregoire finished fourth. Eliseo Salazar drove steadily in Nienhouse Motorsports' G Force to finish fifth, and Unser, despite his lap on three wheels, finished sixth.

The next highest-finishing Goodyear-tired car was Hamilton, three laps down in seventh. "Our tires blistered right from the start," Hamilton said. "The stagger we were running blistered, so we had to go for a small stagger."

Changing the stagger had solved Hamilton's problem. Cheever had no tire problems following the first stop, and Ward also had run strongly on Goodyears. But the best example of making the Goodyear tires work was Scott Goodyear. "We had no problems with tires whatsoever," he said. "We didn't have any blistering. We really concentrated [in preparation] on making the car work on long runs."

OFFICIAL BOX SCORE
PEP BOYS INDY RACING LEAGUE
Longhorn 500 at Texas Motor Speedway
Saturday, June 12, 1999

FP	SP	Car	Driver	Car Name	C/E/T	Laps Comp.	Running/ Reason Out	IRL Pts.	Total IRL Pts.	IRL Standings	IRL Awards	Designated Awards	Total Awards
1	8	4	Scott Goodyear	Pennzoil Panther G Force	G/A/G	208	Running	50	146	1	$102,700	$32,000	$134,700
2	4	2	Greg Ray	Glidden/Menards	D/A/F	208	Running	42	76	8	62,800	25,750	88,550
3	6	99	Sam Schmidt	Sprint PCS/Unistar Auto Insurance	G/A/F	208	Running	35	61	16	49,600	1,450	51,050
4	16	7	Stephan Gregoire	Mexmil/Tokheim/G Force	G/A/F	208	Running	32	66	14	36,400	1,500	37,900
5	20	6	Eliseo Salazar	Nienhouse Motorsports Racing Special	D/A/F	206	Running	30	41	20	31,500	5,000	36,500
6	12	81	Robby Unser	PetroMoly/Team Pelfrey	D/A/F	206	Running	28	71	12	47,600	10,100	57,700
7	15	9	Davey Hamilton	Galles Racing Spinal Conquest	D/A/G	205	Running	26	72	11	46,300	100	46,400
8	1	28	Mark Dismore	MCI WorldCom	D/A/G	205	Running	27	97	3	45,200	12,600	57,800
9	14	12	Buzz Calkins	Bradley Food Marts/Sav-O-Mat	G/A/F	205	Running	22	62	15	45,200	0	45,200
10	2	8	Scott Sharp	Delphi Automotive Systems	D/A/G	203	Running	22	85	6	44,000	0	44,000
11	10	22 R	Ronnie Johncox	ADT Security Systems	D/A/G	203	Running	19	19	31	20,700	0	20,700
12	17	35	Steve Knapp	Delco Remy/Microphonics/ Thermo Tech/ISM Racing	G/A/G	202	Running	18	53	17	41,600	600	42,200
13	9	14	Kenny Brack	AJ Foyt PowerTeam Racing	D/A/G	201	Running	17	83	7	40,400	0	40,400
14	24	91	Buddy Lazier	Delta Faucet/Coors Light/Hemelgarn Racing	D/A/G	200	Running	16	74	9	39,200	0	39,200
15	18	92	Johnny Unser	Tae-Bo/Delta Faucet/Hemelgarn Racing	D/A/G	200	Running	15	16	34	16,000	0	16,000
16	5	51	Eddie Cheever Jr.	The Children's Beverage Group/Team Cheever/Infiniti	D/I/G	188	Electrical	14	89	5	36,800	5,000	41,800
17	25	98	Donnie Beechler	Big Daddy's BBQ Sauce and Spices	D/A/F	179	Contact	13	37	24	13,600	0	13,600
18	7	21	Jeff Ward	Yahoo!/MerchantOnline.com/ Dallara/Olds	D/A/G	176	Running	12	127	2	35,600	0	35,600
19	21	55 R	Robby McGehee	Energizer Advanced Formula	D/A/F	168	Wheel bearing	11	41	20	12,400	0	12,400
20	13	42 R	John Hollansworth Jr.	pcsave.com/Lycos/Dallara	D/A/F	146	Gearbox	10	53	17	33,200	0	33,200
21	3	20	Tyce Carlson	Blueprint-Immke Racing	D/A/F	127	Contact	10	51	19	33,200	0	33,200
22	19	33 R	Jaques Lazier	Truscelli Team Racing/ Warner Bros. Studio Stores	G/A/G	94	Contact	8	10	39	33,200	0	33,200
23	23	3	Raul Boesel	b-Fast Shopper/TransWorld/ Brant Racing R&S MkV	R/A/G	70	Rear suspension	7	67	13	33,200	0	33,200
24	11	11	Billy Boat	Harrah's AJ Foyt Racing	D/A/G	47	Engine	6	96	4	33,200	0	33,200
25	22	30	Jimmy Kite	McCormack Motorsports	G/A/F	19	Oil leak	5	11	37	33,200	0	33,200
26	26	66 R	Scott Harrington	The CertainTeed Building Products Special	D/A/F	0	Did not start	4	39	22	33,200	0	33,200
Team Menard Engines												600	600
Roush Technologies												800	800
											TOTAL 1,000,000	95,500	1,095,500

Time of Race: 2:00:06.816   Average Speed: 151.177 mph   Margin of Victory: 0.888 seconds   Fastest Lap: #99 Sam Schmidt (Lap 199, 215.609)   Fastest Leading Lap: #2 Greg Ray (Lap 137, 215.431)   PPG Pole Winner: #28 Mark Dismore (215.272 mph)   PPG Team Pole Award: #28 MCI WorldCom/Kelley Racing   Coors Light "Pit Performance Award": #4 Scott Goodyear   Firestone First at 99 Award: #81 Robby Unser Delphi   "Leader at Halfway" Award: #2 Greg Ray   MBNA America Lap Leader: #2 Greg Ray   MCI WorldCom Long Distance Award: #6 Eliseo Salazar   Legend: R-Pep Boys Indy Racing League Rookie   Chassis Legend: D-Dallara(17); G- G Force(8); R- Riley&Scott(1)   Engine Legend: A- Oldsmobile Aurora(25); I- Nissan Infiniti(1)   Tire Legend: F- Firestone(12); G- Goodyear(14)

Lap Leaders							Lap Leader Summary				Caution Flags	
Laps	Car#	Driver					Driver	Times	Total		Laps	Reason/Incident
1-28	8	Scott Sharp	66-82	2	Greg Ray		Greg Ray	3	56		26-31	Debris on track
29-33	81	Robby Unser	83-84	99	Sam Schmidt		Scott Goodyear	1	43			#91 B. Lazier, spin pit exit
34-49	98	Donnie Beechler	85-93	33	Jaques Lazier		Scott Sharp	1	28		52-57	#11 Boat, engine failure, stalled on back-stretch
50	81	Robby Unser	94-100	21	Jeff Ward		Donnie Beechler	2	26		96-102	#33 J. Lazier, contact pit exit
51-60	51	Eddie Cheever Jr.	101-137	2	Greg Ray		Sam Schmidt	2	15		104-106	#22 Johncox, #51 Cheever Jr, contact frontstretch
61-62	2	Greg Ray	138-147	98	Donnie Beechler		Eddie Cheever Jr.	2	13		156-161	#81 R. Unser, lost wheel
63-65	51	Eddie Cheever Jr.	148-152	81	Robby Unser		Robby Unser	3	11		179-189	#20 Carlson, accident T2 #98 Beechler, contact with pace car
			153-165	99	Sam Schmidt		Jaques Lazier	1	9		6 caution flags, 39 laps	
			166-208	4	Scott Goodyear		Jeff Ward	1	7			

You'll find our technology on the track and in your garage.

Whether it's a high-speed track of the Indy Racing League, Formula One, CART or NASCAR, you'll find Delphi Automotive Systems technology at work. In the IRL, our advanced electronics provide teams like Delphi/Kelley Racing with optimized engine control, radio telemetry and track condition information. This rugged competition helps us develop race-proven components like Electronic Control Modules that automotive manufacturers put into vehicles around the world. To learn more about us, visit www.delphiauto.com. Or look in your garage. We're probably in your car right now.

DELPHI
Automotive Systems

Driving Tomorrow's Technology.

The official provider of electronics for the IRL.

Greg Ray's Rocky Mountain High

Inset: Race winner Greg Ray hugged his son Winston after a close and emotional victory over Sam Schmidt. "After I saw the checkered flag I wanted to stop and cry," Ray said.

Greg Ray and Team Menard Celebrate First Win

by Tim Tuttle

Somewhere, John Menard was smiling. Because of Menard's hectic lifestyle, the hands-on billionaire businessman was prevented from attending Greg Ray's breakthrough Pep Boys Indy Racing League win in the Radisson 200 at Pikes Peak International Raceway in Fountain, Colorado. The mile-high victory vindicated a myriad of problems Team Menard had suffered up to this stage of the season.

Ray's victory—his first in 19 IRL starts—justified the faith Menard showed in the 32-year-old Texan's ability. When Ray was signed to a 5-year contract to drive the potent Team Menard Dallara-Oldsmobile Aurora that had been vacated by Tony Stewart, critics pointed out that although he was undoubtedly fast, Ray had a propensity for not finishing.

When Ray started the 1999 season with three straight 21st-place finishes (two ending in crashes), the critics repeated: "Fast, yes . . . but see what we told you? You can't win races and you can't become a title contender without getting to the checkered flag."

It was a long time coming, but it finally happened; Greg Ray bagged his first race win. Greg Ray (2) overtakes Jacques Lazier (33) en route to his first IRL victory. Ray, who started from the pole, won by only .120 of a second over runner-up Sam Schmidt.

But something changed. Ray's smooth and superb performance at Pikes Peak—where he led 109 of 200 laps around the slightly banked 1-mile circuit—was his second straight visit to the podium. He finished second in the previous IRL race at Texas Motor Speedway.

"Texas was a big boost for our team," Ray explained. "It gave us some momentum."

Ray and Team Menard kept the momentum going in a big way at Pikes Peak by starting from the pole and scoring the maximum 55 points available for the round. Ray scored only 34 points in the opening three rounds. With the runner-up finish at Texas combined with the PPIR victory, Ray jumped into third place in the championship with 131 points.

Pikes Peak was a two-car race. Runner-up Sam Schmidt, in Treadway Racing's G Force-Aurora, led for 91 laps (Ray led for the other 109 laps) and lost by only .12 of a second. This was a duel to remember between two drivers with similar backgrounds: Before the 1999 campaign, both Ray and Schmidt had driven for teams with limited resources and had shown enough promise to be hired by two of the IRL's well-backed outfits.

Sam Schmidt battled the eventual winner, Greg Ray, for the lead most of the day before falling short and finishing second. Schmidt's disappointment was softened by a check for more than $100,000.

Ray and Schmidt exchanged the lead six times—three in overtaking maneuvers, once in the pits, and twice by employing different pit-stop strategies. Ray led the opening 23 laps before Schmidt passed him while exiting Turn 2. Schmidt led the next 63 laps, all under green flag conditions.

They pitted under caution—brought out by Mark Dismore's contact with the inside wall as he pitted—on Lap 86 and Ray emerged in front. Schmidt regained the lead by overtaking Ray on the outside of Turn 1 on Lap 100, then lost it when Ray passed him on Lap 116 by going underneath in traffic exiting Turn 4.

The race went without a caution for 95 straight laps. Ray extended his lead to 4.2 seconds before pitting for the final time on

Once again, Kelley Racing provided Mark Dismore with a very fast car, but a spin into the pit wall and a loss of brakes spoiled his day. He ran as high as 3rd early on but finished 21st.

Scott Sharp (8), Johnny Unser (92), and Eliseo Salazar (6) demonstrated how tight the racing was through the turns at Pikes Peak International Raceway. Sharp finished 8th, Unser 13th, and Salazar 20th.

Lap 166. Schmidt stayed out through Lap 177. When he pitted, Ray regained the lead by 6.3 seconds.

There were only three cautions, but the final one on Lap 184 set up a mad dash to the checkered flag. The pace car picked up Ray and there were several lapped cars back to Schmidt. Following the Lap 190 restart, Eddie Cheever and Buddy Lazier unlapped themselves. "I didn't want to deal with Lazier or, especially, Cheever," Ray explained. "I let them go."

Schmidt was carving his way through the rest of the traffic, and on Lap 194, he was squarely in Ray's mirrors. They were separated by 1.4 seconds. Steadily, Schmidt gained some ground. At the white flag, his G Force was within striking range, just .525 of a second behind. "I thought I would set him up out of [Turn] 2 on the last lap, and I think I was a little too late getting on the throttle," Schmidt said. "I think it's pretty much impossible because of the [low] banking to get somebody by the [start/finish] line in [Turns] 3 and 4 unless somebody makes them check up. It was real slick out there."

Schmidt managed to get alongside of Ray in the charge to the checkered flag, but was half a car length short. "After I saw the checkered flag, I wanted to stop and cry," Ray said. "My [crew] works so hard, and we've had so much trouble finishing. It's a great feeling to win. Our day was coming. I knew it was coming." But he wasn't sure that this would be the day. "We had oil pressure problems with the engine from the beginning," Ray said. "I don't know how it stayed together. At the end, it started to rattle and I was really worried."

If Schmidt had to finish second, he was happy to see Ray nail down his first win. They've been friends since competing in Formula 2000 at the start of their careers and had agonized together over the problems of finding funding for their IRL efforts. "Last year, I spent a considerable amount of time trying to make deals to get to another race," Schmidt said. "Now, I think about driving the car and working out . . . preparing myself. I think that's really helped make me a better driver this year. This race was fun and I'm really happy to finish second."

Although Scott Harrington didn't get to stand on the podium, his Dallara-Aurora was the third best car in the race. Harrington deserved a Purple Heart for his effort; he was driving wounded. In a crash during practice before the previous round at Texas, Harrington broke his right leg, cracked three ribs, and tore ligaments in both knees. Harrington had John Paul Jr. standing by as replacement if he couldn't compete, but because Harrington made it through practice and qualified eighth, he decided to tackle the race.

"The biggest problem," Harrington explained after qualifying, "are the three cracked ribs when I go over the bumps. It takes your breath away for a second. The bumps hurt my knees, too."

Harrington steadily moved up, passing Dismore's Dallara-Aurora for fourth on Lap 37. He moved up to third by overtaking Cheever's Dallara-Infiniti and to second by overtaking Schmidt in Turn 4 on Lap 151. Harrington was only 5.2 seconds behind Ray when he made his final pit stop on Lap 158. Following the ensuing stops by Schmidt and Ray, he fell back to third. Schmidt's ability to run longer, and turning in fast laps on a lighter fuel load, had allowed him to get out ahead of Harrington.

While trying to overtake the lapped Scott Goodyear on Lap 183, Harrington slapped the wall in Turn 4. His courageous run was

over. "I went down low and thought he was going to give me a way through," Harrington said. "Goodyear came down and I had to roll out of the throttle. The front end washed out worse than it had all day anywhere. I went up the track and hit the wall.

"It was my mistake. In hindsight, I should have bided my time a little more. We had the fastest car out there. That's the tough part. It wasn't that tough making it through the race. The car was unbelievably hooked up. I could drive high or low to pass. It's a bitter pill to swallow when the back luck is self-induced."

Harrington's demise left third place to the steady Davey Hamilton, driving Galles Racing's Dallara-Aurora. Hamilton started ninth and tenaciously clung to the lead lap. By saving fuel, he moved up to third by pitting under the caution started by Dismore's contact after several cars had come in under green.

"It was loose until the first [pit] stop and then we had great balance, a really nice car to drive," Hamilton said. "We actually had

As Buzz Calkins (12) and John Hollansworth Jr. (42) got the half-way signal, Calkins was charging from 24th to a 14th-place finish. Hollansworth, however, started on the front row but finished 16th.

Scott Goodyear (4) couldn't keep pace with Eddie Cheever Jr. (51), who started 11th but finished 4th. Goodyear struggled with his car's handling and took 12th but retained the points lead.

a pretty good race car. I don't know if we could race with the leaders because we never had a chance. We just decided to stay on pace. We had a great race." Hamilton had been nearly a lap down before the caution caused by Harrington's brush with the wall. He finished 15.7 seconds behind Ray at the checkered flag.

Cheever, with the lone Infiniti-powered car in the field, had tried to overtake the other cars early in the race, but circumstances prevented him from challenging for the lead. Starting 11th, Cheever rocketed upward. He passed Dismore for third on Lap 33. Cheever was the first of the front runners to come in for fuel and tires on Lap 75. The Lap 83 caution, allowing Ray, Schmidt, and Hamilton to pit under yellow, dropped him to fifth and to the end of the lead lap.

The 1998 Indianapolis 500 champion hung onto the lead lap for much of the day before going a lap down late in the running. Cheever regained the lead lap on the final restart, Lap 190, and brought it home fourth. "When that yellow came out after our first stop, it put us out of sync and we spent the rest of the day fighting to stay ahead of the leaders," Cheever said.

Cheever also lost the ability to communicate with his crew midway through, hampering his ability to improve the car. "Losing the radio contact with the crew at midpoint, I could not communicate the small adjustments I needed to make to the car," Cheever said. "Making up a lap with no radio is no easy feat."

Cheever was adamant that the Infiniti, winless through 24 races since the inception of the 4-liter normally aspirated formula by the IRL, had the power to take him to Victory Lane. "We had an engine that could have won the race," Cheever said. "Infiniti should feel proud of their engine. We let them down."

Fifth place went to Lazier's Hemelgarn Racing Dallara-Aurora. The 1996 Indy 500 champion's race proceeded in virtually the same manner as Cheever's. Lazier was put nearly a lap down by his first pit stop, then ran out of fuel prior to the second stop and had to coast around. That put him a lap down, and he rebounded to return to the lead lap after the final caution.

"That first yellow killed us," Lazier said. "Then, we were running real strong, trying to make it up. We tried to stretch [the mileage] and ran out of fuel. We're thrilled with a top-five finish, considering we ran out of fuel and lost a lap and a half in the pits. It just didn't go our way."

Robby Unser was sixth in Team Pelfrey's Dallara-Aurora, his third-straight solid finish. He was eighth at Indianapolis and sixth at Texas. "This just builds our momentum," Unser said. "It was a good day. The man that could get through traffic really well is the guy that had the better day. My hat is off to Greg Ray and Team Menard.

"A good finish was very important to me and the team. We came into this weekend with a plan to concentrate on setup and that paid off in the end. I got held up in traffic a little bit, but that's just as much my fault as anyone else's."

Scott Goodyear had won two of the last four races, but he was never in the hunt at Pikes Peak. He finished 12th in Panther Racing's G Force-Aurora, four laps down. "The car got better as we made changes, but we were so far down from the beginning, we couldn't catch up," Goodyear said. "We had struggled since we got here with the [Goodyear] tires and setup, and today that was evident."

Jeff Ward also endured his least competitive outing through five rounds in Pagan Racing's Dallara-Aurora. He finished ninth. "There was so much push that I had to hold back," Ward said. "If it wasn't the wing, it was the crossweight. We just went a little too conservative on that. Traffic wasn't a factor. I just couldn't make it through the corners. Nobody got in the way, nobody was holding me up. I was holding myself up."

Kenny Brack, the defending champion of the race, finished seventh in A. J. Foyt's Dallara-Aurora. He went a lap down when his airjacks failed on his first pit stop and never got back into contention.

Fan-friendly Robby Unser was happy to accommodate well-wishers with autographs prior to the race. He finished sixth—exactly where he started—in his PetroMoly/Team Pelfrey Dallara.

Billy Boat, Foyt's other driver, was caught in the only serious crash of the race. Tyce Carlson, who had started fifth in Blueprint-Immke Racing's Dallara-Aurora, spun in Turn 3 on the opening lap directly in front of Boat. They hit the wall locked together, throwing Carlson's Dallara up on two wheels, but neither driver was injured.

Ray's victory was the first of the 1999 season for Firestone tires. Schmidt and Harrington were also on Firestones, which appeared to have more grip over a long run than the Goodyears. "The Firestone tires were great, absolutely perfect all day," Ray said.

In his fifth start with Menard, Ray had delivered. "It's great to see the pot of gold at the end of the rainbow," Ray said. "John couldn't fly out here and spend so much time away from his business, but I'm sure he's happy about this."

Despite handling woes, Stephan Gregoire persevered and finished 11th, noting: "It was a tough race. It was very slippery and we had no handling. We just wanted to hang in there and go to the end."

OFFICIAL BOX SCORE
PEP BOYS INDY RACING LEAGUE
Radisson 200 at Pikes Peak International Raceway
Sunday, June 27, 1999

FP	SP	Car	Driver	Car Name	C/E/T	Laps Comp.	Running/ Reason Out	IRL Pts.	Total IRL Pts.	IRL Standings	IRL Awards	Designated Awards	Total Awards
1	1	2	Greg Ray	Glidden/Menards	D/A/F	200	Running	55	131	3	$96,200	$50,100	$146,300
2	4	99	Sam Schmidt	Sprint PCS	G/A/F	200	Running	40	101	11	80,100	23,150	103,250
3	9	9	Davey Hamilton	Galles Racing Spinal Conquest	D/A/G	200	Running	35	107	7	68,100	1,850	69,950
4	11	51	Eddie Cheever Jr.	The Children's Beverage Group/Team Cheever/Infiniti	D/I/G	200	Running	32	121	4	56,000	15,100	71,100
5	12	91	Buddy Lazier	Delta Faucet/Coors Light/Hemelgarn Racing	D/A/G	200	Running	30	104	9	51,500	1,100	52,600
6	6	81	Robby Unser	PetroMoly/Team Pelfrey	D/A/F	199	Running	28	99	12	46,100	700	46,800
7	13	14	Kenny Brack	AJ Foyt PowerTeam Racing	D/A/G	199	Running	26	109	5	45,000	100	45,100
8	17	8	Scott Sharp	Delphi Automotive Systems	D/A/G	198	Running	24	109	5	43,900	0	43,900
9	18	21	Jeff Ward	Yahoo!/MerchantOnline.com/ Dallara/Olds	D/A/G	196	Running	22	149	2	43,900	0	43,900
10	23	33 R	Jaques Lazier	Truscelli Team Racing/ Warner Bros. Studio Stores	G/A/G	195	Running	20	30	28	42,900	5,000	47,900
11	15	7	Stephan Gregoire	Mexmil/Tokheim/G Force	G/A/F	195	Running	19	85	13	41,700	0	41,700
12	14	4	Scott Goodyear	Pennzoil Panther G Force	G/A/G	195	Running	18	164	1	40,600	0	40,600
13	16	92	Johnny Unser	Tae-Bo/Delta Faucet/Hemelgarn Racing	D/A/G	194	Running	17	33	26	17,600	0	17,600
14	24	12	Buzz Calkins	Bradley Food Marts/Sav-O-Mat	G/A/F	194	Running	16	78	15	38,400	0	38,400
15	10	30	Jimmy Kite	McCormack Motorsports	G/A/F	194	Running	15	26	31	37,400	0	37,400
16	2	42 R	John Hollansworth Jr.	CompuCom/Lycos	D/A/G	193	Running	16	69	17	36,300	0	36,300
17	21	35	Steve Knapp	Delco Remy/Microphonics/ ThermoTech/ISM Racing	G/A/G	190	Running	13	66	18	35,100	0	35,100
18	20	3	Raul Boesel	b-fast Shopper/Transworld/ Brant Racing R&S MKV	R/A/G	190	Running	12	79	14	35,100	0	35,100
19	8	66 R	Scott Harrington	The Certain Teed Building Products Special	D/A/F	183	Accident	11	50	21	12,100	0	12,100
20	19	6	Eliseo Salazar	Nienhouse Motorsports Racing Special	G/A/F	175	Running	10	51	20	11,000	0	11,000
21	3	28	Mark Dismore	MCI WorldCom	D/A/G	152	Running	10	107	7	33,000	0	33,000
22	22	98	Donnie Beechler	Big Daddy's BBQ Sauce and Spices	D/A/F	113	Handling	8	45	23	11,000	0	11,000
23	5	20	Tyce Carlson	Blueprint-Immke Racing	D/A/F	0	Accident	7	58	19	33,000	0	33,000
24	7	11	Billy Boat	Harrah's AJ Foyt Racing	D/A/G	0	Accident	6	102	10	33,000	0	33,000
25	25	55 R	Robby McGehee	Energizer Advanced Formula	D/A/F	0	Did not start	5	46	22	11,000	0	11,000
			Speedway Engines									800	800
			Team Menard Engines									600	600
											TOTAL- $1,000,000	$98,500	$1,098,500

Fastest Lap: #28 Mark Dismore (Lap 196, 168.721)
PPG Team Pole Award: #2 Glidden/Menards/Team Menard
Delphi "Leader at Halfway" Award: #99 Sam Schmidt
Legend: R-Pep Boys Indy Racing League Rookie
Tire Legend: F- Firestone(12); G- Goodyear(13)

Fastest Leading Lap: #2 Greg Ray (Lap 95, 165.312)
Coors Light "Pit Performance Award": #99 Sam Schmidt
MBNA America Lap Leader: #2 Greg Ray
Chassis Legend: D- Dallara(16); G- G Force(8); R- Riley&Scott(1)

PPG Pole Winner: #2 Greg Ray (176.005 mph)
Firestone First at 99 Award: #2 Greg Ray
MCI WorldCom Long Distance Award: #33 Jaques Lazier
Engine Legend: A- Oldsmobile Aurora(24); I- Nissan Infiniti(1)

Lap Leader Summary:

Driver	Times	Total
Greg Ray	4	109
Sam Schmidt	3	91

Caution Flags:
Laps   Reason/Incident
2-11   #20 Carlson, accident T2, #11 Boat contact T3
83-89   #28 Dismore, spin in pits
184-189   #66 Harrington contact T4
3 caution flags, 23 laps

Scott Sharp Gets His Groove Back

Inset: There's no question who won: Scott Sharp let out a whoop to celebrate the end of a half-season of frustration. The team had struggled at times, but everything meshed in victorious fashion in Atlanta.

Team Kelley Grabs Gold at Atlanta

by Jonathan Ingram

Presented by MCI WORLDCOM

Scott Sharp faked down low and then powered past Robby Unser on the high side to win the Indy Racing League's sixth race of the season at the Atlanta Motor Speedway. The winning move came 31 laps from the checkered flag. But in one important respect, the winning move was in reality made *outside* the cockpit of Sharp's Kelley Racing entry long before the Kobalt Mechanics Tools 500 ever began.

Following the Indianapolis 500, Sharp was dissatisfied with the team's performance and requested that the team switch to another engineer for his Delphi Automotive Systems Dallara-Aurora. His logical choice was Will Moody. The crew chief for Sharp's Trans-Am championships in 1991 and 1993 at American Equipment Racing, Moody had been working in the IRL since its inception. Moody started the season at CBR Cobb Racing with driver Roberto Guerrero, but became available when that team elected to re-group following the Indy 500. Price Cobb, the team owner, allowed Moody to join Sharp at Kelley Racing.

Scott Sharp had a new team manager and a new race car setup for Atlanta, but an old, standby procedure helped him to victory in the Kobalt Tools 500: "I prayed almost every lap," he said.

"We've made some key changes to key people on the team," said Sharp after his fourth career IRL victory. "We basically had to start over in a lot of ways," he continued. That included the team's approach to the Atlanta round, where qualifying became the second priority to finding a car set-up that would be consistent over the long haul on the high banks of the 1.54-mile Atlanta track. "It's hard to develop a new set-up on a race weekend," said Sharp. "We kept digging and digging and we finally got it."

"We changed everything on the car except the engine and tires from the set-up that Scott's used to running," said Moody, who obviously enjoyed the trust of his driver. "There was some confusion about how to adjust the car in the cockpit for things like the changing fuel load. When it actually came time to race at the end, we were ready."

Engineering was the most important component on everybody's team during qualifying at Atlanta. Car set-up is always crucial, but with engines limited to 10,000 rpm and rear-wing angles mandated at 6 degrees, every driver could keep his foot down on the accelerator pedal all the way around the NASCAR-style track for two laps of qualifying. Therefore, trimming the aerodynamic drag out of the car, primarily through ride height, became the most important consideration.

Additionally, teams also needed to get the rear gearing just right to keep from banging into the engine rev limiters. A.J. Foyt hit the jackpot with driver Billy Boat, who clocked an official speed of 215.251 miles per hour in his Harrah's-backed Dallara-Aurora. It was the season's first pole for Boat, whose tail-happy driving style won four straight poles at the end of last year and six overall.

"The last two races, we've had the gear too low," said Boat. "Gearing in qualifying is the most important thing. This time we kind of rolled the dice with a little more gear than we thought we needed and it worked." Foyt said the team wanted to be sure to get the right gear

Not where he wanted to be: Billy Boat started from the pole, but led just two laps and struggled to a 10th-place finish on a night plagued by mechanical troubles.

It may have taken three races for the revival of the Sharp-Moody combination to work, but it seemed only a matter of time. In their two championship seasons, the duo had scored 12 Trans-Am victories and 17 poles. Overall, Sharp scored 14 Trans-Am victories and 24 poles in the three seasons he drove Chevy Camaros prepared by Moody.

In Atlanta, there wasn't much doubt that Moody's involvement led to victory—the first for him as an IRL engineer. Unfortunately, the chassis set-up that Moody gave to Sharp was so unfamiliar to the driver that he struggled to adapt for much of the early part of the race, which left him one lap down near the halfway mark. But fortunately, all's well that ends well.

Billy Boat (11) is overtaken easily by Robby Unser (81), who led as late as Lap 177 (of 208), but finished second to winner Scott Sharp.

combination, which had been a problem previously on the 1.5-mile superspeedways owned by Bruton Smith that are similar to the Atlanta oval. "We realized how far off we were in Charlotte and Texas, so we changed the gears four times during practice," said Foyt.

Another change for Boat in Atlanta came in the budget department. After the Harrah's sponsorship arrived in mid-season, Foyt started investing more money in qualifying and race engines. Just as he had last year with Katech, Foyt began working hand-in-hand with the engine builders at Roush Racing. It also helped that after Round 3 at Indy the IRL reduced maximum engine revs from 10,300 to 10,000, giving the wily Texan an opportunity to exploit new cam profiles.

Late in practice Boat's teammate Kenny Brack ran the gear ratios that Foyt eventually put into Boat's Dallara-Aurora on Goodyears. Brack, unfortunately, was saddled with a new narrow-width rear suspension from Dallara to reduce drag, which the team did not have enough time to sort out. The Swede thus ended up 14th on the grid in his Power Team entry.

The Glidden Dallara-Aurora of Greg Ray, the Sprint PCS G Force-Aurora of Sam Schmidt, the MCI WorldCom Dallara-Aurora of Mark Dismore, and the Pennzoil G Force-Aurora of Scott Goodyear came within a tenth of a second of the pole time. Those who didn't get close to the pole either had gearing or chassis balance problems, or lacked a qualifying engine. But overall, only seven-tenths of a second separated the 25 cars that recorded qualifying times.

After deciding to emphasize the race over Friday's qualifying, Sharp was happy to be in sixth place on the grid, 0.11 of a second from the pole. "We've been fast in qualifying in the past, but we haven't raced well," said Sharp, who opened the season with a pole at the Walt Disney World Speedway. "Now we're trying to put more emphasis on being fast in the race. We haven't been able to do that recently."

Particularly disappointed was Eddie Cheever, the lone entrant powered by an Infiniti V-8. "It was boring and slow, which is not good for qualifying," said Cheever. His Infiniti-powered Dallara would not

come up to speed in short order, a mystifying problem that neither his team nor the Infiniti folks figured out. So after running 214 miles per hour solo during practice, Cheever clocked only 210.674 miles per hour in his solo qualifying run that included one warm-up lap and two under green. That put him 21st on the grid and in search of drafting partners. The track conditions eventually came to the set-up of the Kelley Racing entry, following the transition from a hot, sunny evening into the cooler night. And there were enough crashes and malfunctions among the early front runners to clear the path for Sharp to score his first victory in nearly a year.

The most injurious accident occurred on the 87th lap when Steve Knapp lost control of his G Force in Turn 2, then collected the Dallara of Jeff Ward. A chain reaction resulted in Stephan Gregoire getting hit by rookie Ronnie Johncox. Knapp's car was carried all the

Buddy Lazier's younger brother proved he was capable of running with the top drivers. Jacques Lazier was chasing Kenny Brack for 3rd place when he spun. He recovered to finish in 12th position.

Steve Knapp's day ended when he spun and was collected by Jeff Ward in a hard collision that left Knapp with a fractured vertebrae in his neck.

Scott Sharp's pit crew operated smooth and fast all night, keeping the eventual winner's Delphi Automotive Systems Dallara-Aurora on the track and handling well.

way to the outside wall where the impact left him with a fractured C-7 cervical in his lower neck. "Steve Knapp lost it and Jeff Ward was right behind him," said Gregoire. "I was right behind Ward and got hit in the rear." Knapp was listed in serious condition at the Atlanta Medical Center before being transferred to the Methodist Hospital in Indianapolis for successful surgery.

The incident also turned out to be bad news for Sharp. The four-car accident occurred as leader Ray was being serviced by Team Menard on pit road. Ray emerged from the pits to complete the 88th lap in the lead. Meanwhile five drivers who had pitted earlier all got caught a lap down due to being slowed by the yellow lights before they could get past leader Ray's car in the pits. That group included Unser, Sharp, and Cheever, who would eventually finish a lap down due to gearbox problems.

At the re-start on the 105th lap, second-placed Goodyear suffered serious understeer, enabling the lapped cars ahead of him to

quickly pull away while his Pennzoil machine was swarmed by Schmidt, an oncoming Buddy Lazier, who had started 15th, and Brack. When leader Ray's Menard engine broke its crankshaft and he floated into pit road on Lap 108, Unser and Sharp, among others, were put back on the lead lap. Most significant to the outcome of the race was the subsequent crash of Lazier and Schmidt, who were vying for the lead when a frightful collision occurred at the exit of Turn 2 on the 114th lap.

"You can't just stick your nose in," said an angry Lazier, who was hit from underneath in his left sidepod near the rear by Schmidt as the two drivers entered the back straight. The right front wheel of Schmidt came up onto the sidepod and alongside the cockpit of his Delta Faucet/Coors Light Dallara. Luckily the veteran drivers were able to hold their cars down off the wall and then they slid to the inside apron out of the line of traffic.

Exactly one year after a season-ending racing accident, Eliseo Salazar was extremely impressive in his Nienhouse Motorsports Racing Special G Force-Aurora. The racing veteran qualified 18th, but ran strong to finish 4th.

But Lazier did not attempt to hold his temper in check. "The nature of this track is that you don't run down there on the white line at the bottom [in Turn 2]," he said. "You go in high and then come down." Schmidt evidently thought a gap existed because of Lazier's higher line, but the two then collided under the lights just at dusk. "I'm just not sure what happened out there," said Schmidt, who talked to his friend Lazier once back in the garage. "I will have to watch the replay to determine if there is any blame—but it seems like a racing accident to me."

The ensuing yellow bunched the field and gave new life to Unser and Sharp, who rode in sixth and seventh once the yellow flew. "It was strange," said Sharp's engineer Will Moody. "We had bad luck and then we had good luck and it all balanced out."

With Ray, Lazier, and Schmidt on the sidelines after leading 60 of the first 113 laps, the battle for the lead was left to Goodyear and Brack, who had made quick progress from his 14th starting position. But when Goodyear suffered a broken alternator and Brack broke an exhaust header on his Foyt entry, Sharp was left to do battle with second-year man Unser and rookie Jacques Lazier. For his part, the son of three-time Indy 500 winner Bobby Unser once again proved to be a maturing talent, scoring his second runner-up finish on a high-banked 1.5-mile oval and his third straight finish of sixth or better.

"Scott's car was working up there where no one else was running and he didn't have to stop in traffic," said the Team Pelfrey driver who led twice for 12 laps. "I was married to the bottom of the track."

After passing Unser on Lap 178, Sharp finished only 0.163 of a second ahead of him at the finish. Lazier demonstrated some family traits by leading twice for 24 laps. Due to a late pit stop, the younger Lazier was chasing Brack for third when his Team Truscelli G Force spun three laps from the finish, which dropped the rookie to 12th.

"We had third [place] just in front of us," said Lazier of what might have been. "It was a big carrot for us."

Prior to the Indy 500, the Kelley Racing team, owned by the father and son duo of Jim and Tom Kelley, also made another major shift. Jim Freudenberg was hired as the General Manager from the Arciero/Wells FedEx Championship Team. After that race, in which Sharp retired in 28th place due to a broken transmission, it was decided to release Sharp's engineer, David Cripps, in favor of Moody. Sharp had been uncomfortable with not only his results, but the fact that Cripps worked as the technical director of the team and also oversaw the development of teammate Mark Dismore's Dallara-Aurora entries. With Freudenberg running the overall operation and Moody concentrating solely on Sharp's cars, the result was a sleeker and more efficient operation in a series where the competition had become intensely close.

In light of the 10,000-rpm limit for engines and the third year of standard chassis from Dallara and G Force, details had begun separating

Raised body panels expose the shocks that are at the heart of a handling setup. Team technicians (such as this one from Sam Schmidt's team) adjust the shocks to suit track conditions.

Johnny Unser (92), Ronnie Johncox (22), and Robby McGehee (55) race through Turn 4. Unser and McGehee finished 13th and 14th, respectively, but Johncox saw his day end when he rear-ended Stephan Gregoire.

the winners from losers. "I don't think there's any more closer or competitive racing right now than the IRL," said Sharp.

Sharp vaulted from fifth to second in the points behind Goodyear, who finished 16th since the battery had to be exchanged twice to keep his Pennzoil car going. So Sharp left Atlanta with the season's original goals of being a mainstay in victory lane and in the championship both in place. "I've been so frustrated," he said. "I wanted to do so much more for Kelley Racing. My prayers were answered."

Kenny Brack, the 1999 Indy 500 champion, won the 1998 Atlanta race and ran well enough in 1999 to lead late in the race. But he couldn't keep pace with winner Scott Sharp and had to settle for third.

OFFICIAL BOX SCORE
PEP BOYS INDY RACING LEAGUE
Kobalt Mechanics Tools 500 at Atlanta Motor Speedway
Saturday, July 17, 1999

FP	SP	Car	Driver	Car Name	C/E/T	Laps Comp.	Running/ Reason Out	IRL Pts.	Total IRL Pts.	IRL Standings	IRL Awards	IRL Designated Awards	Total Awards
1	6	8	Scott Sharp	Delphi Automotive Systems	D/A/G	208	Running	50	159	2	$95,500	$25,000	$120,500
2	10	81	Robby Unser	PetroMoly/Team Pelfrey	D/A/F	208	Running	40	139	7	79,200	6,750	85,950
3	14	14	Kenny Brack	AJ Foyt PowerTeam Racing	D/A/G	208	Running	35	144	5	67,100	2,050	69,150
4	18	6	Eliseo Salazar	Nienhouse Motorsports Racing Special	G/A/F	208	Running	32	83	16	33,100	500	33,600
5	20	12	Buzz Calkins	Bradley Food Marts/Sav-O-Mat	G/A/F	208	Running	30	108	13	50,700	100	50,800
6	21	51	Eddie Cheever Jr.	The Children's Beverage Group/ Team Cheever/Infiniti	D/I/G	207	Running	28	149	4	45,300	5,100	50,400
7	7	9	Davey Hamilton	Galles Racing Spinal Conquest	D/A/G	207	Running	26	133	8	44,200	100	44,300
8	27	98	Donnie Beechler	Big Daddy's BBQ Sauce and Spices	D/A/F	207	Running	24	69	19	21,100	5,000	26,100
9	11	30	Jimmy Kite	Team Losi/Fastrod/ McCormack Motorsports	G/A/F	207	Running	22	48	25	43,100	0	43,100
10	1	11	Billy Boat	Harrah's AJ Foyt Racing	D/A/G	207	Running	23	125	9	42,000	12,500	54,500
11	25	3	Raul Boesel	b-fast Shopper/Brant Racing R&S MKV	R/A/G	207	Running	19	98	14	40,900	0	40,900
12	16	33 R	Jaques Lazier	Warner Bros. Studio Store/ Warner Bros. Studio Team Racing	G/A/G	206	Spin	18	48	25	39,800	0	39,800
13	22	92	Johnny Unser	Tae-Bo/Delta Faucet/Hemelgarn Racing	D/A/G	206	Running	17	50	24	16,800	0	16,800
14	23	55 R	Robby McGehee	Energizer Advanced Formula	D/A/F	205	Running	16	62	23	15,600	0	15,600
15	12	66 R	Scott Harrington	CertainTeed Building Products Special	D/A/F	204	Running	15	65	22	14,600	0	14,600
16	5	4	Scott Goodyear	Pennzoil Panther G Force	G/A/G	200	Running	16	180	1	35,500	10,000	45,500
17	4	28	Mark Dismore	MCI WorldCom	D/A/G	186	Running	13	120	10	34,300	0	34,300
18	19	17	Dr. Jack Miller	Mayfield/Aramark/Folgers Coffee	D/A/G	184	Engine	12	13	39	12,300	0	12,300
19	9	42 R	John Hollansworth Jr.	CompuCom/Lycos/TeamXtreme	D/A/F	169	Running	11	80	17	33,300	0	33,300
20	26	20	Tyce Carlson	Immke Auto Group/ Hubbard Photographics	D/A/F	156	Clutch	10	68	21	32,200	0	32,200
21	15	91	Buddy Lazier	Delta Faucet/Coors Light/ Hemelgarn Racing	D/A/G	113	Accident	9	113	11	32,200	10,000	42,200
22	3	99	Sam Schmidt	Sprint PCS	G/A/F	113	Accident	9	110	12	32,200	0	32,200
23	2	2	Greg Ray	Glidden/Menards	D/A/F	108	Electrical	9	140	6	32,200	10,000	42,200
24	13	7	Stephan Gregoire	Dick Simon Racing/Mexmil/ Tokheim/Viking Air Tools	G/A/F	87	Accident	6	91	15	32,200	0	32,200
25	17	22 R	Ronnie Johncox	The Home Depot	D/A/G	87	Accident	5	24	32	10,200	0	10,200
26	8	21	Jeff Ward	Yahoo!/MerchantOnline.com/ Dallara/Olds	D/A/G	83	Accident	4	153	3	32,200	0	32,200
27	24	35	Steve Knapp	Delco Remy/Microphonics/Fuz.com/ SM Racing/G Force	G/A/G	57	Accident	3	69	19	32,200	0	32,200
			Brayton Engineering									1,000	1,000
			Katech Engineering									400	400
											TOTAL—$1,000,000	$88,500	$1,088,500

Time of Race: 2:12:15.235   Average Speed: 141.546 mph   Margin of Victory: 0.163 seconds (under caution)

Fastest Lap: #33 Jaques Lazier (Lap 3, 215.097 mph, 25.105 sec.)   Fastest Leading Lap: #4 Scott Goodyear (Lap 47, 214.584 mph, 25.165 sec.)

PPG Pole Winner: #11 Billy Boat (215.251 mph, 25.087 sec.)   PPG Team Pole Award: #11 Harrah's AJ Foyt Racing

Firestone First at 99 Award: #2 Greg Ray Delphi   "Leader at Halfway" Award: #91 Buddy Lazier

MBNA America Lap Leader: #4 Scott Goodyear   MCI WorldCom Long Distance Award: #98 Donnie Beechler

Legend: R-Pep Boys Indy Racing League Rookie   Chassis Legend: D- Dallara(18); G- G Force(8); R- Riley&Scott(1)

Engine Legend: A- Oldsmobile Aurora(26); I- Nissan Infiniti(1)   Tire Legend: F- Firestone(12); G- Goodyear(15)

Lap Leaders

Laps	Car#Driver
1-2	#11 Billy Boat
3-13	#2 Greg Ray
14-31	#99 Sam Schmidt
32-81	#4 Scott Goodyear
82-107	#2 Greg Ray
108	#14 Kenny Brack
109-113	#91 Buddy Lazier
114-123	#14 Kenny Brack
124-142	#33 Jaques Lazier
143-144	#4 Scott Goodyear
145-149	#33 Jaques Lazier
150	#9 Davey Hamilton
151-161	#8 Scott Sharp
162-164	#81 Robby Unser
165-168	#14 Kenny Brack
169-177	#81 Robby Unser
178-208	#8 Scott Sharp

16 Lead changes among 10 drivers

Lap Leader Summary:

Driver	Times	Total
Scott Goodyear	2	52
Scott Sharp	2	42
Greg Ray	2	37
Jaques Lazier	2	24
Sam Schmidt	1	18
Kenny Brack	3	15
Robby Unser	2	12
Buddy Lazier	1	5
Billy Boat	1	2
Davey Hamilton	1	1

Caution Flags:

Laps	Reason/Incident
29-35	#42 Hollansworth accident T2
51-55	#35 Knapp tow-in
88-104	#22 Johncox, #35 Knapp, #21 Ward, #7 Gregoire, accident T2
114-119	#99 Schmidt, #91 B. Lazier, accident backstraight
166-169	#66 Harrington, spin pit exit
188-191	#17 Miller, blew engine
207-208	#33 J. Lazier, spin backstraight

7 caution flags, 45 laps

FIREHAWK®
BORN AT INDY.
DRIVEN EVERYWHERE™.

FIRESTONE ACCEPTS THE CHALLENGE...
AND YOU WIN!

THE LESSONS WE LEARN ON RACE DAY ARE IN THE TIRES YOU COUNT ON EVERY DAY.

With a record 50 wins at the Indy 500,® Firestone knows Indy® racing like no other tire company. And if we can develop the kind of quick acceleration, grip and stability required for Indy racing tires, just imagine how well our line of Firehawk® street performance radials will perform for you. Firehawk performance tires are speed rated from S to Z and specifically engineered for crisp handling and legendary performance. We now offer two Firehawk tires with **UNI-T**®, the **U**ltimate **N**etwork of **I**ntelligent **T**ire **T**echnology—

Firestone® Firehawk® SH30®
With UNI-T®
High-Performance Street Tire

the Firehawk® SZ50® and the Firehawk® SH30®. The Firehawk SH30 with **UNI-T** is an H-rated high-performance tire designed to deliver outstanding wet performance, especially wet cornering, while still providing excellent dry performance. Stop by your local Firestone retailer and check out the complete Firehawk line today. And congratulations to all teams racing on Firestone Firehawk tires. We wish you much success.

uni·T
Ultimate Tire Technology

Race-Winning Firestone® Firehawk®
Indy Racing Slick &
Firestone® Firehawk® SS10® Street Tire

Firestone®
America's Tire Since 1900

Race-Winning Firestone® Firehawk®
Indy Racing Rain Tire &
Firestone® Firehawk® SZ50® With UNI-T®
Ultra-High Performance Street Tire

Indy 500® and Indy® are registered trademarks of the Indianapolis Motor Speedway.

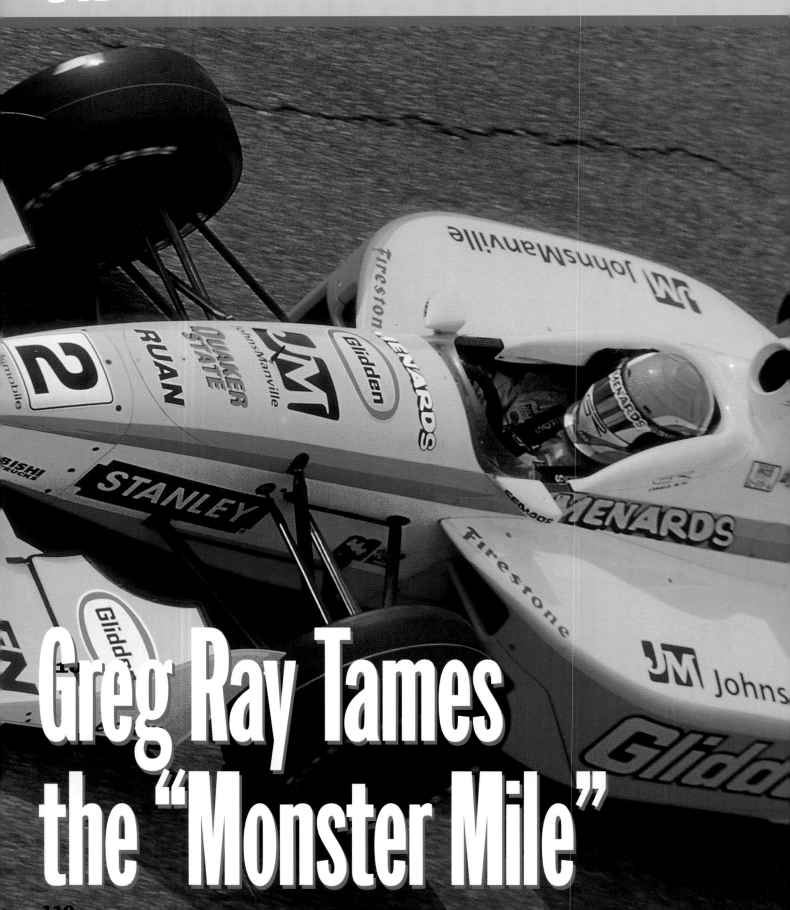

Greg Ray Tames the "Monster Mile"

Inset: Race winner Greg Ray (center) hoisted hardware with runner-up Buddy Lazier (left) and third-place finisher Kenny Brack (right) after the MBNA Mid-Atlantic 200. The win boosted Ray to second in points.

Team Menard Notches Win Number 2

by Tim Tuttle

Greg Ray didn't have the fastest car in the MBNA Mid-Atlantic 200 at Dover Downs International Speedway (the fastest cars belonged to Kelley Racing teammates Scott Sharp and Mark Dismore who combined to lead for a total of 125 laps). The Menard team didn't have the best pit strategy for Ray, either, but Ray and his Dallara-Aurora were superior at passing in traffic and that ability proved to be the most important of all.

The 33-year-old Texan capitalized on prime moments of opportunity to earn his second Pep Boys Indy Racing League victory of the season. Ray is known for his aggression, but he tempered it at Dover with a touch of conservatism that pointed to his improving maturity. Ray's triumph, by .731 of a second over Buddy Lazier, was likely to be the finest drive of his career. Mistake free, it bordered on perfection.

The Kelley Racing duo of Dismore and Sharp filled the front row and Ray occupied the third spot on the grid. Because of Dover's 24-degree banking in the corners and the IRL-mandated 62-degree setting of the rear wing, chassis setups for qualifying were funda-

To win at the "Monster Mile," you must have durability and patience. Greg Ray displayed both qualities as he bided his time and methodically picked off cars to work his way through traffic. In the final stages of the race, he bolted past Mark Dismore and Sam Schmidt to assume the lead and take the win.

Schmidt tried to go around the heavy traffic on the outside in Turn 2 and found his lane blocked. Dismore exited Turn 2 and was balked by a slower car. Ray darted to the far inside and, in a flash on the back straight, went from fourth to second. "It was pretty simple," Ray said. "It was the first time I had to deal with a lot of traffic. Everybody was on cold tires. One car backpedaled and then another car backpedaled and they went up the track. We'd been working the low line and I drove it on in. I don't know how many cars I passed, but it had to be seven or eight. I thought getting by Dismore was the pass of the race. He was a 10th [of a second per lap] quicker all day."

Ray had, in reality, cleared seven cars. Remaining in front were Scott Harrington, nearly a lap down, and Gregoire. Gregoire couldn't find a way around Harrington and Ray took advantage to pass the Frenchman for the lead on the inside of Turn 1 on Lap 173. "Harrington must have thought he was in the lead," Ray said. "Harrington was running real defensive and Thomas Knapp said not to do anything crazy. I stuck with them and finally got a good run off [Harrington and Gregoire] in Turn 4 and passed [Gregoire] into Turn 1."

Eddie Cheever Jr. and Robby Unser accosted rookie driver Scott Harrington (66) after the race, blaming him for causing their crashes. Both apologized in the following week, but were still fined by the IRL.

mentally the same as for the race. These factors would make passing extremely difficult.

Sharp passed polesitter Dismore on the outside of Turn 1 at the start and stayed in front for 34 straight laps. Dismore was second, running in tandem and slowly pulling away from Ray, who was 1.5 seconds behind. "We knew the two Kelley cars were going to be tough to beat," Team Menard manager and engineer Thomas Knapp said. "They were just about where we thought they'd be."

But Sharp's right rear tire deflated on Lap 35—a debris-caused puncture was suspected—and he spun rear-wing first into the outside wall in Turn 4 ending his race. Dismore moved to the front and led 87 straight laps, through the first round of scheduled pit stops. The leaders pitted for routine service on Lap 121 with Dismore 2.6 seconds ahead of Ray.

Gregoire stretched his G Force-Aurora's fuel mileage to reach Lap 123 before stopping, and Schmidt's G Force-Aurora, which assumed the lead, went to Lap 128. The cars of Robby McGehee, Buddy Lazier, Jimmy Kite, and Scott Harrington had undertaken a pit strategy that was out of sequence with the leaders and that put them in front of Dismore on the track. But McGehee, the leader from Laps 129 to 145, ran out of fuel on Lap 146, and the others were forced to come in for service.

Still recovering from a broken leg, getting into and out of his race car was no simple feat for Scott Harrington, yet he managed to enjoy a laugh while squeezing into the cockpit.

Dismore returned to the front on Lap 147, with Ray in second, but the track went under full caution on that very same lap. Dismore and Ray needed to stop again to reach the finish and they came into the pits on Lap 151. Gregoire, believing he could go the distance, stayed out and took the lead. Schmidt was in second. Dismore emerged from his stop in third, followed by Ray. In front of them were four cars on the tail of the lead lap, directly behind the pace car. It was a situation that lent itself to both a chaotic and exciting restart on Lap 160 and that's what happened.

Ray was able to pass Harrington two laps later in Turn 1 and went unchallenged to the checkered flag. "We stayed with our strategy the whole time," Ray said. "We were going to use our top gear, use the draft and stay out of trouble. I wasn't antsy to lead; I just wanted to stay out of trouble."

For Ray, winning his second race felt every bit as good as his first. "I remember how it felt going into those closing laps at Pikes Peak," Ray said. "It was very emotional, getting goose bumps, almost breaking out in tears, smiling, just trying to stay focused. I had more of it this time. This was a hard race. It was very emotional for me in the car. It's a feeling I want to feel a lot more.

"It seems like we've won the two most difficult races of the year. [Dover] is called the Monster Mile for good reason. I think winning the first race helps your confidence. I've always had a lot of self confidence, but knowing you can do it is one thing, and going out there and doing it, is all together something else."

Although he had been a contender in several other IRL races this season prior to Dover, Lazier's runner-up was his best result of the year. He found wrestling his Hemelgarn Racing Dallara-Aurora around the high banks in near 100-degree heat to be hard work.

"This place is so grueling," Lazier said. "By the fifth lap, your arms and every muscle in your body is burning. I think it has a lot to do with the concrete [surface], the Gs you're pulling, the awe-some grip you have. And, then, with this heat, it's enough to pretty much kill you. You've got to be tough to be able to finish this thing, let alone finish at speed."

Lazier also finished second at Dover in 1998. "It's such a wonderful thing to be second for the second time here, but, of course, we'd like to be one position better," he said. "We had a good car, capable of winning if things had gone our way." Starting from 17th on the grid, Lazier climbed into eighth position by the race's third caution on Lap 71. Luckless Eliseo Salazar's rear wing had collapsed in Turn 2, sending him hard into the outside wall. The equally unfortunate John Hollansworth Jr., came around the corner, drove over a glut debris, clipped Salazar's demolished G Force, and promptly exited the race. Neither driver was injured.

The cleanup would take 18 laps, setting up the chance for an alternative pit-stop strategy. McGehee's Conti Racing Dallara-Aurora came in on Lap 84. Hemelgarn waited until the end of the caution, bringing in Lazier on Lap 88. When Schmidt made his second stop on Lap 128, McGehee took the lead. Lazier was second.

McGehee ran out of fuel on Lap 146. Lazier had pitted a lap previously. And on the next lap, the caution came out for Kite's stranded-on-course G Force-Aurora. Lazier barely stayed on the lead lap. "We'd have been a lap up on most of the field if the [Lap 147] caution had come out a lap or two earlier before we had to pit,"

Jeff Ward (21) leads a pack of racers down one of the straights of Dover. Runner-up Buddy Lazier (91) pursues Ward along with Billy Boat (11), Tyce Carlson (20), and Jimmy Kite (30).

going to go around a lot of cars on the outside. But a black car [McGehee] drove me up high and into the marbles. It wasn't his fault; I know he didn't know I was there. But I got all that build up [spent rubber] on my tires and had to really get off the throttle in Turn 1."

Lazier fell back to fifth position. Schmidt began showing he had the speed to lead when he passed Dismore for third on the outside in Turn 2 on Lap 172. Four laps later, Schmidt moved into second by overtaking Gregoire on the outside entering Turn 1.

Schmidt was within a couple of car lengths of Ray when a front-wing flap fell off in Turn 1. Schmidt was forced to slow dramatically and it took him several laps to regain confidence in the handling of his G Force. Schmidt did manage to stay on the lead lap and finished fifth. With Schmidt off the pace, Ray had a 2.8-second lead over Gregoire, who was still trying to get past Harrington.

Dismore was in fourth. On Lap 190, Dismore tried to get underneath Gregoire exiting Turn 4. They touched wheels, collided, and went into the wall. Gregoire had accepted the fact that Ray had used the traffic, in the form of Harrington, to pass him for the lead, but he was angered that Harrington, once he was a lap down, didn't allow he and Dismore past to race for the lead.

"Ray used the traffic and got a good run on me exiting Turn 4," Gregoire said, "and got me. I guarantee that if Harrington hadn't been blocking me, I'd have won the race. I had a little push in traffic, but

Stephan Gregoire (7) led Laps 151 through 172 before being passed in thrilling fashion by winner Greg Ray. Gregoire later collided with Mark Dismore, taking both cars out of the race and leaving Gregoire 14th.

Lazier said, "but we had to for fuel and then the yellow came out. That was unfortunate, but we were also fortunate that we got out in time to avoid going down a lap."

For the Lap 160 restart, Lazier was lined up in third position, but with the lapped McGehee car directly in front of him. Lazier was the eighth car in running order on the track, also behind the four cars almost a lap down, Gregoire, and Schmidt.

"On that restart, I had a great run going into Turn 4," Lazier said. "I was a full gear, 20 miles per hour, ahead of everybody else. I was

The banking of "The Monster Mile" at Dover is shown in this shot of rookie Robby McGehee's Dallara-Aurora. The first-year IRL racer led Laps 129 through 145 and came home ninth.

the car was perfect in clean air. I wasn't quite fast enough to make a move on [Harrington]. He makes a move sometimes you don't expect and I'm not crazy. We wanted to finish the race. But I have to give credit to Ray for using the traffic."

Gregoire charged Harrington with weaving and said it was the cause of the crash with Dismore. "[Harrington] was driving all over the place," Gregoire said. "I was upset nobody showed him the black flag. Harrington was shown the blue flag [an advisory signal that the leaders are directly behind] lap after lap to let the leaders through. And he didn't take any notice of it. He cost me many positions."

With Gregoire and Dismore eliminated, Lazier moved up to second and Kenny Brack, in A.J. Foyt's Dallara-Aurora, finished third.

Brack had qualified 14th and advanced to 9th when Sharp crashed. He gained four positions on his first pit stop to fourth and was third, behind Dismore and Ray, on Lap 150. Brack fell to sixth when he made his final pitstop and gained positions as Schmidt, Dismore, and Gregoire had problems over the final 20 laps.

"I never thought we'd get as far up to third in the race from where we started," Brack said. "We've got to be happy with third. We didn't have the speed in the car we needed. We were lacking two-tenths [of a second] per lap. We were a little short of top gear. We had a little luck, too. We didn't make any mistakes and a couple of people made mistakes and we took advantage of them."

Billy Boat finished fourth in Foyt's Dallara-Aurora. "We had a pretty good car," Boat said. "This Monster Mile is a tough place to pass. We were geared a little too short and it hurt us in the draft. We finished fourth, still rolling. Anytime you can say you finished in the top five and put the car in the transporter, that's saying something."

When the race was over, Eddie Cheever Jr., and Robby Unser confronted Harrington in his pit. Cheever chased Harrington, still slowed by his broken right leg suffered in June at Texas Motor Speedway, around his car and put his hands around Harrington's neck area. One witness said Cheever had also tried to punch Harrington, but missed. Cheever and Unser were upset over what they said was Harrington's role in a Lap 57 crash that knocked out Cheever. Cheever had been attempting to pass Unser, who was behind Harrington. Cheever said Harrington's blocking had forced Unser up the track in Turn 2 into Cheever's way. Cheever, forced to brake, was hit from behind by Hollansworth.

"I lost Phoenix [this year] because of that moron and he was doing the same thing here," Cheever said. "He was going high, low, high down the back straight. It's ridiculous. He's changing his lane in the middle of the corner. Harrington was blocking Robby and moving all over the place. I don't know if [Harrington] has epileptic fits in the cockpit or he's deliberately trying to block."

Billy Boat started on the pole at Atlanta and went steadily backward in the race. At Dover he started 16th, but moved up smoothly to finish 4th, putting him 7th in the points race.

Kenny Brack never led a lap at Dover, but he avoided trouble and piloted his AJ Foyt PowerTeam Racing Dallara-Aurora to a third-place finish.

For his part, Unser said, "It was wrong for us to do that, but something had to be done. I had to sit and watch it [Harrington's alleged blocking] all day." Harrington denied he was blocking or that he played any part in Cheever's wreck. "I maintained my line and the cars behind me could pass me if they wanted to," Harrington said. "Our car was set up to run the low line and I maintained my line all day. I don't even think I played a role in Eddie's accident."

The IRL fined Cheever and Unser $5,000 each for unsportsmanlike conduct and conduct detrimental to the sport of auto racing for their actions. "It was inexcusable what I did," Cheever said. "I should have let the sanctioning body address the situation. That's what they are for."

Ray had no trouble passing Harrington, or anybody else. "This is, by far, the best year of my life," he said.

Jeff Ward (21) finished 13th but came away from the grueling race 4th in points. "It was just a matter of survival," said Ward, shown here passing Davey Hamilton, who crashed after 12 laps.

OFFICIAL BOX SCORE
PEP BOYS INDY RACING LEAGUE
MBNA Mid-Atlantic 200 at Dover Downs International Speedway
Sunday, August 1, 1999

FP	SP	Car	Driver	Car Name	C/E/T	Laps Comp.	Running/ Reason Out	IRL Pts.	Total IRL Pts.	IRL Standings	IRL Awards	Designated Awards	Total Awards
1	3	2	Greg Ray	Glidden/Menards	D/A/F	200	Running	51	191	2	$105,100	$37,660	$142,700
2	17	91	Buddy Lazier	Delta Faucet/Coors Light/ Hemelgarn Racing	D/A/G	200	Running	40	153	9	87,300	19,550	106,850
3	14	14	Kenny Brack	AJ Foyt PowerTeam Racing	D/A/G	200	Running	35	179	3	73,700	2,050	75,750
4	16	11	Billy Boat	Harrah's AJ Foyt Racing	D/A/G	200	Running	32	157	7	60,200	100	60,300
5	4	99	Sam Schmidt	Sprint PCS	G/A/F	200	Running	30	140	10	55,200	100	55,300
6	5	66 R	Scott Harrington	The CertainTeed Building Products Special	D/A/F	199	Running	28	93	17	27,100	100	27,200
7	22	33 R	Jaques Lazier	Warner Bros. Studio Stores/ Truscelli Team Racing	G/A/G	199	Running	26	74	22	47,800	100	47,900
8	12	12	Buzz Calkins	Bradley Food Marts/Sav-O-Mat	G/A/F	199	Running	24	132	13	46,600	0	46,600
9	10	55 R	Robby McGehee	Energizer Advanced Formula	D/A/F	198	Running	22	84	21	24,600	0	24,600
10	20	98	Donnie Beechler	Big Daddy's BBQ Sauce and Spices	D/A/F	198	Running	20	89	19	23,400	0	23,400
11	11	20	Tyce Carlson	Hubbard Photographics Inc./ Immke Auto Group	D/A/F	198	Running	19	87	20	22,100	0	22,100
12	13	81	Robby Unser	PetroMoly/Team Pelfrey	D/A/F	197	Running	18	157	7	42,900	0	42,900
13	7	21	Jeff Ward	Yahoo!/MerchantOnline.com/ Dallara/Olds	D/A/G	195	Running	17	170	4	41,700	0	41,700
14	9	7	Stephan Gregoire	Dick Simon Racing/Mexmil/ Tokheim/Viking Air Tools	G/A/F	189	Accident	16	107	14	40,400	0	40,400
15	1	28	Mark Dismore	MCI WorldCom	D/A/G	189	Accident	20	140	10	39,200	32,500	71,700
16	15	30	Jimmy Kite	Team Losi/Fast Rod/ McCormack Motorsports	G/A/F	144	Brakes	14	62	25	38,100	0	38,100
17	18	4	Scott Goodyear	Pennzoil Panther G Force	G/A/G	143	Timing chain	13	193	1	36,700	0	36,700
18	21	6	Eliseo Salazar	Nienhouse Motorsports Racing Special	G/A/F	69	Accident	12	95	16	36,700	0	36,700
19	6	42 R	John Hollansworth Jr.	CompuCom/Lycos/TeamXtreme	D/A/F	69	Accident	11	91	18	35,600	0	35,600
20	23	22 R	Ronnie Johncox	Technique Inc.	D/A/G	66	Engine	10	34	29	12,400	0	12,400
21	19	51	Eddie Cheever Jr.	The Children's Beverage Group/Team Cheever/Infiniti	D/I/G	56	Accident	9	158	6	34,400	5,000	39,400
22	2	8	Scott Sharp	Delphi Automotive Systems	D/A/G	35	Accident	10	169	5	34,400	0	34,400
23	8	9	Davey Hamilton	Galles Racing Spinal Conquest	D/A/G	12	Engine	7	140	10	34,400	0	34,400
			Speedway Engines									800	800
			Team Menard Engines									600	600
										TOTAL	$1,000,000	$98,500	$1,098,500

Time of Race: 1:45:01.503
Fastest Lap: #28 Mark Dismore (Lap 116, 182.325 mph, 19.745 sec.)
PPG Pole Winner: #28 Mark Dismore (182.639 mph, 19.711 sec.)
Delphi "Leader at Halfway" Award: #28 Mark Dismore
Legend: R-Pep Boys Indy Racing League Rookie
Tire Legend: F- Firestone(12); G- Goodyear(11)

Average Speed: 114.258 mph
Fastest Leading Lap: #28 Mark Dismore
PPG Team Pole Award: #28 MCI WorldCom/Kelley Racing
MBNA America Lap Leader: #28 Mark Dismore
Chassis Legend: D- Dallara(16); G- G Force(7)

Margin of Victory: 0.731 sec.
(Lap 116, 182.325 mph, 19.745 sec.)
Firestone First at 99 Award: #2 Greg Ray
MCI WorldCom Long Distance Award: #91 Buddy Lazier
Engine Legend: A- Oldsmobile Aurora(22); I- Nissan Infiniti(1)

Lap Leaders:
Laps	Car#	Driver
1-34	#8	Scott Sharp
35-121	#28	Mark Dismore
122-128	#99	Sam Schmidt
129-145	#55	Robby McGehee
146	#66	Scott Harrington
147-150	#28	Mark Dismore
151-172	#7	Stephan Gregoire
173-200	#2	Greg Ray

7 Lead changes among 7 drivers

Lap Leader Summary:
Driver	Times	Total
Mark Dismore	2	91
Scott Sharp	1	34
Greg Ray	1	28
Stephan Gregoire	1	22
Robby McGehee	1	17
Sam Schmidt	1	7
Scott Harrington	1	1

Caution Flags:
Laps	Reason/Incident
35-44	#8 Sharp accident T4
57-64	#51 Cheever accident T2
71-88	#7 Salazar, #42 Hollansworth, accident T2
147-159	#30 Kite tow-in
190-196	#7 Gregoire, #28 Dismore, accident front straight

5 caution flags, 56 laps

Coors LIGHT

THERE'S THUNDER COMING FROM THE ROCKIES

 The Official Beer of The Indy 500® and The Pep Boys® Indy Racing League

Greg Ray Shines Through

Inset: Greg Ray hoists the winner's trophy high over his head on the victory podium. Ray not only won the Colorado Indy 200, but he stretched his lead points over Panther Racing's Scott Goodyear. It was the Team Glidden/Menard driver's third win in four IRL races.

Team Menard's Savvy Drive to Glory

by Tim Tuttle

Don't let the margin of victory (.445 of a second) deceive you; Greg Ray was in complete control during the Colorado Indy 200. The Texan had 'em covered with a smooth, calculated, and mistake-free performance in Team Menard's Glidden Dallara-Aurora.

Ray was in front for stretches of 46 and 74 laps and led a total of 146. That is impressive, but even more telling of Ray's turn-around in the second half of the Pep Boys Indy Racing League campaign was his coolness under fire in the closing laps when Ray had traffic in front of him and the very hungry Davey Hamilton challenging from behind.

Ray's aggressive style has been both an attribute and a liability throughout his up-and-down career. He was able to hold off Hamilton, in Galles Racing's Spinal Conquest G Force-Aurora, by properly applying the concept of risk management. Control like that is a sure sign of growth, and it's an area where Ray has made large strides in 1999.

Just as he did in June, Greg Ray (2) held off tough challengers to win at Pikes Peak International Raceway. This time the threat came from Davey Hamilton, whom Ray beat to the checkered flag by just .445 of a second.

119

a race until after Indy. Now, we're finishing. We're not doing anything different now than we did at the start of the season. Things are just going our way."

In terms of preparation and effort, Ray's self appraisal of Team Menard was on the money. But, in the last five races since the Indy 500, he has also eliminated the mistakes that took him out of potential victories at Phoenix and Indianapolis. Ray could have easily run into trouble down the stretch at the second Pikes Peak race because there were eight cars—some lapped, some fighting to stay on the lead lap—ahead of Ray during a restart with 17 laps remaining, and Hamilton was directly in his mirrors.

Hamilton tried to pass Ray on the outside on the restart, but was forced to back off in Turn 2. Hamilton kept the heat on until the checkered flag. "In the open air, I could go flat out, but as soon as I got in the dirty air, it shut down the front end," Hamilton said. "I got up next to him on the outside after the last restart and lost the front end. We really need to win a race and I want my first [in the IRL], and I was doing everything possible to get past him. I was even shifting for the last 10 laps, sixth gear down the back straight and fifth in the turns. There were a few times when I had a run, but he had something to block me. He blocked me with 10 laps to go, but I would have done the same thing if I'd been him."

Ray's skill at carving through the traffic was critical to keeping Hamilton at bay. Ray came up behind Scott Harrington's Dallara-Aurora on Lap 189. Harrington, on the lead lap, defended his position and Ray was momentarily bottled up. Hamilton tried to overtake him on the outside in Turn 3, but was forced to back off the throttle to turn the car away from the approaching wall. Three laps later, Ray made a well-timed slingshot maneuver out of Turn 4 and passed

"Ray has learned how to finish," Rick Galles said. "Davey was right behind him and Ray was patient. He didn't put himself in a bad position by doing that. Ray didn't let the pressure get to him."

Ray's triumph in the IRL's second race of the season at Pikes Peak International Raceway provided further and compelling evidence of his new-found maturity. He won both of the 1999 races on PPIR's 1-mile oval, and claimed a third victory at Dover in between. With three triumphs out of four races, Ray soared into the IRL championship lead by 44 points over Scott Goodyear (246 points to 202 points). It is a long way from where Ray and the Thomas Knapp—directed Menard team were after the Indianapolis 500.

"It feels good to be in the position we're in," Ray said. "We've felt capable of winning every race this season, but we hadn't finished

There was fierce racing even well back in the pack. Eddie Cheever Jr. (51) overtook Billy Boat (11) here and finished 11th, while Boat took 13th and Jaques Lazier (33) was 12th.

Robby McGehee (55) welcomed back chief mechanic Steve Fried, who was injured in a pit-road accident at the Indianapolis 500. "[Fried's] presence means so much to us," said McGehee, who finished seventh in Colorado.

Sam Schmidt (99) and Greg Ray posted the exact same qualifying times, but since Ray qualified before Schmidt, Ray was awarded the pole position on a tiebreaker. Ray won while Schmidt took fifth.

Harrington on the inside of Turn 1. Harrington, no longer on the lead lap, properly allowed Hamilton past a couple of turns later.

Within several laps, Hamilton had Ray squarely in his sights again. Ray was gaining on Sam Schmidt, running fifth and on the end of the lead lap in Treadway Racing's G Force-Aurora. Ray decided he couldn't afford to allow Schmidt to dictate the pace.

"I was quicker than Sam was and I ran up on him," Ray explained. "I had to back up, because I didn't want to get next to him and create a hole for Davey to come in. I decided to pass Sam with two laps to go and I put both left-side wheels below the white line to do it."

Going that far to the inside, across that slippery painted line, was dangerous territory and Ray knew it. "I didn't really want to, but I thought I had to do it to win," Ray said. "I was thinking about the points and the championship, because a lot of our competition had trouble in the race. We needed to win."

Ray's daring maneuver closed out any hopes Hamilton had over the final 1 1/2 laps. Ray's other duel took place with Schmidt at the start of the race. Schmidt and Ray had tied for the fastest lap in qualifying, averaging 176.263 miles per hour. It was the first time in IRL history the pole had to be decided by the tie-breaking procedure (Rule 6.7), which states that whomever had gone out first was the pole winner. The luck of the draw went to Ray.

The pole is worth $10,000 and three points. "The championship points for the end of the year are more important than the money," Ray said. Schmidt couldn't quite believe they ran the same

time of 20.424 seconds. "It's amazing to me and a little frustrating," Schmidt said. "I'm more disappointed for the team than for myself."

Schmidt led the opening 28 laps, including 12 that were run under caution. He went side-by-side with Ray through Turns 1 and 2 and down the back straight and finally made the pass on the outside entering Turn 3.

At the end of the first lap, Jeff Ward, who qualified 10th, spun exiting Turn 4 and hit the outside wall with the back of his Pagan Racing Dallara-Aurora. Moments later, Ronnie Johncox had the rear of his Tri Star Motorsports Dallara-Aurora step out and into the middle of the Turn 4 wall. Neither driver was injured.

"The car just got loose," Ward said. "I mean, I've never had it happen like that before. It slowly just rotated and came around. There were a lot of guys in front of me that could've taken the air from me. I wasn't pushing that hard for the car to come around like that."

Johncox, who qualified 18th, lifted when he saw Ward spinning and it cost him. "I checked up and tried to turn to avoid it," he said. "I don't know exactly what happened other than the back end just came around real fast and I crashed."

These crashes would prove to be the only hard wall-banging incidents of the race. Schmidt held the lead after the Lap 14 restart and began encountering slower cars on Lap 25. Entering Turn 1 on Lap 29, Schmidt came upon a group that was running two abreast. "I chose

the outside and it was the wrong choice," Schmidt said. Ray went low and darted past Schmidt exiting Turn 2 and led the next seven laps.

Schmidt regained the lead in the same way he'd lost it. Ray was forced to slow for a cluster of lapped cars in Turn 4 and Schmidt went inside in Turn 1 on Lap 36. They traded places a third time in the same circumstances on Lap 39 when Ray went inside Schmidt in Turn 1. Ray led the next 46 laps.

"The traffic was Schmidt's downfall. He fell back to eighth by Lap 51." The car was great when we were by ourselves, but in traffic we'd lose the front end going into a turn and the back would snap around on an exit," Schmidt explained. "It was like a big circle we couldn't get out of."

By Lap 50, Ray had built up an 8.6-second lead over Hamilton, who had started fifth and moved up steadily. He made his first pit stop on Lap 84 and Hamilton came in one lap later. Schmidt was getting tremendous fuel mileage with his Comptech-built Aurora and stayed out until Lap 92. The extra distance promoted Schmidt into the lead for seven laps.

When Schmidt came in for service on Lap 93, Ray regained the lead. He stayed there for 74 straight laps, including six under caution for debris. Ray led by 12.3 seconds over Hemelgarn Racing's Buddy Lazier after 100 laps, but saw it evaporate for the caution that began on Lap 109.

Jimmy Kite (30), who started 16th, finished 8th in his Team Losi/Fastrod/McCormack Motorsports entry. It was a significant improvement over his 15th-place finish in the June race at Pikes Peak.

Team technicians make a pre-race check of the suspension and tire pressure of the Dick Simon Racing/Mexmil G Force/Aurora/Firestone car. Stephan Gregoire started 21st in this car but brought it home in 14th.

There were seven cars separating Ray and Lazier for the Lap 115 restart. Lazier's Dallara-Aurora began overtaking the cars and gaining on Ray. By Lap 140, Lazier trailed by 2.7 seconds. The margin fluctuated in the ebb-and-flow of traffic and was at 4 seconds when Lazier lost power on the front straight on Lap 158. The team had miscalculated the fuel mileage and left him out one lap too long. Lazier managed to coast around to his pit, but fell to the tail of the lead lap.

Hamilton regained second place. He was 1.4 seconds behind Ray before coming in for his second pit stop on Lap 164. Ray made his second scheduled stop on Lap 166. Suddenly, Kelley Racing teammates Mark Dismore and Scott Sharp were running 1 and 2. Dismore and Sharp had pitted during the Lap 109-114 caution period, hoping that more yellow-flag laps would allow them to go the distance. Dismore had started third in his Dallara-Aurora and stayed in the hunt throughout the race. Sharp had gone a lap down at one-third distance, but the strategy and an improved car had moved him back into contention.

Hamilton, on warmer tires, was nearly able to overtake Ray on Lap 169 on the inside of Turn 1. Ray hung tough and Hamilton was forced to abandon the effort. Dismore held a 14.2-second lead on Lap 173 and Ray was third, 18.5 seconds back. The caution that Dismore and Sharp desperately needed never appeared. Sharp pitted on Lap 174. The green-flag stop put him a lap down. On Lap 180, Sharp grazed the wall in Turn 4, bringing out a caution. Sharp was able to limp his Dallara-Aurora into the pits, making for a three-lap yellow period.

The caution period had come too late for Dismore, who pitted on Lap 182. It dropped him to third behind Ray and Hamilton, and he remained there until the checkered flag. Dismore's trip to the podium was his first in the IRL. "I'm happy," Dismore said. "It's great to be on the podium. I have no complaints. We had a little push in the car and I couldn't really do much in the straights. Greg and Davey aren't dummies and they weren't going to leave the door open. It was all a momentum deal and the opportunity to pass never presented itself."

Lazier brought it home fourth; the final car on the lead lap and angry and frustrated over the fuel snafu that cost him so much time. "We threw away all that we worked for," said Lazier, who finished 7 seconds behind the winner. Lazier had qualified ninth. He gained four positions on the first lap and was up to third by Lap 36.

Schmidt was next across the line. "I'm happy with fifth," he said. "From Lap 40 to our first pit stop, our car was really bad. We changed it on the first pit stop and it was perfect after that. But I was 10 or 12 cars back and couldn't make up the ground."

Harrington was sixth. He'd been the fastest in all three practices prior to qualifying, but started from fourth on the grid. Harrington's race started with a near disaster; he accidentally hit the engine kill switch approaching the green flag. Harrington was fortunate that the cars around him avoided him.

Harrington bump-clutch started his engine, but dropped to ninth by the end of the first lap. "We chased the setup all day," Harrington said. "We're just happy to bring the car home in sixth. It's another strong run."

Conti Racing had two reasons to be happy at Pikes Peak: Robby McGehee had his best run since Indianapolis by finishing seventh, and injured crew chief Steve Fried had returned to the team. Fried suffered near fatal injuries when he was run over by Jimmy Kite (who was knocked into him after a collision with Jeret Schroeder) on the pit lane at Indianapolis. Fried's recovery wasn't complete and the injuries restricted his ability to function at Pikes Peak, but his presence was welcomed by the team. "Steve is such a key part of our team, such a leader," McGehee said. "Him just being here is a huge deal for our team."

Scott Harrington (right) appears skeptical about the topic he is discussing during pre-race driver introductions with Scott Sharp (left) and the race's eventual runner-up, Davey Hamilton (center).

Kite, driving McCormack Motorsports' G Force-Dallara, charged from 16th on the grid to finish 8th. Robby Unser had his fifth top-10 in eight races by taking 9th in Pelfrey Racing's Dallara-Aurora.

Kenny Brack struggled to 10th, two laps down, in A.J. Foyt's Dallara-Aurora. "It's the worst car we've had in two years," Brack said. "It was loose in the beginning. We adjusted, but never really got into the ballpark. It was decent, but we never got something we could race."

But the driver and team who had the most discouraging race of all was Goodyear and Panther Racing. Goodyear qualified 11th, but was never in contention and finished 21st. He'd been forced to make a long pit stop at the halfway point for a broken radiator hose fitting. "I'm disappointed," Goodyear said, "but at this point we've got to take it race by race."

Eddie Cheever also had mechanical problems. His Dallara-Infiniti dropped a cylinder when he was running fifth on Lap 168. Cheever finished 11th. Ray was, of course, at the other end of the spectrum. His car had run flawlessly and he had driven it forcefully and skillfully.

OFFICIAL BOX SCORE
PEP BOYS INDY RACING LEAGUE
Colorado Indy 200 at Pikes Peak International Raceway
Sunday, August 29, 1999

FP	SP	Car	Driver	Car Name	C/E/T	Laps Comp.	Running/ Reason Out	IRL Pts.	Total IRL Pts.	IRL Standings	IRL Awards	Designated Awards	Total Awards
1	1	2	Greg Ray	Glidden/Menards	D/A/F	200	Running	55	246	1	$97,700	$61,300	$159,000
2	5	9	Davey Hamilton	Galles Racing Spinal Conquest	D/A/G	200	Running	40	180	5	81,300	3,550	84,850
3	3	28	Mark Dismore	MCI WorldCom	D/A/G	200	Running	36	176	10	69,000	11,450	80,450
4	9	91	Buddy Lazier	Delta Faucet/Coors Light Hemelgarn Racing	D/A/G	200	Running	32	185	4	56,700	1,900	58,609
5	2	99	Sam Schmidt	Sprint PCS	G/A/F	199	Running	32	172	12	52,100	10,100	62,200
6	4	66 R	Scott Harrington	The Certain Teed Building Products Special	D/A/F	199	Running	28	121	15	46,600	1,200	47,800
7	8	55 R	Robby McGehee	Energizer Advanced Formula	D/A/F	199	Running	26	110	16	23,400	0	23,400
8	16	30	Jimmy Kite	Team Losi/Fast Rod/ McCormack Motorsports	G/A/F	199	Running	24	86	23	44,400	100	44,500
9	12	81	Robby Unser	PetroMoly/Team Pelfrey	D/A/F	199	Running	22	179	6	44,400	0	44,400
10	13	14	Kenny Brack	AJ Foyt Power Team Racing	D/A/G	198	Running	20	199	3	43,300	0	43,300
11	20	51	Eddie Cheever Jr.	The Children's Beverage Group/Team Cheever/Infiniti	D/I/G	197	Running	19	177	7	42,100	10,000	52,100
12	17	33 R	Jaques Lazier	Warner Bros. Studio Stores/ Truscelli Team Racing	G/A/G	197	Running	18	92	22	41,000	0	41,000
13	14	11	Billy Boat	Harrah's AJ Foyt Racing	D/A/G	196	Running	17	174	11	39,900	0	39,900
14	21	7	Stephan Gregoire	Dick Simon Racing/Mexmil/ Tokheim/Viking Air Tools	G/A/F	196	Running	16	123	14	38,700	0	38,700
15	15	12	Buzz Calkins	Bradley Food Marts/Sav-O-Mat	G/A/F	194	Running	15	147	13	37,700	0	37,700
16	7	42 R	John Hollansworth Jr.	CompuCom/Lycos/TeamXtreme	D/A/F	192	Running	14	105	18	36,600	0	36,600
17	19	20	Tyce Carlson	Hubbard Photographics Inc./ Immke Auto Group	D/A/F	190	Running	13	100	19	13,400	0	13,400
18	23	26 R	Bobby Regester	Truscelli Team Racing	G/A/G	189	Running	12	12	40	13,400	0	13,400
19	22	6	Eliseo Salazar	Nienhouse Motorsports Racing Special	G/A/F	187	Running	11	106	17	34,300	0	34,300
20	24	98	Donnie Beechler	Big Daddy's BBQ Sauce and Spices	D/A/F	187	Running	10	99	20	33,200	0	33,200
21	11	4	Scott Goodyear	Pennzoil Panther G Force	G/A/G	184	Running	9	202	2	33,200	0	33,200
22	6	8	Scott Sharp	Delphi Automotive Systems	D/A/G	178	Accident	8	177	7	33,200	0	33,200
23	10	21	Jeff Ward	Yahoo!/MerchantOnline.com/ Dallara/Olds	D/A/G	0	Accident	7	177	7	33,200	0	33,200
24	18	22 R	Ronnie Johncox	Technique Inc./Tri Star Motorsports Inc.	D/A/G	0	Accident	6	40	27	11,200	0	11,200
			Speedway Engines									800	800
			Team Menard Engines									600	600
											TOTAL- $1,000,000	$101,000	$1,101,000

Time of Race: 1:28:35.633
Fastest Lap: #91 Buddy Lazier (Lap 198, 172.084 mph, 20.920 sec.)
PPG Pole Winner: #2 Greg Ray (176.263 mph, 20.424 sec.)
Delphi "Leader at Halfway" Award: #2 Greg Ray
MCI WorldCom Long Distance Award: #51 Eddie Cheever Jr.
Engine Legend: A- Oldsmobile Aurora(23); I- Nissan Infiniti(1)

Average Speed: 135.450 mph
Fastest Leading Lap: #2 Greg Ray (Lap 194, 170.374 mph, 21.130 sec.)
PPG Team Pole Award: #2 Glidden/Menards
Coors Pit Performance: #99 Treadway Racing
Legend: R-Pep Boys Indy Racing League Rookie
Tire Legend: F- Firestone(12); G- Goodyear(12)

Margin of Victory: 0.445 sec.
Firestone First at 99 Award: #2 Greg Ray
MBNA America Lap Leader: #2 Greg Ray
Chassis Legend: D-Dallara(16); G- G Force(8)

Lap Leaders:

Laps	Car#	Driver
1-28	#99	Sam Schmidt
29-35	#2	Greg Ray
36-38	#99	Sam Schmidt
39-84	#2	Greg Ray
85	#9	Davey Hamilton
86-92	#99	Sam Schmidt
93-166	#2	Greg Ray
167-181	#28	Mark Dismore
182-200	#2	Greg Ray

8 Lead changes among 4 drivers

Lap Leader Summary:

Driver	Times	Total
Greg Ray	4	146
Sam Schmidt	3	38
Mark Dismore	1	15
Davey Hamilton	1	1

Caution Flags:

Laps	Reason/Incident
2-13	#21 Ward, #22 Johncox, accident T4
109-114	Debris
181-183	#8 Sharp, accident T4

Sam Schmidt's
One Bold Move

Inset: A triumphant Sam Schmidt hoists the spoils of victory—his first in the IRL. The win also catapulted him and his Sprint PCS G Force/Aurora/Firestone from 12th to 3rd in the points race.

Treadway Racing Takes Victory with Decisive Pass

by Tim Tuttle

I n 1996, Sam Schmidt was an aspiring Pep Boys Indy Racing League driver who wasn't on any team's radar screen. He'd won races, first in amateur competition (where he was the 1993 Formula Continental national champion), then in two Formula Ford 2000 professional series, but it was still quite a leap into Indy cars.

"I knew I had to be in the cars and get the experience before anyone would hire me," Schmidt said. "There are lots of guys walking around in the garages looking for jobs. You've got to be able to show an owner what you can do or you're going to be left on the outside."

Schmidt took the initiative of investing in himself. A successful businessman—he holds a master's degree in international finance from Pepperdine University in Malibu, California—Schmidt spent $400,000 to purchase a Dallara and two Oldsmobile Aurora engines. Only part of the money came from sponsorship.

It was a weekend of glorious firsts for hometown boy Sam Schmidt. He won his first-ever IRL pole, then overtook Kenny Brack with three laps left to earn his first victory in the IRL.

A familiar position: Kenny Brack (14) led three times for 118 laps, including diving first into a corner ahead of a pack that included Greg Ray (2), Scott Goodyear (4), and Scott Sharp (8).

Schmidt took his equipment and forged out a cooperative agreement with teams to run him in 1997, initially with Blueprint Racing for two races, and then with LP Racing for the final four races of 1997 and all 11 of the 1998 races. It was low budget, at best. "I spent most of the time between races on the phone trying to find enough sponsorship to get to the next race," Schmidt said.

The final race of the 1998 campaign was a turning point for Schmidt. Using a borrowed engine, after his race engine was lost in shipping, Schmidt finished second to Arie Luyendyk at Las Vegas Motor Speedway.

That breakthrough—it was his first trip to the IRL podium—led to Schmidt being hired as Luyendyk's replacement at Treadway Racing,

one of the IRL's best-funded and best-run operations, for the 1999 season. Schmidt was a surprising selection to most in the IRL paddock, but he filled Luyendyk's seat with admirable effectiveness. In the Vegas.com 500, Schmidt—like Luyendyk before him—took Treadway to the top of the mountain with a hard-fought victory. "I always had the confidence that Sam was a good driver," owner Fred Treadway said.

Schmidt, driving the same G Force chassis that Luyendyk had at Las Vegas in 1998, made a hair-raising pass of Kenny Brack with 2 1/2 laps remaining to capture his first IRL triumph. It came in his 26th start. "I think, internally, we knew we could accomplish what we have accomplished, but a lot of people on the outside didn't think we could," Schmidt said. "You work all your career to get in the position to be hired by a team like Treadway. That's why I went out and bought that car [in 1997], so I could get the experience."

Schmidt is a Las Vegas resident and he approached the race weekend with hometown style: Schmidt showed up dressed for a pre-race party as an Elvis look-a-like, his blonde hair and long sideburns dyed jet-black. "After this," Schmidt said, "I'm working on a second occupation [as an Elvis impersonator]. This is just huge. Winning here is the next best thing to winning at Indy."

Schmidt's celebration actually began during qualifying, where he averaged 209.465 miles per hour to capture the first pole of his career. When the green flag dropped for the start of the race, Schmidt was passed for the lead on the second lap by Kelley Racing's Mark Dismore, who qualified on the outside of the front row, but Schmidt regained it on Lap 13.

Dismore jumped back in front by overtaking Schmidt following a Lap 27 restart. Schmidt dropped to sixth, then rebounded to third before a caution slowed the pace and sent the leaders in for their first pit stops. Trying to exit his pit box Schmidt stalled and emerged in 10th position. "I wasn't sure if we'd be able to come back from that," he said. "It took us a while to get back up there."

In a race riddled with cautions for a bevy of crashes, Schmidt steadily moved forward. When he passed Buzz Calkins' G Force on Lap 136, Schmidt had climbed to fourth. Ten laps later, he went under Jaques Lazier in Turn 2 and set his sights on Brack, who had been out front since Lap 73.

Schmidt looped around the outside of Brack's G Force in Turns 1 and 2 to take the lead on Lap 150 and established a 2.5-second advantage over the next 10 laps. Under caution, Schmidt and Brack made their final pit stops on Lap 165. The AJ Foyt crew put Brack in front and the Swede bolted away from Schmidt on the Lap 170 restart.

Brack's car was superb on fresh Goodyear tires, but the Firestones used by Schmidt maintained a better level of grip for an extended run. Brack opened up a 2.1-second gap to Schmidt by Lap 175, then began to lose ground. Within six laps, Schmidt was only a car length behind. The pace slowed for two more cautions, setting

Rookie Ronnie Johncox stays cool during practice as he listens to team owner Larry Curry (right) while Robbie Buhl listens in (left). Johncox tagged the wall on Lap 163 of the race and suffered a broken foot.

up a final—and deciding—restart at the end of Lap 202. Six laps remained. Brack had blitzed Schmidt on the previous two restarts, but this time the 35-year-old was ready to respond.

"Kenny was accelerating hard down the back straight," Schmidt said. "The restart was all or nothing. If I wasn't right on his gearbox, I wasn't going to have a chance to get him." Schmidt shadowed Brack for three laps. Entering Turn 1, with three laps remaining, Schmidt decided it was now or never.

"I drove hard into [Turn] 1," Schmidt said. "Maybe Kenny didn't pick the throttle up as soon as usual, because I got a run on him to the outside. I was really hanging the car out, so much that I might have brushed the [outside] wall in Turn 2. Kenny does a great job of driving clean, but using [the track] all up. He gets into the corner low and carries a smooth line through the corner to the outside. He doesn't leave much room."

Schmidt powered off Turn 2 and tucked in behind Brack down the back straight. Going into Turn 3, Schmidt darted to the inside and passed Brack for the lead. "I knew I wasn't going to lift going in Turn 3 and thank God that Kenny gave me room," Schmidt said.

Brack was unable to mount a counterattack, finishing .617 of a second behind Schmidt. Foyt had decided to put Brack in a G Force for the first time in 1999 at Las Vegas. That decision was based primarily on evidence that the G Force had been easier on the Goodyear tires than the Dallara on the 1.5-mile tracks. Brack had qualified

third, his best starting position of the season. Foyt then worked his magic on the race setup. "I put a lot of downforce on the car for the race, 250 [more] pounds, " Foyt explained. "We knew the track was going to get slick. We drove those tires into the ground."

The reigning Indianapolis 500 champion stayed near the front in the early going before taking the lead on Lap 73. He set the pace for 117 of the final 126 laps. "We found a good setup and the car was balanced throughout the race," Brack said. "The only problem we had was with a vibration we picked up during the run. I drove hard all the way. I was flat at the end, but he had extra speed. Our cars were equal. The difference was in the tires. Mine were vibrating and that not only hurts your vision, but also the car's performance. I don't think our [Goodyears] were as good as [Schmidt's] Firestones through a fuel run."

Robbie Buhl (22) started 21st but ran strong to take 3rd. "To think we would be on the podium after Friday was a nice surprise . . . the guys did a great job working with the car and the tires. It showed today."

A smooth pit stop for Scott Sharp (8) was typical of his steady weekend; he qualified sixth and finished fourth, moving him into fourth place in the points standings.

Kenny Brack (14) led the most laps, but finished a frustrating second to Sam Schmidt, who took the lead just three laps from the checkered flag. Still, Brack moved into second in points with one race remaining.

Blistering, mid-day desert heat in Las Vegas poses a severe challenge to tires, especially in race conditions. A Firestone engineer is seen checking the tire temperature during practice on Robby McGehee's car.

Brack added, "We're happy with second. Of course, you want to win, but this was the best we could do. We closed the gap on [championship leader] Greg Ray."

Robbie Buhl finished a remarkable third after starting 21st. He hadn't driven since Indianapolis and arrived at Las Vegas without having tested Tri Star Motorsports' Dallara. "It feels good," Buhl said. "To come from where we were on Friday [22nd and 26th in the two practices], we came a long way. We walked out after Friday kind of scratching our heads, but we made a big gain on Saturday morning. The car came good in the race, just kept getting better. I had no complaints with the [Goodyear] tires and was really happy with the grip and balance of our car."

Buhl finished third at Phoenix for Sinden Racing Services and sixth at Indy for a combined Sinden/Foyt entry, but the Sinden team ran out of sponsorship and suspended operations. "I really wanted to do the last two races of the season," Buhl said. "Larry [Curry] called me a couple of weeks ago and asked me to do Las Vegas. [Ronnie] Johncox is a good driver, but he's a rookie and Larry was looking for somebody with experience that could give them some feedback on the car."

Curry, the team's manager and engineer, and former IRL driver Tony Stewart (now in NASCAR's Winston Cup) are part of the Tri Star ownership group. Buhl had driven for Curry at Team Menard in 1997 and 1998. "It's funny to drive for Tony and Larry in a different scenario," Buhl said. "I appreciate the opportunity they gave me." Buhl's path to third, the first podium for the first-year Tri Star team, was cleared by a rash of crashes that eliminated Team Menard's Ray, Panther Racing's Scott Goodyear, Galles Racing's Davey Hamilton, and Dismore.

Eddie Cheever Jr., using the lone Nissan Infiniti-powered engine in the field, Team Pelfrey's Robby Unser, and Jaques Lazier were contenders before mechanical failures eliminated them. Goodyear's string of second-half misfortunes continued when his G Force snapped sideways in Turn 4 on Lap 48 and put him into the outside wall. He was running sixth. A post-race inspection by the Panther team determined a chassis component failure was the cause. "I was running well and just biding our time, waiting to race in the second half of the race," said Goodyear, who suffered a slight fracture of the left leg in the impact.

Ray had entered Las Vegas with a 44-point lead over Goodyear. With him out, Ray was driving his Dallara conservatively. Ray was running eighth when he saw an opportunity to pass Dismore for position at the race's halfway point. "I was just taking it easy since this is a 500K race," Ray said. "Mark Dismore had a hard time with Turn 4. I had a run on him, but he blocked me low. I went to the high side and showed him my nose. I have no idea why he came into me. I was clearly there on the high side. He just moved up and bumped me."

Ray slid into the gray and managed to maintain control without hitting the wall. The brilliant save did him little good. "For some reason, the impact broke the [engine's] timing chain," Ray said.

Dismore didn't expect Ray to try to pass him on the outside. "At that point in the corner, I didn't expect anyone to be there," Dismore said. "I don't want to get into [a disagreement] with Greg, but his left front tire hit my sidepod. I think I was in the right position." Dismore soon became a casualty, too.

Ray didn't know the timing chain had been damaged. He pitted and returned for the next restart. But when he tried to accelerate, nothing happened. Ray moved down low in Turn 1 as the field streamed past.

Billy Boat, a lap down in AJ Foyt's Dallara, slowed for Ray. John Hollansworth Jr., in TeamXtreme's Dallara, didn't and hit Boat in the back. They spun out of control. Dismore tried to out-run the two cars as they went up the track to the outside, but ran out of room and crashed into them.

Hamilton had a marvelous run, rising from the 26th (and last) starting position to fourth. But on Lap 192, Kelley Racing's Scott Sharp went under Hamilton's Dallara in Turn 3 and they touched. Hamilton went into the outside wall; Sharp continued. "Sharp had his eyes closed or lost his brain," Hamilton said. "I'm pretty upset with what happened because it was completely unnecessary. He could have raced me clean."

Sharp disagreed. "He cut me off," he said. "He did it to me and others all day."

Starting 18th, Cheever had another of those impressive charges cut short by an engine failure. He climbed to third by Lap 16 and took the lead on Lap 31, passing Dismore on the inside of Turn 3. Cheever's Dallara led 32 of 42 laps before Brack passed him for the lead on

Lap 73. Cheever was still in second when he fell out on Lap 138.

"When I passed all those cars in the beginning to take the lead, I can't tell you how much fun that was," Cheever said. "I really thought we had it. That charge at the beginning of the race was because of the power of the Infiniti. You could literally see its horsepower. We've been trying new bits in the engine and we may have pushed the envelope too far."

Robby Unser had an extremely competitive race in his Dallara. From 13th, he moved up to fourth by Lap 33 and was second on Lap 41. Unser was running fourth when a fuel pump failure stopped him on Lap 139. "The car was awesome," he said. "Of all the chances [of winning] we've had this year, this one was the best."

Jaques Lazier, driving Truscelli Racing's G Force, also ran as high as second. He was third in the closing stages when he slowed on course, from a fuel pickup problem. He coasted into the pits and lost three laps, but still finished seventh.

"I could go high, low, and wherever I wanted to go," Lazier said. "In my mind, we were the fastest car out there . . . I really thought we had a chance to win. I was just pacing myself."

Despite leading twice for 32 laps and running well early, Eddie Cheever Jr. (51) finished 17th. "The engine blew. Before that, it was going great. We've been road testing a lot of different things. Today, it wasn't enough."

A run-in with Mark Dismore and eventual engine woes ended Greg Ray's day after just 110 laps. Despite finishing 21st, Ray maintained a 13-point lead over Kenny Brack heading into the season-ending shootout at Texas.

Sharp brought his Dallara home in fourth, the final car on the lead lap. "I'm quite pleased with a fourth-place finish," Sharp said. "The car ended the race being quite consistent. We had to make a few adjustments throughout the race, but we were able to get the car to do what we wanted."

Bradley Motorsports provided Calkins with position-gaining pit stops and a solid car and he finished fifth. Calkins won a late-race duel with Conti Racing's Robby McGehee. "That was a lot of fun," Calkins said. "It's the most fun I've had racing in some time. We ran very strong in the opening segments, then developed a problem with too much drag midway through. After we got that cleared up,

we really got going toward the end. I'm pretty pleased to be fifth."

Willy T. Ribbs made his return to Indy car racing at Las Vegas after a five-year absence. He spun on Lap 17 and hit the wall in McCormack Motorsports' G Force. Ribbs became the first African-American to compete in the IRL.

Schmidt's victory, the fifth for Treadway in the IRL, did not come easy. He'd put himself in a hole with the gaff on his first pit stop and had to climb out of it. And the pass of Brack at the end was clear evidence that he was deserving of a chance to replace Luyendyk.

"I had to take a really big risk to pass Kenny," Schmidt said, "but we didn't come here to finish second."

OFFICIAL BOX SCORE
PEP BOYS INDY RACING LEAGUE
Vegas.com 500 at Las Vegas Motor Speedway
Sunday, September 25, 1999

FP	SP	Car	Driver	Car Name	C/E/T	Laps Comp.	Running/ Reason Out	IRL Pts.	Total IRL Pts.	IRL Standings	IRL Awards	Designated Awards	Total Awards
1	1	99	Sam Schmidt	Sprint PCS	G/A/F	208	running	53	225	3	$96,700	$49,500	$146,200
2	3	14	Kenny Brack	A.J. Foyt Power Team Racing	G/A/G	208	running	43	242	2	80,200	45,350	125,550
3	21	22	Robbie Buhl	Tri Star Motorsports Inc.	D/A/G	208	running	35	108	22	46,000	8,450	54,450
4	6	8	Scott Sharp	Delphi Automotive Systems	D/A/G	208	running	32	209	4	55,700	100	55,800
5	16	12	Buzz Calkins	Bradley Food Marts/Sav-O-Mat	G/A/F	207	running	30	177	13	51,200	0	51,200
6	19	55 (R)	Robby McGehee	Energizer Advanced Formula	D/A/F	207	running	28	138	15	45,700	400	46,100
7	20	33 (R)	Jaques Lazier	Warner Bros. Studio Stores/Truscelli Team Racing	G/A/G	205	running	26	118	19	44,600	600	45,200
8	11	7	Stephan Gregoire	Dick Simon Racing/Mexmil/ Tokheim/Viking Air Tools	G/A/F	205	running	24	147	14	43,500	100	43,600
9	7	20	Tyce Carlson	Hubbard Photographics/ Immke Auto Group	D/A/F	205	running	122	12	18	21,500	100	21,600
10	17	21	Jeff Ward	Yahoo!/MerchantOnline.com/Dallara/Olds	D/A/G	204	running	20	197	7	42,400	0	42,400
11	10	91	Buddy Lazier	Delta Faucet/Coors Light/ HemelgarnRacing	D/A/G	199	running	19	204	6	41,200	0	41,200
12	22	6	Eliseo Salazar	Nienhouse Motorsports Racing Special	G/A/F	196	running	18	124	17	40,200	0	40,200
13	26	9	Davey Hamilton	Galles Racing Spinal Conquest	D/A/G	191	accident	17	197	7	39,100	0	39,100
14	12	66 (R)	Scott Harrington	The CertainTeed Building Products Special	D/A/F	156	running	16	137	16	37,900	0	37,900
15	23	17 (R)	Ronnie Johncox	Technique Inc./Tri Star Motorsports Inc.	D/A/G	154	accident	15	55	27	14,800	0	14,800
16	13	81	Robby Unser	Team Pelfrey/PetroMoly	D/A/F	139	fuel pressure	14	193	9	35,800	0	35,800
17	18	51	Eddie Cheever Jr.	The Children's Beverage Group/ TeamCheever/Infiniti	D/I/G	138	engine	13	190	10	34,600	5,000	39,600
18	15	98	Donnie Beechler	Big Daddy's BBQ Sauce and Spices	D/A/F	121	accident	12	111	21	12,600	0	12,600
19	8	42 (R)	John Hollansworth Jr.	CompuCom/Lycos/TeamXtreme	D/A/F	110	accident	11	116	20	33,500	2,500	36,000
20	2	28	Mark Dismore	MCI World Com	D/A/G	110	accident	12	188	11	32,400	0	32,400
21	4	2	Greg Ray	Glidden/Menards	D/A/F	110	engine	9	255	1	32,400	0	32,400
22	9	11	Billy Boat	Harrah's A.J. Foyt Racing	D/A/G	109	accident	8	182	12	32,400	0	32,400
23	14	92	Johnny Unser	Tae-Bo/Delta Faucet/Hemelgarn Racing	D/A/G	90	accident	7	57	26	10,400	0	10,400
24	25	27 (R)	Niclas Jonsson	Blueprint Racing/ZMax/Firestone	G/A/F	85	engine	6	6	44	10,400	0	10,400
25	5	4	Scott Goodyear	Pennzoil Panther G Force	G/A/G	47	accident	5	207	5	32,400	0	32,400
26	24	30	Willy T. Ribbs	Cole Bros. Water/Team Losi/Fast Rod	G/A/F	16	accident	4	4	45	32,400	0	32,400
				Brayton Engineering								600	600
				Roush Engineering								400	400
				Comptech Engines								400	400
											TOTAL - $1,000,000	$113,500	$1,113,500

Time of Race: 2:29:50.204   Average Speed: 124.936 mph   Margin of Victory: 0.617 sec.   Fastest Lap: #20 Tyce Carlson (Race lap 33, 205.152 mph, 26.322 sec.)
Fastest Leading Lap: #99 Sam Schmidt (Lap 151, 202.422 mph, 26.677 sec.)   PPG Pole Winner: #99 Sam Schmidt (209.465 mph, 25.780 sec.)   PPG Team Pole Award: #99 Treadway Racing
Firestone First at 99 Award: #99 Sam Schmidt   Delphi "Leader at Halfway" Award: #14 Kenny Brack Coors Pit Performance: #99 Treadway Racing
MBNA America Lap Leader: #14 Kenny Brack   MCI WorldCom Long Distance Award: #22 Robbie Buhl
Legend: R-Pep Boys Indy Racing League Rookie   Chassis Legend: D-Dallara(17); G- G Force(9)
Engine Legend: A- Oldsmobile Aurora(25); I- Nissan Infiniti(1)   Tire Legend: F- Firestone(13); G- Goodyear(13)

Lap Leaders:			Lap Leader Summary			95-101	#92 J. Unser, accident T4
Laps	Car#	Driver	Driver	Times	Total	105-109	#2 Ray, #28 Dismore, touch T1
1-1	#99	Sam Schmidt	Kenny Brack	3	118	111-121	#11 Boat, #42 Hollansworth,
2-12	#28	Mark Dismore	Sam Schmidt	4	35		#28 Dismore, accident T1
13-27	#99	Sam Schmidt	Eddie Cheever Jr.	2	32	125-132	#98 Beechler, accident T4
28-30	#28	Mark Dismore	Mark Dismore	2	14	163-169	#17 Johncox, accident T2
31-49	#51	Eddie Cheever Jr.	Stephan Gregoire	1	9	193-196	#9 Hamilton, #8 Sharp, accident T3
50-50	#14	Kenny Brack				198-201	#6 Salazar, spin T4
51-59	#7	Stephan Gregoire	Caution Flags:				
60-72	#51	Eddie Cheever Jr.	Laps	Reason/Incident			
73-149	#14	Kenny Brack	1-5	#98 Beechler, spin backstretch		11 caution flags, 70 laps	
150-165	#99	Sam Schmidt		#7 Gregoire, #66 Harrington, accident T3			
166-205	#14	Kenny Brack	8-8	#92 J. Unser, spin T4			
206-208	#99	Sam Schmidt	18-26	#30 Ribbs, accident T4			
11 Lead changes among 5 drivers			49-57	#4 Goodyear, accident T4			

prepare for rush hour

And if you think these guys are rushing, what about you? All those stop lights, short trips, stop signs and the rush hour traffic. That kind of stop-and-go driving is brutal on your engine, no matter what kind of vehicle you drive. That's why Pennzoil® motor oils are designed to protect your engine in rigorous, stop-and-go driving conditions. The kind of driving you do every day.

PENNZOIL

Stop. Go. Pennzoil.™

THE GRAND FINALE

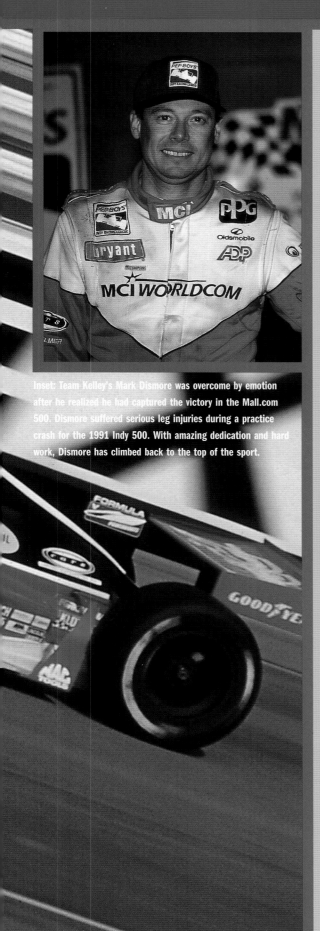

Inset: Team Kelley's Mark Dismore was overcome by emotion after he realized he had captured the victory in the Mall.com 500. Dismore suffered serious leg injuries during a practice crash for the 1991 Indy 500. With amazing dedication and hard work, Dismore has climbed back to the top of the sport.

MARK DISMORE WINS THE BATTLE; GREG RAY WINS THE WAR

BY JOHN STURBIN

WWW.MALL.COM
TEXAS MOTOR SPEEDWAY
OCTOBER 17, 1999

For many drivers, the 1999 Pep Boys Indy Racing League season proved to be either feast or famine. IRL's formula for close, competitive racing translated into sterling racing over the course of the entire season. It produced 7 different race winners and 3 championship point leaders at various stages of the season. At the first race, Walt Disney World, Panther Racing's Scott Goodyear came out of the gate strong, taking second. He grabbed victory at the next race held at Phoenix and followed it up with a win in the Long Horn 500 at Texas Motor Speedway. But by mid-season, his championship charge started to unravel. Three consecutive finishes outside of the top 10 dropped him out of the points lead.

While Goodyear's effort was stalling, Team Menard's Greg Ray was building momentum. After dismal 21st-place finishes in the first three races, the 33-year-old Texan languished near the bottom of the

Mark Dismore had shown incredible speeds during the season by winning two poles. But he had been unable to match his speed with consistency in the races. At the Mall.com 500, it all came together and the former Formula Atlantic great took his first IRL career win and won by a one lap margin.

Before qualifying began for the Mall.com 500, six drivers were in mathematical contention for the championship. Those drivers (from left to right: Buddy Lazier, Scott Sharp, Kenny Brack, Greg Ray, Sam Schmidt, and Scott Goodyear) posed for a photograph with the ultimate prize, the Pep Boys Indy Racing League Cup.

points table. But by mid-season, Ray came alive. The team had gelled, and they found the setup, speed, and, most importantly, the consistency to win. Never lacking confidence or the ability to stand on the gas, Ray led the league in the highly visible categories of poles (4), victories (3), and laps-led (464). He won the first Pikes Peak race, then the Dover Downs race, and finally the second Pikes Peak race. The victory total was almost spot-on the preseason prediction he had made after signing a five-year contract with Menard in October 1998. Ray's job was to replace Tony Stewart, the league's 1997 champion and original poster boy, in the multicolored Team Menard Dallara-Aurora.

Native son Greg Ray from nearby Plano, Texas, was in a dream situation. He was leading in points, and was poised to win the championship at his home track. The series leader by a scant 13 points as qualifying began on the 1.5-mile TMS quad-oval, Ray preserved a wild race in which he

When the green flag fell, Kenny Brack and Sam Schmidt stood in the way of Greg Ray claiming the Pep Boys Indy Racing League Championship. After his car was damaged by debris, Ray drove a calculated, conservative race to place third and claim the championship.

clinched his first major championship with a third-place finish after a rain-delayed and drawn-out day.

But Ray's championship victory wasn't the only big story of the day. Team Kelley's Mark Dismore finally scored his elusive first IRL victory. In so many races dating back to the series inception, he had been in the hunt for the win only to lose out in the waning stages

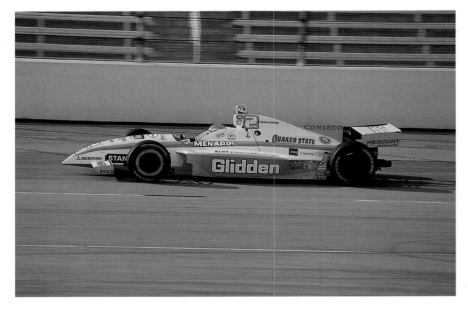

Last year Kenny Brack dominated the championship, winning three consecutive races on his way to the 1998 IRL driver's championship. During the 1999 season, he hadn't shown the same kind of dominance, but he did show dogged consistency. With only a single win, one second, and two third place finishes, Brack kept in contention for the championship until the final round.

of the race. Anxious to rack up his first IRL win, Dismore finally did it in Texas, and he did it in dominant fashion. Starting in second position, he won the rain-delayed race by a one-lap margin over second place Davey Hamilton.

Ray celebrated his championship by spinning off a pair of victory donuts at both ends of the track's frontstretch dogleg, then joined team owner John Menard to collect the Pep Boys Million, a $1 million bonus to be split evenly by owner and driver.

Ray, only the fifth man to call himself an IRL champion, was asked how it felt to rub shoulders with fellow champions from his home state, Foyt and Rutherford. "I am a Texan and I am an Indy-car driver, so I'm in that group," said Ray. "Am I in the Johnny Rutherford or by

any means the A.J. Foyt [group]? No way. I mean, those guys are living legends. One championship doesn't make a career. Those guys had many, many years of that. So those are guys you aspire to be like."

When Ray began the season with three consecutive 21st-place finishes for arguably the IRL's strongest outfit, his critics were quick to zing him. "Well, we always have very high expectations of ourselves, and we thought a realistic goal was to win four races," Ray said. "And if we could do that, we could win the championship. We won three races and threatened to win a bunch more. We didn't achieve all our goals but I think we really came together as a team."

Ray, the odds on favorite for the championship after Round 9 at Las Vegas Motor Speedway, added that he hoped this season had

Up until the Mall.com 500, John Hollansworth Jr.'s best result of the season was 13th at the Indy 500. Driving a Dallara/Aurora/Firestone machine, he sliced his way through the field from an 18th starting position to finish 5th.

After a brilliant start to the season with two wins and a second place, it all started to unravel for Scott Goodyear and the Panther Racing team. After the second Pikes Peak race, he lost the points lead. In the last two races of the season, his championship challenge was thwarted by crashes.

Indianapolis Motor Speedway President Tony George and A.J. Foyt discuss business. Foyt's driver, Kenny Brack, won the biggest race of them all, the Indy 500, and challenged for the championship until the end of the season.

earned something other than a passing grade in team chemistry. "You want to be respected [by] your peers," said Ray, who began seizing the title when he qualified on the pole at TMS at 216.107 miles per hour. "It's much more gratifying for me to be respected by car owners, engineers, and other drivers than it is by the media—because those guys don't drive race cars, no offense. To be respected by your peers is more important than anything."

"I think all you can do is focus on who you are and work real hard towards that. The nice thing is you can go back and analyze and make changes, you can become a better person, you can become a better driver. And I've become both of those."

Ray also can do the math. After squandering a chance to clinch the previous round in Las Vegas with another 21st-place finish, Ray knew that Kenny Brack, Sam Schmidt, Scott Sharp, Scott Goodyear, and Buddy Lazier were championship-eligible under the IRL's points system. Brack, the reigning series champion in the AJ Foyt Power Team G Force-Aurora, was 13 points back. Schmidt's first career IRL victory before his hometown fans in Vegas had advanced him from 12th to 3rd, only 30 points out. Sharp, who shared the first IRL title with Buzz Calkins, was 46 points behind. Goodyear had slipped from 2nd to 5th, 28 points behind Ray, after finishing 25th at Vegas. Lazier was a true longshot, 51 points out under a system that allows any driver to score a maximum of 55 points in qualifying and during the race.

Qualifying day sliced the field of contenders neatly in half. Ray bagged the maximum three points for the pole with his hot lap. Neither Brack, who qualified fifth, nor Schmidt, fourth-fastest in his Sprint PCS G Force-Aurora, earned any of the remaining three qualifying points.

Goodyear did collect one point for qualifying his Pennzoil Panther Racing G Force-Aurora third, but even that was not enough to keep him from elimination for the title. Also mathematically eliminated were Sharp, who qualified his Delphi Automotive Systems Dallara-Aurora in seventh, and Lazier, whose Delta Faucet Dallara-Aurora wound up 16th on the grid.

"The three weeks from Las Vegas to this race was difficult," Ray said. "I really felt like the championship was ours to win or ours to lose, because we had the points advantage. It's hard to put the whole weight of the entire championship season on one night. That's what it came down to."

Ray's front-row starting mate was Mark Dismore, pole-sitter for the IRL's Longhorn 500 at TMS in June at 215.272 miles per hour. His best of two laps this time was 216.071 miles per hour, 0.004 of a second behind Ray. "I'll take second [place in qualifying] if I can win Sunday," said Dismore, winless in 29 career IRL starts. "I want to get a win. I'm really sick of not winning one of these things."

There would be no secret to Dismore's race-day strategy. "Go like hell. Hopefully the car will be good all day and I can drive it hard," Dismore said. "And that's what I plan on doing."

As predicted by the weather forecasters all week, race-day greeted the teams and a crowd anticipated in excess of 70,000 with a cold rain and raw north wind. The ambient temperature was in the mid-50s when the 26-car field rolled off 3 hours and 55 minutes after its scheduled 1 P.M. start.

Concerned about the championship, four drivers contending for the Rookie of the Year title, the debut of 19-year-old Sarah Fisher, and cold tires, IRL officials began the race under the first of a series of green-yellow flags. The single-file order allowed drivers to build up in their tires on a track where temperatures were measured at 60 degrees Fahrenheit.

With the safety-first rule in effect, the championship contenders began sorting themselves out. Schmidt's shot at the title ended when he and Sharp collided on a restart down the front straight on Lap 126. The crash punted Schmidt into the outside retaining wall, causing heavy front-end damage to a car he was fighting to keep in eighth place.

Schmidt exited the track on race-day after suffering a fractured and dislocated left foot and an open-toe fracture on his right foot. He, in fact, shared a helicopter ride to Parkland Hospital in Dallas with Goodyear, who had made driver's-side contact with the Turn 4 wall on Lap 116 after his car's rear end broke loose and did a half-spin. To that point, Goodyear had led 65 of the scheduled 208 laps.

Schmidt's exit reduced the championship chase to a one-on-one featuring Brack and Ray. When the race went back to green on Lap 140, Brack, Ray, and Dismore held their positions as the only drivers on the lead lap until Sharp's blown engine brought out the day's fifth yellow flag.

On Lap 154, Brack pitted for tires and fuel and handed the lead to Ray. Dismore made his final stop on Lap 161, allowing Brack to recycle his way into second behind Ray. The Texan was working on a 1.333-second lead on Lap 182 when Brack's car slowed dramatically down the backstretch. "It's all over for us," Foyt said as his crew hustled to replace a broken right rear wheel bearing.

"Hopefully we can salvage a second in the points."

With both his championship contenders disabled, Ray turned his attention to a front nose section on his car that had been damaged by debris from Schmidt's crash. "I'm not sure exactly what it was," said Ray, who led twice for a total of 56 laps. "It was something pretty big. I could hear things sticking to the bottom of the car and the car jumped. So I knew it was some metal parts. There was this really big piece of carbon fiber—part of a cowling, or something—that hit the nose and the wing and the suspension. It definitely changed how the car handled, but it didn't hold us back."

On Lap 187, Ray pitted for tires and fuel and the reassurance from Menard that the flapping carbon fiber would hold up. "You learn to keep your emotions somewhat in check," said Menard, the home building supply magnate from Eau Claire, Wisconsin. "I probably have just enough Norwegian heritage to keep the emotions under control."

Ray later kidded his boss when he said, "You show emotions from time to time. You got on the radio and said, 'Stay calm out there. Stay . . . just . . . just . . . just stay calm out there!' I'm fine. You just calm down."

"That's true," Menard said.

Ray went down a lap during that stop, allowing Dismore and Hamilton to move past. Ray's fourth victory of the season was not going to happen here.

Beginning with Lap 187, Dismore's MCI WorldCom Dallara-Aurora was the only car on the lead lap. Dismore—who led three times for a total of 31 laps—became the fifth and final driver to pace the race. Dismore's victory, in his 30th start, marked the longest streak between the first career start and first career victory in the IRL's four-year history. In Victory Lane, Dismore's emotions finally caught up with him.

"I was just thinking about things," said Dismore, a 43-year-old resident of Greenfield, Indiana, "My dad has [prostate] cancer, and it's been on my mind. But I don't need that reason to win a race. I've been ready for a long time." Dismore, who averaged 135.246 miles per hour and ran Goodyear Eagle racing radial tires, earned $130,500 for himself and team-owner Tom Kelley. Dismore also apparently has come full-circle from a crash during practice at the Indianapolis Motor Speedway in May 1991 that nearly ended his career.

Two-time Pep Boys IRL series runner-up Davey Hamilton finished out the season with a fine second place standing. Hamilton and the Galles Racing Spinal Conquest car placed fourth in this year's final point standings.

"I knew I could win," said Dismore, the fourth first-time IRL winner in 1999. Ray, Goodyear, and Schmidt were the others. "We all knew I could win, for a long time now. But when you don't, there is some doubt," said Dismore, who became only the second driver in series history to win a race by one lap. Arie Luyendyk captured the 1997 True Value 500 at TMS in June 1997 by that margin. "I'm a pretty motivated guy. But this win helps my guys and gets them pumped. This was a tough one. I think the others will come easier."

Hamilton, meanwhile, extended a pair of personal records in the Galles Racing Dallara-Aurora. He is the only driver to have competed in every IRL race run to-date, 34. And he finished in the top five for the 13th time in his league career, a series record. "We fought all day and had a great car, but just came home one shy again," said Hamilton, who along with car-owner Rick Galles, scrambled to secure proper funding from Spinal Conquest to run the entire schedule. "Next year we'll be more organized and put together a stronger effort. There's some tough guys out there who haven't won yet. But we'll get there." Galles said, "My team is incredible. They stayed together, even though I tried to run them off."

Ray, a Firestone Firehawk racing radial loyalist, joined Hamilton one lap down in the final standings. Finishing fourth, also one lap down, was Eddie Cheever Jr. in the Team Cheever Dallara powered by the lone Nissan Infiniti Indy V-8 in the series. John Hollansworth Jr. of Dallas was the top finishing rookie in the TeamXtreme Dallara-Aurora, registering a career-best fifth. That easily eclipsed his previous best of 13th at Indianapolis.

But sixth-place Scott Harrington, who began the race trailing Robby McGehee by one point, outscored McGehee, 28 to 18, to secure rookie of the year honors by nine points, 165 to 156. Harrington collected a $50,000 bonus from Sprint PCS. "We weren't just shooting for the rookie of the year title," said Harrington, driver of the Harrington Motorsports Dallara-Aurora. "We wanted to win the race. We gambled once, and ran out of fuel."

Sarah Fisher became the youngest driver to start an IRL event and only the fifth woman to take the green flag in a major North American open-wheel race. After qualifying 17th, she completed 66 laps before a broken timing chain relegated the "Petty Blue" Team Pelfrey Dallara-Aurora to 25th. "I think I was doing my job well, even though we went a lap down," said Fisher, of tiny Commercial Point, Ohio. "I'm a little upset now, but I really like the people I'm around and I'm looking forward to racing next year."

Tyce Carlson completed an emotionally trying weekend with a 13th-place finish. Eleven people—including nine crewmen from Carlson's Blueprint-Immke Racing Dallara-Aurora—were injured when rookie Niclas Jonsson veered left into Carlson's pit in the waning minutes of Saturday's final practice. Crewman Tracy Hash suffered the most serious injury, a complex compound fracture of the left leg above the ankle. Carlson's replacement race-day crew came from Jonsson's Blueprint Racing Enterprises G Force-Aurora entry, which was too badly damaged to compete.

Ray compiled 293 championship points, ahead of Brack who finished 16th in the race and ended the season with 256 points. Dismore placed third with 240 championship points, followed by Hamilton with 237 and Schmidt with 233.

"We had a good chance," said Brack, the native of Sweden who added an Indy 500 victory to his resume in May. "Mechanical failures will happen, and it was nobody's fault really. You just got to go on." Brack spoke from the rear of Foyt's trailer as Ray's championship celebration was beginning to crest on a temporary stage in front of the frontstretch grandstands. The title also was the second in three seasons for Menard, who first entered the Indy 500 in 1979 and is still searching for his first victory at the famed Speedway.

"You cannot put into words how great it feels to finally have some success after you tried so hard for so long," said Menard, 59. "This is a business where success is very elusive. I think I'm happier this time than I was the first time, and I didn't think I could be happier. But next year when we win the third one, we'll be even happier."

Ray said that winning the Indy 500 for himself and Menard will become the focus for the defense of their championship in 2000. "I questioned why we didn't win the championship last year and also the Indy 500 this year," Ray said. "You just have to be patient and work hard and give it your all. You have to make sacrifices to reach a goal."

OFFICIAL BOX SCORE
PEP BOYS INDY RACING LEAGUE

Mall.com 500 at Texas Motor Speedway
Sunday, October 17, 1999

FP	SP	Car	Driver	Car Name	C/E/T	Laps Comp.	Running Reason Out	IRL Pts.	Total IRL Pts.	IRL Standings	IRL Awards	Designated Awards	Total Awards
1	2	28	Mark Dismore	MCI World Com	D/A/G	208	Running	52	240	3	$95,500	$35,000	$130,500
2	6	9	Davey Hamilton	Galles Racing Spinal Conquest	D/A/G	207	Running	40	237	4	79,200	5,750	84,950
3	1	2	Greg Ray	Glidden/Menards	D/A/F	207	Running	38	293	1	67,100	25,550	92,650
4	20	51	Eddie Cheever Jr.	The Children's Beverage Group/ Team Cheever/Infiniti	D/I/G	207	Running	32	222	7	55,100	20,900	76,000
5	18	42 R	John Hollansworth Jr.	CompuCom/Lycos/TeamXtreme	D/A/F	206	Running	30	146	17	28,700	1,600	30,300
6	8	66 R	Scott Harrington	CertainTeed Building Products Special	D/A/F	206	Running	28	165	14	45,300	700	46,000
7	23	33 R	Jaques Lazier	Warner Bros. Studio Stores/ Truscelli Team Racing	G/A/G	206	Running	26	144	18	44,200	100	44,300
8	19	12	Buzz Calkins	Bradley Food Marts/Sav-O-Mat	G/A/F	206	Running	24	201	13	43,100	0	43,100
9	25	11	Billy Boat	Harrah's AJ Foyt Racing	D/A/G	205	Running	22	204	12	43,100	0	43,100
10	16	91	Buddy Lazier	Delta Faucet/Coors Light/Hemelgarn Racing	D/A/G	204	Running	20	224	6	42,000	0	42,000
11	22	98	Donnie Beechler	Big Daddy's BBQ Sauce and Spices	D/A/F	203	Running	19	130	21	18,900	0	18,900
12	14	55 R	Robby McGehee	Energizer Advanced Formula	D/A/F	202	Running	18	156	16	39,800	0	39,800
13	9	20	Tyce Carlson	Hubbard Photographics/ Immke Auto Group	D/A/F	198	Running	17	139	19	38,800	0	38,800
14	11	81	Robby Unser	Team Pelfrey/PetroMoly	D/A/F	194	Engine	16	209	10	37,600	0	37,600
15	13	7	Stephan Gregoire	Dick Simon Racing/Mexmil/ Tokheim/Viking Air Tools	G/A/F	191	Running	15	162	15	36,600	0	36,600
16	5	14	Kenny Brack	AJ Foyt Power Team Racing	G/A/G	186	Running	14	256	2	35,500	0	35,500
17	10	6	Eliseo Salazar	Nienhouse Motorsports Racing Special	G/A/F	166	Running	13	137	20	34,300	0	34,300
18	26	30	John Paul Jr.	Big Daddy's Beef Jerky/Cole Bros. Water	G/A/F	166	Running	12	39	28	34,300	0	34,300
19	7	8	Scott Sharp	Delphi Automotive Systems	D/A/G	151	Engine	11	220	8	33,300	0	33,300
20	21	43 R	Doug Didero	Mid America Freight Systems/Western Star Trucks	D/A/F	149	Electrical	10	10	42	10,200	0	10,200
21	12	21	Jeff Ward	Yahoo!/MerchantOnline.com/ Dallara/Olds	D/A/G	143	Engine	9	206	11	32,200	0	32,200
22	4	99	Sam Schmidt	Sprint PCS/Mall.com	G/A/F	124	Accident	8	233	5	32,200	0	32,200
23	3	4	Scott Goodyear	Pennzoil Panther G Force	G/A/G	115	Accident	10	217	9	32,200	10,000	42,200
24	15	22	Robbie Buhl	Tristarmall.com/Tri Star Motorsports Inc.	D/A/G	99	Suspension	6	114	22	10,200	0	10,200
25	17	48 R	Sarah Fisher	Team Pelfrey	D/A/F	66	Timing chain	5	5	46	10,200	0	10,200
26	24	17 R	Ronnie Johncox	Technique Inc./Tristarmall.com	D/A/G	41	Ignition	4	59	26	10,200	0	10,200
27	27	27 R	Niclas Jonsson	Blueprint Racing/ZMax/Firestone	G/A/F	0	Did not start	3	9	43	10,200	0	10,200
			Brayton Engineering									400	400
			Team Menard Engines									400	400
			Speedway Engines									600	600
										TOTAL- $1,000,000		$101,000	$1,101,000

Time of Race: 2:14:15.722   Average Speed: 135.246 mph   Margin of Victory: one lap
Fastest Lap: #4 Scott Goodyear (Race lap 91, 217.579 mph, 24.074 sec.)   Fastest Leading Lap: #4 Scott Goodyear (Lap 52, 216.769 mph, 24.164 sec.)

PPG Pole Winner: #2 Greg Ray (216.107 mph, 24.238 sec.)   PPG Team Pole Award: #2 Team Menard   Firestone First at 99 Award: #2 Greg Ray
Delphi "Leader at Halfway" Award: #28 Mark Dismore   Coors Pit Performance: #51 Team Cheever   MBNA America Lap Leader: #4 Scott Goodyear
MCI WorldCom Long Distance Award: #51 Eddie Cheever Jr.

Legend: R-Pep Boys Indy Racing League Rookie   Chassis Legend: D-Dallara(18); G- G Force(9)   Engine Legend: A- Oldsmobile Aurora(26); I- Nissan Infiniti(1)
Tire Legend: F- Firestone(15); G- Goodyear(12)

Lap Leaders:

Laps	Car#	Driver
1-24	#2	Greg Ray
25-31	#28	Mark Dismore
32-89	#4	Scott Goodyear
90-103	#14	Kenny Brack
104-105	#28	Mark Dismore
106-108	#8	Scott Sharp
109-115	#4	Scott
116-154	#14	Kenny Brack
155-186	#2	Greg Ray
187-208	#28	Mark Dismore

9 Lead changes among 5 drivers

Lap Leader Summary:

Driver	Times	Laps
Scott Goodyear	2	65
Greg Ray	2	56
Kenny Brack	2	53
Mark Dismore	3	31
Scott Sharp	1	3

Caution Flags:

Laps	Reason/Incident
1-19	#30 Paul, Spin T2
53-64	#22 Buhl, Tow-in
116-124	#4 Goodyear, Accident T4
126-139	#99 Schmidt, #8 Sharp, Accident frontstretch
152-164	#8 Sharp, blown engine, spin frontstretch
196-206	#82 Unser, Accident T2

6 caution flags, 78 laps

REVERSAL OF FORTUNE

GREG RAY AND TEAM MENARD CAPTURE THE CHAMPIONSHIP

by Jonathan Ingram

Greg Ray is a profile in perseverance. Before he joined Team Menard for his third IRL season, Ray had experienced more ups and downs in his career than a helicopter pilot. As it turned out, the immensely talented driver's struggles over the years were good preparation for the 1999 Indianapolis Racing League season with Team Menard. A season that had as many lows as it had highs. But after a slow start and an accident in the penultimate round in Las Vegas, Ray clinched the Pep Boys Indy Racing League championship in the season finale at the Texas Motor Speedway, just about a cow chip's toss from his home in Plano, Texas.

Although a devout Christian, Ray is hardly pious in his perseverance and instead exemplifies the transcendentalist poet Ralph Waldo Emerson's creed of "Nothing great was ever achieved without enthusiasm." At the end of a grueling campaign in which he battled Scott Goodyear, Scott Sharp, and finally defending champion Kenny Brack to win the championship, Ray's emotions were a mixture of ecstasy and homily. "To be part of this team and win the championship here at my home track is a dream come true," he said. "I questioned why we didn't win the championship last year and also the Indy 500 this year. You just have to be patient and work hard and give it your all. You have to make sacrifices to reach your goal."

Typical of his season, he won three races and four poles but success was constantly thwarted or was followed by adversity. Ray clinched the title on a long and demanding day. Rain postponed the start of the race, giving Ray more time to think about that accident in Las Vegas, where he might have clinched the title. "That was a tough time between Las Vegas and the Texas race," Ray

After a disastrous start to the season with three consecutive 21st place finishes, Greg Ray and the Menard team turned their fortunes around. With the right race strategy and Greg Ray's superb driving, the team vaulted to the front of the field. Finally, Ray was able to showcase his considerable talent by winning four poles, three races, and then took the big prize—the Pep Boys Indy Racing League Championship.

The Team Menard/Greg Ray storm rolled over the competition at the Radisson 200, held at Pikes Peak International Raceway. Everything was clicking for the team. Ray staged a masterful performance, patiently yet aggressively carving through the pack for the win.

admitted. "I could think about it every morning, every afternoon, and every evening."

During the race weekend, competitor and friend Sam Schmidt stayed at Ray's home. He had gone jogging with Ray that morning before the race and suffered a crash during the race that sent him to the hospital with a severely broken foot. A piece of metal struck Ray's Glidden/Menard Dallara-Aurora, which radically affected the car's handling. "After that," said Ray, who eventually finished third, "it pulled hard to the left."

When the chassis of Brack, his closest pursuer in the points, suffered a problem in the rear suspension, Ray was almost home free. Not long after the presentation of the championship trophy, which carries a $1 million bonus from Pep Boys, Ray suffered yet another setback. He was picked out of a line of traffic for a speeding ticket as he drove home. "I didn't argue with the guy," said Ray, whose boundless energy and optimism had uncharacteristically reached their limits. "I was too tired and too happy and just wanted to go home."

Let's take a step back. Ray entered 1999 with great enthusiasm after landing a front-line ride in a major racing series for the first

time, joining the team of John Menard that won the championship in the 1996-1997 season. He was stepping into the cockpit previously occupied by the IRL's most prominent personality and one of its most talented racers, Tony Stewart. With one front row start at the Indy 500 and no victories to his credit, Ray talked his way into the ride with Menard. He used the same conviction and confidence he displayed at his first driving school, where at age 25 he declared, "I'm going to win the Indy 500."

The 1999 Indy 500 became one of the low points of Ray's championship campaign. A pit road crash resulting from no radio communication put him on the sidelines after leading 31 laps and setting the fastest lap. That was Round 3 of the 10-race season, and the accident constituted the fourth straight setback for Ray, not counting a bid for the pole at the Brickyard that also went awry.

In Round 1 at the Walt Disney World Speedway, Ray ran with the leaders for 163 laps until he was sidelined with gearbox failure. In Round 2 at the Phoenix International Raceway, Ray was dicing at the front when a collision with a lapped car took him out of the race. The Texan bounced back at the Charlotte Motor Speedway to win the pole and was leading the race when the tragic accident that claimed the lives of three spectators occurred, forcing the event to be cancelled. Then came the disappointment at Indy.

Through it all, Ray remained undaunted. "I don't think I ever had the mindset that the victories or a championship wasn't going to happen," said the 33-year-old Ray. "I kept on telling people that I knew we were working hard at the shop, and we demonstrated at every track that in each qualifying session and each race that we were fast. I knew our day was coming. That's what I kept saying. We were running strong and had a good team. We had the ability. I thought our day would come before it did. But that's one thing about racing and the Indy Racing League. If you're not the best example that day, then you're not going to win because it's so competitive."

Ray was no stranger to adverse circumstances. The first hurdle he had to overcome was an extremely late start to his racing career. The son of a boat dealer, Ray was a successful entrepreneur by age 25, starting several different companies. But driving a business from behind a desk left Ray unsatisfied. So he decided to enter a sport where most of the successful participants start during their teen years, and some of them are in go-karts and quarter midgets before they get out of grade school.

"One thing that allowed me to be so successful so quickly at my age: I had already graduated from college, and already had been running my own businesses, and had already had a lot of failures and successes," said Ray. "I knew about people and chemistry and how hard work pays off. I had the dream and the desire and felt like I had the belief in myself. Some people take me as a cocky or arrogant person. But I think once you get to know me, I'm not about that at all. I love what I do and have a lot of confidence."

In many respects, the Pep Boys IRL championship was similar to the first time Ray became a motor racing champion—at age 27. He had to come back from severe adversity to win the Formula Atlantic title at the Sports Car Club of America's annual Runoffs at Road Atlanta. In his second year of driving, Ray arrived at the Georgia track with seven victories in his Divisional races, eight poles, and eight track records. He won the pole for the race that would include competitors from the entire country and would determine the national champion. Then disaster struck.

The night before the race, Ray planned to spend a relaxing evening in the hot tub at his hotel. At the hotel, he dropped his room key and leaned over to pick it up, bracing his right hand on the door jamb. An improvident draft of air blew the door shut, slamming it on his middle finger and fracturing it at the metacarpal joint. Ray spent the eve of the championship race at the hospital. A splint was fitted that would allow him to drive, despite the 300-plus shifts required during the required 18 laps around Road Atlanta. Then disaster struck again.

On the warm-up lap, the unfamiliar splint on his hand caused Ray to inadvertently shut off the fuel pump and his Swift DB-4 sputtered to a halt. The crew told him via radio to try the auxiliary fuel pump. By the time the engine in Ray's Swift found new life, the field had escaped. He started at the back of the pack, moved to fifth by the end of five laps, and took the lead one lap later. By race's end, Ray had a 22-second margin. He was given the Mark Donohue Award for Outstanding Performance and tabbed as a sure-bet in the professional ranks.

The following year, Ray nearly won the professional Toyota Atlantic championship, stunning veterans with three wins and four poles in his first four races for Genoa Racing. But then a flood of over-driving, spins, and crashes followed. Ray's trademark enthusiasm behind the wheel did not undermine him in as much as a lack of experience. The desire to always be at the front of the field was not yet tempered by the inevitable realities of racing where sometimes a driver has to settle for a solid finish if his equipment is not up to winning. "If desire alone could win races," *On Track Magazine* reported, "Ray would be undefeated."

In effect, Ray was trying to win races on his own. "I've been self-proclaimed as an aggressive driver for years," said Ray. "I like to go fast and I like to push the equipment right to the edge.

Personally, that's what I get out of it. When I started racing, it was for what's behind my left chest, my heart. It's a great emotional release to feel those feelings and to be in control and I like the aggressive style."

As an indication of his future success at the Indy 500 and in the IRL, Ray won all three poles on the oval tracks during the 1994 Toyota Atlantic season. Alas, an engine failure while leading in the penultimate round at Nazareth, Pennsylvania, ended any championship hopes in a series where he competed against future IRL drivers Richie Hearn and Mark Dismore. Nevertheless, Ray finished a remarkable third in the championship during his lone rookie season in the series.

Typical for an open-wheel driver with talent but not enough financial backing, Ray disappeared from racing for one year, then spent a season in the Indy Lights series with Team Green, finishing 12th in points. When the IRL started up in 1996, Ray found the opportunity to make it to a major series and the Indy 500. He teamed up with Thomas Knapp Motorsports, starting 30th that year at Indy and finishing 25th. The team started four other IRL events with a finish of eighth at Texas; the best effort. Ray spent much of his non-racing time trying to locate sponsorship for the under-financed team of Knapp, often showing up at races to ply the paddock and let people know that the team was looking for more financial backing and then would be back.

In 1998, the combination of Knapp's chassis expertise and Ray's driving stunned observers at the Indy 500, where Ray qualified his under-funded Dallara-Aurora second and started in the middle of the front row. Incredibly, the team arrived with one qualifying engine, one race engine, and no sponsor after a company backed out of its obligation. The team skipped two days of practice, then tried to generate sponsor support by turning a quick time on the third day. Ray

Greg Ray celebrates his second win at Pikes Peak with his son Winston. Under the guidance of Team Manager Thomas Knapp and the financial resources of John Menard, the team overcame problems experienced early in the season.

clocked 219.952 miles per hour, but the only response was limited support from Indianapolis-area businesses. They kept running nevertheless and recorded a speed of 222.717 miles per hour in just 95 laps of practice, third fastest of the opening six days.

On Pole Day, the team waited until Happy Hour, when the shadows grew longer and the air cooler. With 45 minutes remaining until the 6 p.m. deadline, Ray averaged 221.125 miles per hour in his four laps to take the middle of the front row. Notably, he qualified ahead of both the Team Menard entries driven by Stewart and Robbie Buhl. Ray then led 18 laps in the race, further heightening the awareness of his skills, before falling out eventually with gearbox problems.

Ray's now obvious ability at Indy led to a two-race deal with A.J. Foyt as a substitute for the injured Billy Boat. More importantly, that Indy performance helped launch the behind-the-scenes discussions with Menard, who knew he would have to find a replacement for the departing Tony Stewart, who was bound for NASCAR's Winston Cup. Those discussions eventually led to a meeting between Menard, Ray, and Knapp in Eau Claire, Wisconsin, at a restaurant near the headquarters for the team owner's chain of lumber and home improvement stores. It was from discussions at this meeting that Menard decided he wanted to hire Ray as his driver for the IRL program in 1999 and to bring Knapp on board as the team manager.

"Greg and I talked at racetracks throughout the summer of '98," said Menard. "Greg's very confident. I've been around enough race car drivers. I didn't think he was that cocky, but Greg certainly has self-confidence and that's a very necessary ingredient. Let's face it, racing is about aggression. You don't get behind the wheel of a race car if you're going to succeed and be a non-aggressive person. That's what I'm looking for. When you're out of the car and how you handle, that is also important. Hopefully you can be a reasonably

normal human being. Greg's certainly a very delightful person to be around when he's out of the car. But if you go wheel-to-wheel with him in a corner, you'd have to regard him differently."

For his part, Ray relied on the salesmanship he had learned in his entrepreneur days and on his natural enthusiasm. "Tom and I were all looking at the meeting as giving us a high possibility of working together with John," said Ray. "John was looking at the direction the team was going to go and his whole future. I felt like I needed to make a statement, let him know what I was thinking. I think I did that in pretty aggressive form. He has 120 stores and 20,000 employees. He's a very busy and successful person. I knew I only had so much of his time. We had only two hours and I talked for an hour and 45 minutes. I was definitely trying to get my point across."

The duo succeeded in convincing Menard they could sustain the success of his IRL program, where Stewart had followed his championship season with two victories in 1998. For his part, Menard had already decided on making major changes. When team manager Larry Curry was discovered to be using an illegal rear wing on the team's Dallara's earlier that summer at the Pikes Peak International Raceway, Menard knew he wanted to take a different direction for his team. "You can't be cheating," said Menard. "That was a defining moment for me. That's when I decided to either get out of racing or change my management structure to something more technically excellent to win races fair and square."

Ironically, that decision finally came to a successful conclusion at the same Pikes Peak track. That's where Ray won his first race in Round 5, after finishing less than a second behind Scott Goodyear at Texas in Round 4. Ray started on the Pikes Peak pole and led 109 of the 200 laps at the 1.0-mile oval, beating Schmidt by 0.12 seconds. With Knapp as his engineer and a front-line budget that provided first-class

engines from Butch Meyer, Ray had finally reached the summit. "After I saw the checkered flag, I wanted to stop the car and cry," he said.

The team then went on to win Round 7 at Dover's Monster Mile and returned to capture Round 8 at Pikes Peak from the pole again. "I think Butch Meyer puts together an awfully good engine for the altitude of Pikes Peak and the 1-mile tracks," said Menard about the three-out-of-four victory streak. "I think it helped us that those tracks came later in the season. We came together later in the season with momentum and drive."

The three victories in four races launched Ray into the championship lead. At the other race in that skein, Ray was leading at the Atlanta Motor Speedway when a timing chain broke in his engine.

"I think if you look at how we qualified and the race laps we led at all the tracks, we had the potential to win every single race, including the first race at Orlando," said Ray. "I was the most conservative driver I've ever been at Orlando and had a conservative set-up. We were still in a position in the last 30 laps to win that race when I had a gearbox problem. From there on, we had the speed and should have and could have won all the races."

"But the series is so competitive and we're pushing this equipment right to the very edge," continued Ray. "Certainly, I made mistakes and had some bad luck and have had some mechanical problems. But when we get it all right, when it all comes together we've got a very strong package."

One thing Ray learned to get right was keeping his enthusiasm for speed in check and paying more attention to plotting a strategic approach to races. "Certainly, there's a lot of confidence in the people around me now," said Ray. "I may not feel the need to show that I'm the fastest guy on the track at every single second. These races are 200 miles and 500 miles and it's about speed and game plan and making smart decisions. I think I'm learning when to pick my times and show my cards when I need to. Each race I won was by less than a second. I could have lapped everybody and instead I dropped off three quarters of a second a lap to conserve the car. I like being aggressive and winning these races is a great feeling. I feel like I found a zone."

Indeed. It's called being the champion.

Greg Ray confers with John O'Gary in the pits at the first Pikes Peak race. Their diligent work to get the car properly set up paid off with a triumphant win.

Engine builder Butch Meyer, Greg Ray, and John Menard proudly accept the $10,000 check for qualifying on the pole for the season finale at Texas Motor Speedway. Greg Ray drove a steady race to third place in the championship while championship challenger Kenny Brack faltered and finished 16th.

THE 1999 PEP BOYS INDY RACING LEAGUE CHAMPIONSHIP SERIES

IN FACTS, FIGURES, AND STATISTICS

Race & PPG Pole Winners

		Race Winner	Average Speed	PPG Pole	Speed
WDWS	Jan. 24, 1999	Eddie Cheever Jr.	118.538 mph	Scott Sharp	171.371 mph
PIR	Mar. 28, 1999	Scott Goodyear	102.856	Greg Ray	177.139
IMS	May 30, 1999	Kenny Brack	153.176	Arie Luyendyk	225.179
TMS 1	June 12, 1999	Scott Goodyear	151.177	Mark Dismore	215.272
PPIR 1	June 27, 1999	Greg Ray	134.111	Greg Ray	176.005
AMS	July 17, 1999	Scott Sharp	141.546	Billy Boat	215.251
DDIS	Aug. 1, 1999	Greg Ray	114.258	Mark Dismore	182.639
PPIR 2	Aug. 29, 1999	Greg Ray	135.450	Greg Ray	176.263
LVMS	Sept. 26, 1999	Sam Schmidt	124.936	Sam Schmidt	209.465
TMS 2	Oct. 17, 1999	Mark Dismore	135.246	Greg Ray	216.107

Top 5 Finishers

	First	Second	Third	Fourth	Fifth
WDWS	Cheever	Goodyear	Ward	Sharp	Boesel
PIR	Goodyear	Ward	Buhl	Boat	Harrington
IMS	Brack	Ward	Boat	Gordon	McGehee
TMS 1	Goodyear	Ray	Schmidt	Gregoire	Salazar
PPIR 1	Ray	Schmidt	Hamilton	Cheever	B. Lazier
AMS	Sharp	R. Unser	Brack	Salazar	Calkins
DDIS	Ray	B. Lazier	Brack	Boat	Schmidt
PPIR 2	Ray	Hamilton	Dismore	B. Lazier	Schmidt
LVMS	Schmidt	Brack	Buhl	Sharp	Calkins
TMS 2	Dismore	Hamilton	Ray	Cheever	Hollansworth

Race Statistics

	Starters	Running at Finish	On Lead Lap	Leaders	Lead Changes	Yellows	Laps Under Yellow	Time of Race	Margin of Victory
WDWS	28	20	4	5	10	7	48	1:41:14.800	5.148 sec.
PIR	27	14	5	5	5	8	62	1:56:40.052	4.738
IMS	33	16	4	7	17	8	42	3:15:51.182	6.562
TMS 1	25	16	4	9	15	6	33	2:00:06.816	.888
PPIR 1	24	20	5	2	6	3	23	1:29:28.676	.120
AMS	27	17	5	10	16	7	45	2:12:15.235	.163 (UC)
DDIS	23	13	5	7	7	5	56	1:45:01.503	.731
PPIR 2	24	21	4	4	8	3	21	1:28:35.633	.445
LVMS	26	13	4	5	11	11	70	2:29:50.204	.617
TMS 2	26	17	1	5	9	6	78	2:14:15.722	One Lap

Key: WDWS-Walt Disney World Speedway; PIR-Phoenix International Raceway; IMS-Indianapolis Motor Speedway; TMS-Texas Motor Speedway; PPIR-Pikes Peak International Raceway; AMS-Atlanta Motor Speedway; DDIS-Dover Downs International Speedway; LVMS-Las Vegas Motor Speedway.

(UC) - Race ended under caution

Car	Driver	Car Name	C/E/T	Entrant
2	Greg Ray	Glidden/Menards	D/A/F	Team Menard, Inc.
2T	Greg Ray	Glidden/Menards	D/A/F	Team Menard, Inc.
3	Andy Michner	Brant Racing R&S MKV	R/A/G	Brant Racing
3T	Andy Michner	Brant Racing R&S MKV	R/A/G	Brant Racing
4	Scott Goodyear	Pennzoil Panther G Force	G/A/G	Panther Racing
4T	Scott Goodyear	Pennzoil Panther G Force	G/A/G	Panther Racing
5	Arie Luyendyk	Sprint PCS/Meijer	G/A/F	Treadway Racing LLC
5T	Arie Luyendyk	Sprint PCS/Meijer	G/A/F	Treadway Racing LLC
6	Eliseo Salazar	Nienhouse Motorsports Racing Special	G/A/F	Nienhouse Motorsports
6T	Eliseo Salazar	Nienhouse Motorsports Racing Special	G/A/F	Nienhouse Motorsports
7	Stephan Gregoire	Mexmil/Tokheim G Force	G/A/F	Dick Simon Racing LLC
7T	Stephan Gregoire	Mexmil/Tokheim G Force	G/A/F	Dick Simon Racing LLC
8	Scott Sharp	Delphi Automotive Systems	D/A/G	Kelley Racing
8T	Scott Sharp	Delphi Automotive Systems	D/A/G	Kelley Racing
10	John Paul Jr.	Jonathan Byrd's Cafeteria/VisionAire	G/A/F	Jonathan Byrd Cunningham Racing LLC
10T	John Paul Jr.	Jonathan Byrd's Cafeteria/VisionAire	G/A/F	Jonathan Byrd Cunningham Racing LLC
11	Billy Boat	AJ Foyt Racing	D/A/G	AJ Foyt Enterprises
11T	Billy Boat	AJ Foyt Racing	D/A/G	AJ Foyt Enterprises
12	Buzz Calkins	Bradley Food Marts/Sav-O-Mat	D/A/F	Bradley Motorsports
12T	Buzz Calkins	Bradley Food Marts/Sav-O-Mat	G/A/F	Bradley Motorsports
14	Kenny Brack	AJ Foyt PowerTeam Racing	D/A/G	AJ Foyt Enterprises
14T	Kenny Brack	AJ Foyt PowerTeam Racing	D/A/G	AJ Foyt Enterprises
15	Jaques Lazier (R)	Tivoli Hotel/G Force	G/I/G	DR/Lazier Racing
15T	Jaques Lazier (R)	Tivoli Hotel/G Force	G/A/G	DR/Lazier Racing
17	Jack Miller	Dean's Milk Chug	D/A/G	Tri Star Motorsports Inc.
18	Mike Borkowski (R)	PDM Racing	G/A/G	PDM Racing, Inc.
18T	Mike Borkowski (R)	PDM Racing	G/A/G	PDM Racing, Inc.
19	Stan Wattles	Metro Racing Systems/NCLD	D/A/G	Metro Racing Systems, Inc.
19T	Stan Wattles	Metro Racing Systems/NCLD	R/A/G	Metro Racing Systems, Inc.
20	Tyce Carlson	Blueprint-Immke Racing	D/A/F	Blueprint-Immke Racing
20T	Tyce Carlson	Blueprint-Immke Racing	D/A/F	Blueprint-Immke Racing
21	Jeff Ward	Pagan Racing Dallara-Oldsmobile	D/A/G	Pagan Racing
21T	Jeff Ward	Pagan Racing Dallara-Oldsmobile	D/A/G	Pagan Racing
22	Tony Stewart	The Home Depot	D/A/G	Tri Star Motorsports, Inc.
22T	Tony Stewart	The Home Depot	D/A/G	Tri Star Motorsports, Inc.
23	Robby Gordon	Johns Manville/Menards/Duracell	G/E/F	Team Gordon, Inc.
23T	Robby Gordon	Johns Manville/Menards/Duracell	G/A/F	Team Gordon, Inc.
25	Davey Hamilton	Barnhart Galles Motorsports Spinal Victory	D/A/G	Barnhart Galles Motorsports
25T	Davey Hamilton	Barnhart Galles Motorsports Spinal Victory	D/A/G	Barnhart Galles Motorsports
28	Mark Dismore	MCI WorldCom	D/A/G	Kelley Racing
28T	Mark Dismore	MCI WorldCom	D/A/G	Kelley Racing
30	Raul Boesel	TransWorld Racing/McCormack Motorsports	G/A/F	McCormack Motorsports
30T	Raul Boesel	TransWorld Racing/McCormack Motorsports	G/A/F	McCormack Motorsports
32	TBA	Glidden/Menards	D/A/F	Team Menard, Inc.

Car	Driver	Car Name	C/E/T	Entrant
32T	TBA	Glidden/Menards	G/A/F	Team Menard, Inc.
33	Roberto Moreno	Truscelli Team Racing/Warner Bros.	G/A/G	Truscelli Team Racing
33T	Roberto Moreno	Truscelli Team Racing/Warner Bros.	G/A/G	Truscelli Team Racing
34	Jimmy Kite	Team Coulson Dallara	D/A/tba	Team Scandia
35	Steve Knapp	Thermo Tech Prolong ISM Racing G Force Goodyear	G/A/G	ISM Racing Corp.
35T	Steve Knapp	Thermo Tech Prolong ISM Racing G Force Goodyear	G/A/G	ISM Racing Corp.
41	TBA	AJ Foyt Racing	D/A/G	AJ Foyt Enterprises
41T	TBA	AJ Foyt Racing	D/A/G	AJ Foyt Enterprises
42	John Hollansworth Jr. (R)	Pcsave.com/Lycos Dallara	D/A/F	TeamXtreme Racing, LLC
42T	John Hollansworth Jr. (R)	Pcsave.com/Lycos Dallara	D/A/F	TeamXtreme Racing, LLC
43	Dave Steele (R)	Pennzoil Panther G Force	G/A/G	Panther Racing
43T	Dave Steele (R)	Pennzoil Panther G Force	G/A/G	Panther Racing
44	Robbie Buhl	Dreyer & Reinbold Racing Dallara Infiniti	D/I/F	Sinden Racing Service
44T	Robbie Buhl	Dreyer & Reinbold Racing Dallara Infiniti	D/I/F	Sinden Racing Service
48	TBA	Team Pelfrey	D/A/F	Team Pelfrey
50	Roberto Guerrero	Cobb Racing/G Force/Infiniti	G/I/F	Cobb Racing/Price Cobb
50T	Roberto Guerrero	Cobb Racing/G Force/Infiniti	G/I/F	Cobb Racing/Price Cobb
51	Eddie Cheever Jr.	Team Cheever/The Children's Beverage Group/Dallara	D/I/G	Team Cheever
51T	Eddie Cheever Jr.	Team Cheever/The Children's Beverage Group/Dallara	D/I/G	Team Cheever
52	Wim Eyckmans (R)	EGP/Team Cheever	D/A/G	Team Cheever
52T	Wim Eyckmans (R)	EGP/Team Cheever	G/A/G	Team Cheever
54	TBA	Beck Motorsports	D/A/F	Beck Motorsports
54T	TBA	Beck Motorsports	D/A/F	Beck Motorsports
55	Robby McGehee (R)	Conti Racing	D/A/F	Conti Racing
66	Scott Harrington	Harrington Motorsports	D/I/F	Harrington Motorsports
66T	Scott Harrington	Harrington Motorsports	D/I/F	Harrington Motorsports
70	TBA	Chitwood Motorsports	D/A/G	Chitwood Motorsports Inc.
77	TBA	Chastain Motorsports	G/A/G	Chastain Motorsports
81	Robby Unser	PetroMoly/Team Pelfrey	D/A/F	Team Pelfrey
91	Buddy Lazier	Delta Faucet/Coors Light/Tae-Bo/Hemelgarn Racing	D/A/G	Hemelgarn Racing Inc.
91T	Buddy Lazier	Delta Faucet/Coors Light/Tae-Bo/Hemelgarn Racing	D/A/G	Hemelgarn Racing Inc.
92	Johnny Unser	Tae-Bo/Hemelgarn Racing/Homier Tool/Delta Faucet	D/A/G	Hemelgarn Racing Inc.
92T	Johnny Unser	Tae-Bo/Hemelgarn Racing/Homier Tool/Delta Faucet	D/A/G	Hemelgarn Racing Inc.
93	TBA	Hemelgarn Racing	D/A/G	Hemelgarn Racing Inc.
93T	TBA	Hemelgarn Racing	D/A/G	Hemelgarn Racing Inc.
96	Jeret Schroeder (R)	Purity Farms Cobb Racing G Force Infiniti Firestone	G/I/F	Cobb Racing
98	Donnie Beechler	Cahill Racing/Firestone/Oldsmobile/Dallara	D/A/F	Cahill Racing, Inc.
98T	Donnie Beechler	Cahill Racing/Firestone/Oldsmobile/Dallara	D/A/F	Cahill Racing, Inc.
99	Sam Schmidt	Unistar Auto Insurance	G/A/F	Treadway Racing LLC
99T	Sam Schmidt	Unistar Auto Insurance	G/A/F	Treadway Racing LLC

Legend: Chassis: D=Dallara, G=G Force, R=Riley & Scott.
Engine: A=Oldsmobile Aurora, I=Nissan Infiniti.
Tire: F=Firestone, G=Goodyear. R=Rookie.
Entry List as of April 15, 1999

The Indianapolis Motor Speedway and participating sponsors in the 83rd Indianapolis 500 are pleased to offer the following qualifying incentives.

PPG Industries returns to present the PPG Pole Award, worth $100,000 to the pole position winner plus **Chevrolet** will present the pole winner with a 1999 Camaro.

GTE awards each front row qualifier with $10,000, **Daktronics** pays $10,000 to the last driver to be bumped on the last day of qualifying. **Ferguson Steel** also presents $10,000 for consistency in qualifying. **Ameritech** presents the youngest starting driver with $7,500.

PPG Pole Award
$100,000
PPG INDUSTRIES

**CHEVROLET
OFFICIAL CAR AWARD**
1999 Chevrolet Camaro
(pole winner)

GTE "Front Runner" Award - $30,000
$10,000 awarded to each front row driver
GTE

Daktronics "My Bubble Burst" Award - $10,000
awarded to the last driver to be bumped on the last day of qualifying
Daktronics

Ameritech "Youngest Starting Driver" Award - $7,500
AMERITECH

**Buckeye Machine/
Race Spec
"Final Measure"
Award - $5,000**
awarded to last team to pass inspection
and qualify for the race
**BUCKEYE MACHINE/
RACE SPEC**

**COLD FIRE
"Hottest Pit Crew"
Award - $5,000**
awarded to the pit crew of the
highest qualifying rookie
FIREFREEZE WORLDWIDE

**Ferguson Steel
"Most Consistent Qualifier"
Award - $5,000**
awarded to the veteran who records
the most consistent qualifying laps
**FERGUSON STEEL
COMPANY, INC.**

**Ferguson Steel "Most Consistent
Rookie Qualifier"
Award - $5,000**
awarded to the rookie who records
the most consistent qualifying laps
**FERGUSON STEEL
COMPANY, INC.**

**Mi-Jack "Top Performer"
Award - $5,000**
awarded to the driver recording
the fastest single qualifying lap
MI-JACK PRODUCTS

**Snap-On/CAM "Top
Wrench" Award - $5,000**
recognizes mechanical excellence by
a chief mechanic during practice and
qualifying
SNAP-ON/CAM

**T.P. Donovan
"Top Starting Rookie"
Award - $5,000**
**T.P. DONOVAN
INVESTMENTS**

PPG Industries leads the way for all participating Contingency Awards sponsors of the 1999 Indianapolis 500 with their posting of $495,000 divided equally among each of the 33 starting drivers. PPG also presents each starting driver with a special PPG Starters' Ring.

Pennzoil follows PPG with a posting of $150,000. Other leading Accessory Award sponsors include the Robert Bosch Corporation offering $45,000 and Nissan, Oldsmobile and Raybestos each post $30,000. First Brands/STP Racing offers $26,000.

$495,000 $150,000

| BOSCH $45,000 | OLDSMOBILE $30,000 | NISSAN $30,000 | RAYBESTOS BRAKE PARTS $30,000 | FIRST BRANDS STP RACING $26,000 |

SIMPSON HELMETS $10,000

MOBIL OIL $10,000

EARL'S PERFORMANCE PRODUCTS $13,000

PREMIER FARNELL CORP. $10,000

BELL HELMETS $6,000

FIRST GEAR $5,000

KLOTZ SPECIAL FORMULA PRODUCTS $5,000

CANON $5,000

HYPERCO INC. $5,000

CHAMPION $5,000

IDEAL DIVISION STANT CORP. $5,000

STANT MFG. $5,000

EMCO GEARS, INC. $5,000

KECO COATINGS $5,000

WISECO PISTON $5,000

The 1999 Indianapolis 500 Mile Race purse exceeded **8 million dollars** for the fifth time in Speedway history. While the Indianapolis Motor Speedway contributed over 6 million dollars to this purse, over 50 participating sponsors posted over $1 million in cash and prizes.

Borg-Warner leads the postings for Race Day awards with $130,000 in cash for the winner and a $100,000 bonus if a back-to-back win is recorded. **Coors Brewing Company** has posted $80,000 for their Carburetion Day Coors Indy Pit Stop Challenge. **Acordia Motorsports Insurance** offers $50,000 in race day awards.

The 1999 race winner will also receive a 2000 Monte Carlo from **Chevrolet.**

BORG-WARNER TROPHY AWARD
$130,000 plus trophy replica
$100,000 bonus if the 1998 winner repeats his victory
($20,000 added to the bonus each year until a back-to-back win is recorded)
Borg-Warner Automotive, Inc.
(race winner)

$80,000 - Coors Brewing Company
(contest held May 27, 1999)

BANK ONE "ROOKIE OF THE YEAR" AWARD
$25,000 - Bank One, Indianapolis

GT INTERACTIVE "FASTEST RACE LAP" AWARD
$25,000 - GT Interactive

MCI WorldCom "LONG DISTANCE" AWARD
$20,000 - Delphi Automotive Systems
(awarded to the driver who most improves their position during the race)

DELPHI AUTOMOTIVE SYSTEMS "LEADER AT HALFWAY" AWARD
$20,000 - Delphi Automotive Systems

CHEVROLET OFFICIAL PACE CAR AWARD
2000 Chevrolet Monte Carlo
(race winner)

ACORDIA MOTORSPORTS INSURANCE
$50,000
(two $25,000 awards to be presented on race day)

SCOTT BRAYTON DRIVERS TROPHY
$25,000 - Royal Purple Motor Oil
(awarded to the driver who most exemplifies the attitude, spirit and competitive drive of Scott Brayton)

FIRESTONE "FIRST AT 99" AWARD
$20,000 - Bridgestone/Firestone Inc.
(awarded to the highest running driver at Lap 99 using Firestone tires)

UNION PLANTERS BANK "LEADERS' CIRCLE" AWARD
$20,000 - Union Planters Bank

AMERICAN DAIRY AWARDS
$10,750 - American Dairy Association
(winner, fastest rookie, winning chief mechanic, each qualifying rookie)

NATIONAL CITY BANK "CHECKERED FLAG" AWARD
$10,000 - National City Bank, Indiana
(race winner)

MBNA MOTORSPORTS "LAP LEADER" AWARD
$10,000 - MBNA

MARSH "MOST IMPROVED POSITION" AWARD
$10,000 - Marsh Supermarkets

KODAK "PHOTO FINISH" AWARD
$10,000 - Eastman Kodak Company
(race winner)

C & R RACING "TRUE GRIT" AWARD
$5,000 - C & R Racing, Inc.
(awarded to the mechanic that exemplifies outstanding achievement and excellence in preparation and management)

CLINT BRAWNER "MECHANICAL EXCELLENCE" AWARD
$5,000 - Clint Brawner Mechanical Excellence Foundation

"CRAFTSMAN TRACTOR" AWARD
$5,000 - Frigidaire Home Products
(awarded to the highest finishing team using the Craftsman Tractor during the entire month of May at the Speedway)

DAMON'S AWARD
$5,000 - Damon's Barbeque Ribs
(race winner)

GOODYEAR "WINNING CAR OWNER" AWARD
$5,000 plus ring - The Goodyear Tire and Rubber Co.

INDIANA OXYGEN "PERSEVERANCE" AWARD
$5,000 - Indiana Oxygen
(presented to the team on race day that exemplifies the most exceptional sportsmanship in a non-winning effort)

LINCOLN ELECTRIC "HARD CHARGER" AWARD
$5,000 - Lincoln Electric
Racing's #1 Choice in Welding
(awarded to the lowest qualifier to lead the race)

MOTORSPORTS SPARES INT'L "PERSISTENCE PAYS" AWARD
$5,000 - Motorsports Spares Int'l., Inc.
(awarded to the highest finishing last day qualifier)

PREMIER/D-A "MECHANICAL ACHIEVEMENT" AWARD
$5,000 - Premier Farnell Corp.

OFFICIAL SPONSORS OF THE 1999 INDIANAPOLIS 500

Blue Star	Official Battery
Canon	Official Camera
Chevrolet	Official Car, Pace Car & Truck
	Official Vehicle of the Indianapolis Motor Speedway
Clarian Health	Official Healthcare Provider for the Indianapolis Motor Speedway
Coors Light	Official Beer
DAMON'S	Official Barbeque Rib
EAR	Official Earplug
Emergency One	Official Fire Truck of the Indianapolis Motor Speedway
FireFreeze	Official Fire Fighting Agent
Kidde	Official Fire Extinguisher
Kroger	Official Supermarket
Kodak	Official Film & Single Use Camera
MBNA	Official Credit Card
MCI WorldCom	Official Long Distance, Calling Card, Pre-paid Calling Card & Local Service Provider
Pennzoil	Official Motor Oil
Pep Boys	Official Auto Parts Store
Pepsi	Official Soft Drink
Sprint PCS	Official PCS Provider
Vulcan	Official Race Recovery Vehicle of the Indianapolis Motor Speedway

OFFICIAL SPONSORS

Official Battery

Official Camera

Official Trailers

Official Clothier

KIDDE
Official Fire Extinguisher

MBNA Motorsports
Official Sponsor

NORTEL
Technical Consultant & Provider
Advanced Internet Solutions

Oldsmobile
Official Vehicle, Car & Pace Car

Official Sponsor

 Official Fuel Certification

Indianapolis 500 Scoring Positions at 10-Lap

POS	Driver	SP	1	10	20	30	40	50	60	70	80	90	100	110	120	130	140	150	160	170	180	190	200	Driver
1	Arie Luyendyk	5	5	5	5	5	5	2	14	14	14	2	5	5	2	14	14	14	14	14	32	32	14	Kenny Brack
2	Greg Ray	2	2	2	2	2	2	5	2	2	2	5	2	2	14	51	21	21	21	21	21	14	21	Jeff Ward
3	Billy Boat	11	11	11	14	14	99	99	5	5	5	14	14	51	21	21	11	11	11	11	14	21	11	Billy Boat
4	Robby Gordon	32	32	28	11	11	14	14	99	4	4	4	51	14	11	11	55	55	28	32	11	11	32	Robby Gordon
5	Mark Dismore	28	28	14	28	51	22	22	22	55	55	51	4	11	84	55	28	28	55	84	55	84	55	Robby McGehee
6	Scott Sharp	8	21	32	21	28	55	55	55	33	51	55	55	28	28	28	32	84	84	55	84	55	84	Robbie Buhl
7	Sam Schmidt	99	14	21	51	21	3	33	33	22	33	22	11	21	51	84	84	32	32	96	91	91	91	Buddy Lazier
8	Kenny Brack	14	4	4	4	99	33	51	51	51	22	84	84	55	55	51	51	81	81	81	81	81	81	Robby Unser
9	Scott Goodyear	4	99	51	99	4	12	81	9	9	11	11	28	22	22	22	51	91	91	42	22	22	22	Tony Stewart
10	Hideshi Matsuda	54	54	54	54	54	51	4	11	11	9	9	22	32	32	96	81	81	9	9	9	9	54	Hideshi Matsuda
11	Davey Hamilton	9	9	99	32	32	81	11	84	84	84	21	21	96	96	91	91	22	22	54	54	54	9	Davey Hamilton
12	John Hollansworth Jr.	42	51	9	81	42	21	21	21	21	21	28	9	9	91	81	81	42	9	3	3	3	3	Raul Boesel
13	Steve Knapp	35	81	81	9	9	4	3	81	28	28	32	32	33	81	3	22	3	3	54	42	42	42	John Hollansworth Jr.
14	Jeff Ward	21	42	42	42	20	11	84	8	32	32	33	52	81	3	42	3	42	42	3	42	20	20	Tyce Carlson
15	Tyce Carlson	20	20	20	20	98	42	9	28	8	8	35	33	3	42	42	54	54	54	20	20	96	96	Jeret Schroeder
16	Eddie Cheever Jr.	51	6	35	98	22	84	42	21	35	35	52	96	42	54	54	20	20	20	28	28	28	28	Mark Dismore
17	Robby Unser	81	35	22	35	50	9	28	32	52	52	96	81	20	20	20	51	51	51	51	51	51	19	Stan Wattles
18	Eliseo Salazar	6	91	91	50	84	28	98	32	96	96	81	3	5	33	33	33	33	33	19	19	19	51	Eddie Cheever Jr.
19	Donnie Beechler	98	98	33	55	98	98	8	96	3	3	50	42	54	2	2	2	2	2	33	12	12	12	Buzz Calkins
20	Stan Wattles	19	96	96	91	81	52	20	35	81	81	3	54	20	5	5	5	5	5	2	33	33	33	Robert Moreno
21	Jeret Schroeder	96	19	50	84	35	32	52	3	91	3	33	33	52	52	52	52	52	5	5	2	2	2	Greg Ray
22	Buddy Lazier	91	12	84	55	8	91	81	52	50	42	42	54	4	4	4	50	4	52	52	5	5	5	Arie Luyendyk
23	Roberto Moreno	33	50	12	12	52	50	35	20	20	54	54	50	50	50	35	30	50	19	50	50	52	52	Wim Eyckmans
24	Tony Stewart	22	33	52	50	12	35	96	50	42	20	20	35	35	35	30	30	30	50	30	50	30	30	Jimmy Kite
25	Roberto Guerrero	50	52	19	3	3	96	91	42	54	98	8	8	8	8	8	35	19	4	12	12	50	50	Roberto Guerrero
26	Buzz Calkins	12	22	3	33	96	91	50	54	98	8	98	98	98	30	8	12	35	35	4	4	35	35	Steve Knapp
27	Robby McGehee	55	55	96	55	19	19	19	99	91	99	99	19	19	19	19	8	12	12	35	35	4	4	Scott Goodyear
28	Jimmy Kite	30	30	55	19	8	50	54	19	19	19	19	19	30	98	98	12	8	8	8	8	8	8	Scott Sharp
29	Wim Eyckmans	52	84	30	12	91	54	12	12	12	12	30	30	99	99	12	98	98	98	98	98	98	98	Donnie Beechler
30	Johnny Unser	92	92	92	92	17	17	17	30	30	30	12	12	12	12	99	99	99	99	99	99	99	99	Sam Schmidt
31	Jack Miller	17	3	8	17	30	30	30	17	17	17	17	17	17	17	17	17	17	17	17	17	17	17	Jack Miller
32	Robbie Buhl	84	8	6	6	92	92	92	92	92	92	92	92	92	92	92	92	92	92	92	92	92	92	Johnny Unser
33	Raul Boesel	3	17	17	17	6	6	6	6	6	6	6	6	6	6	6	6	6	6	6	6	6	6	Eliseo Salazar
	Race Average Speed:		199.397	161.383	131.795	150.684	141.190	150.933	158.165	145.037	150.902	155.610	149.259	147.202	147.965	144.396	147.588	150.461	152.447	150.311	148.730	151.095	153.176	

	WDWS		PIR		IMS		TMS 1		PPIR 1		AMS		DDIS		PPIR 2		LVMS		TMS 2	
	SP	FP	SP	FP	SP	FP	SP	FP	SP	FP	SP	FP	SP	FP	SP	FP	SP	FP	SP	FP
Beechler, Donnie	22	26	7	11	19	29	25	17	22	22	27	8	20	10	24	20	15	18	22	11
Boat, Billy	14	9	23	4	3	3	11	24	7	24	1	10	16	4	14	13	9	22	25	9
Boesel, Raul	3	5	10	19	33	12	23	23	20	18	25	11	-	-	-	-	-	-	-	-
Brack, Kenny	5	22	21	24	8	1	9	13	13	7	14	3	14	3	13	10	3	2	5	16
Buhl, Robbie	26	20	17	3	32	6	-	-	-	-	-	-	-	-	-	-	21	3	15	24
Calkins, Buzz	11	17	12	14	26	19	14	9	24	14	20	5	12	8	15	15	16	5	19	8
Carlson, Tyce	9	12	9	23	15	14	3	21	5	23	26	20	11	11	19	17	7	9	9	13
Cheever, Eddie	13	1	18	17	16	18	5	16	11	4	21	6	19	21	20	11	18	17	20	4
Didero, Doug	-	-	-	-	-	-	-	-	-	-	-	-	-	-	-	-	-	-	21	20
Dismore, Mark	10	6	2	7	5	16	1	8	3	21	4	17	1	15	3	3	2	20	2	1
Eyckmans, Wim	-	-	-	-	29	23	-	-	-	-	-	-	-	-	-	-	-	-	-	-
Fisher, Sarah	-	-	-	-	-	-	-	-	-	-	-	-	-	-	-	-	-	-	17	25
Goodyear, Scott	4	2	3	1	9	27	8	1	14	12	5	16	18	17	11	21	5	25	3	23
Gordon, Robby	-	-	-	-	4	4	-	-	-	-	-	-	-	-	-	-	-	-	-	-
Greco, Marco	-	-	22	12	-	-	-	-	-	-	-	-	-	-	-	-	-	-	-	-
Gregoire, Stephan	25	16	19	10	-	-	16	4	15	11	13	24	9	14	21	14	11	8	13	15
Guerrero, Roberto	12	13	11	16	25	25	-	-	-	-	-	-	-	-	-	-	-	-	-	-
Hamilton, Davey	20	8	27	27	11	11	15	7	9	3	7	7	8	23	5	2	26	13	6	2
Harrington, Scott	28	25	8	5	-	-	-	-	8	19	12	15	5	6	4	6	12	14	8	6
Hollansworth, John	18	19	16	15	12	13	13	20	2	16	9	19	6	19	7	16	8	19	18	5
Johncox, Ronnie	-	-	-	-	-	-	10	11	-	-	17	25	23	20	18	24	23	15	24	26
Jonsson, Niclas	-	-	-	-	-	-	-	-	-	-	-	-	-	-	-	-	25	24	-	-
Kite, Jimmy	-	-	-	-	28	24	22	25	10	15	11	9	15	16	16	8	-	-	-	-
Knapp, Steve	17	7	24	25	13	26	17	12	21	17	24	27	-	-	-	-	-	-	-	-
Lazier, Buddy	8	10	15	18	22	7	24	14	12	5	15	21	17	2	9	4	10	11	16	10
Lazier, Jaques	-	-	-	-	-	-	19	22	23	10	16	12	22	7	17	12	20	7	23	7
Leffler, Jason	15	28	-	-	-	-	-	-	-	-	-	-	-	-	-	-	-	-	-	-
Luyendyk, Arie	-	-	-	-	1	22	-	-	-	-	-	-	-	-	-	-	-	-	-	-
Matsuda, Hideshi	-	-	-	-	10	10	-	-	-	-	-	-	-	-	-	-	-	-	-	-
McGehee, Robby	-	-	-	-	27	5	21	19	-	-	23	14	10	9	8	7	19	6	14	12
Michner, Andy	27	18	26	13	-	-	-	-	-	-	-	-	-	-	-	-	-	-	-	-
Miller, Dr. Jack	-	-	-	-	31	31	-	-	-	-	19	18	-	-	-	-	-	-	-	-
Moreno, Roberto	-	-	4	6	23	20	-	-	-	-	-	-	-	-	-	-	-	-	-	-
Paul, John	19	11	25	22	-	-	-	-	-	-	-	-	-	-	-	-	-	-	26	18
Ray, Greg	2	21	1	21	2	21	4	2	1	1	2	23	3	1	1	1	4	21	1	3
Regester, Bobby	-	-	-	-	-	-	-	-	-	-	-	-	-	-	23	18	-	-	-	-
Ribbs, Willy T.	-	-	-	-	-	-	-	-	-	-	-	-	-	-	-	-	24	26	-	-
Salazar, Eliseo	-	-	14	20	18	33	20	5	19	20	18	4	21	18	22	19	22	12	10	17
Salles, Gaulter	23	23	-	-	-	-	-	-	-	-	-	-	-	-	-	-	-	-	-	-
Schmidt, Sam	7	27	20	9	7	30	6	3	4	2	3	22	4	5	2	5	1	1	4	22
Schroeder, Jeret	-	-	-	-	21	15	-	-	-	-	-	-	-	-	-	-	-	-	-	-
Sharp, Scott	1	4	6	8	6	28	2	10	17	8	6	1	2	22	6	22	6	4	7	19
Stewart, Tony	-	-	-	-	24	9	-	-	-	-	-	-	-	-	-	-	-	-	-	-
Tyler, Brian	24	14	-	-	-	-	-	-	-	-	-	-	-	-	-	-	-	-	-	-
Unser, Johnny	-	-	-	-	30	32	18	15	16	13	22	13	-	-	-	-	14	23	-	-
Unser, Robby	21	15	13	26	17	8	12	6	6	6	10	2	13	12	12	9	13	16	11	14
Ward, Jeff	6	3	5	2	14	2	7	18	18	9	8	26	7	13	10	23	17	10	12	21
Wattles, Stan	16	24	-	-	20	17	-	-	-	-	-	-	-	-	-	-	-	-	-	-

	Entrant	WDWS	PIR	IMS	TMS 1	PPIR 1	AMS	DDIS	PPIR 2	LVMS	TMS 2	Total
1	Team Menard, #2	11	12	11	42	55	9	51	55	9	38	293
2	A.J. Foyt Enterprises, #14	8	6	52	17	26	35	35	20	43	14	256
3	Kelley Racing, #28	28	28	14	27	10	13	20	36	12	52	240
4	Galles Racing, #9	24		19	26	35	26	7	40	17	40	234
5	Treadway Racing, #99	3	22	1	35	40	9	30	32	53	8	233
6	Hemelgarn Racing, #91	20	12	26	16	30	9	40	32	19	20	224
7	Team Cheever, #51	50	13	12	14	32	28	9	19	13	32	222
8	Kelley Racing, #8	37	24	2	22	24	50	10	8	32	11	220
9	Panther Racing, #4	40	53	3	50	18	16	13	9	5	10	217
10	Team Pelfrey, #81	15	4	24	28	28	40	18	22	14	16	209
11	A.J. Foyt Enterprises, #11	22	32	36	6	6	23	32	17	8	22	204
12	Bradley Motorsports, #12	13	16	11	22	16	30	24	15	30	24	201
13	Truscelli Team Racing, #33	16	28	10	8	20	18	26	18	26	26	196
14	Pagan Racing, #21	40	40	12	22	4	17	7	20	9		171
15	Harrington Motorsports, #66	5	30		4**	11	15	28	28	16	28	165
16	Dick Simon Racing, #7	14	20		32	19	6	16	16	24	15	162
17	Conti Racing, #55			30	11	5***	16	22	26	28	18	156
18	TeamXtreme Racing, #42	11	15	17	10	16	11	11	14	11	30	146
19	McCormack Motorsports, #30	31	11	6	5	15	22	14	24	4	12	144
20	Blueprint-Immke Racing, #20	18	7	16	10	7	10	19	13	22	17	139
21	Nienhouse Motorsports, #6		10	1	30	10	32	12	11	18	13	137
22	Cahill Racing, #98	4	19	1	13	8	24	20	10	12	19	130
23	Tri Star Motorsports, #22	7		22	19		5	10	6	35	6	110
24	Brant Racing, #3	12	17	18	7	12	19					85
25	ISM Racing, #35	35	5	4	18	13	3					78
26	Hemelgarn Racing, #92			1	15	17	17			7		57
27	Sinden Racing Services, #44	10	35									45
28	Cobb Racing, #50	17	14	5								36
29	Team Menard, #32		32								32	
30	Tri Star Motorsports, #17			1			12			15	4	32
31	A.J. Foyt Enterprises, #84			28								28
32	Jonathan Byrd-Cunningham Racing, #10	19	8									27
33	PDM, #18	26										26
34	Beck Motorsports, #54			20								20
35	Metro Racing, #19	6		13								19
36	Phoenix Racing, #16		18									18
37	Cobb Racing, #96		15								15	
38	Treadway Racing, #5	2		11								13
39	Truscelli Team Racing, #26								12			12
40	Mid American Motorsports, #43									10	10	
41	Blueprint Racing Ent., LLC									6	3****	9
42	Team Cheever, #52		7									7
43	Team Pelfrey, #48									5	5	
44	Barnhart Motorsports, #25		3									3
45	DR Motorsports, #15		2*									2

Key: WDWS-Walt Disney World Speedway; PIR-Phoenix International Raceway; IMS-Indianapolis Motor Speedway; TMS-Texas Motor Speedway; PPIR-Pikes Peak International Raceway; AMS-Atlanta Motor Speedway; DDIS-Dover Downs International Speedway; LVMS-Las Vegas Motor Speedway

* Was awarded money and points for 28th finishing position but did not start the race.

** Was awarded money and points for 26th finishing position but did not start the race.

*** Was awarded money and points for 25th finishing position but did not start the race.

**** Was awarded money and points for 27th finishing position but did not start the race.

Year	St. Pos.	Car #	Driver	Car Name & Sponsor Chassis/Engine	Qualify Speed	Race Time	Race Speed
1911	28	32	Ray Harroun	Nordyke & Marmon / Marmon / Marmon	6:42:08.000		74.602
1912	7	8	Joe Dawson	National Motor Vehicle / National / National	86.130	6:21:06.000	78.719
1913	7	16	Jules Goux	Peugeot / Peugeot / Peugeot	86.030	6:35:05.000	75.933
1914	15	16	Rene Thomas	L. Delage / Delage / Delage	94.540	6:03:45.000	82.474
1915	2	2	Ralph DePalma	Mercedes/E.C. Patterson / Mercedes / Mercedes	98.580	5:33:55.510	89.840
1916	4	17	Dario Resta	Peugeot Auto Racing / Peugeot / Peugeot	94.400	3:34:17.000	84.001 a
1919	2	3	Howdy Wilcox	Peugeot/Indpls Spdway Team / Peugeot / Peugeot	100.010	5:40:42.870	88.050
1920	6	4	Gaston Chevrolet	Monroe/William Small / Frontenac / Frontenac	91.550	5:38:32.000	88.618
1921	20	2	Tommy Milton	Frontenac/Louis Chevrolet / Frontenac / Frontenac	93.050	5:34:44.650	89.621
1922	1	35	Jimmy Murphy	Jimmy Murphy / Duesenberg / Miller	100.500	5:17:30.790	94.484
1923	1	1	Tommy Milton	H.C.S. Motor / Miller / Miller	108.170	5:29:50.170	90.954
1924	21	15	L.L. Corum-J. Boyer	Duesenberg / Duesenberg / Duesenberg	93.330	5:05:23.510	98.234
1925	2	12	Peter DePaolo	Duesenberg / Duesenberg / Duesenberg	113.080	4:56:39.460	101.127
1926	20	15	Frank Lockhart	Miller/Peter Kreis / Miller / Miller	95.780	4:10:14.950	95.904 b
1927	22	32	George Souders	Duesenberg/William White / Duesenberg / Duesenberg	111.550	5:07:33.080	97.545
1928	13	14	Louie Meyer	Miller/Alden Sampson, II / Miller / Miller	111.350	5:01:33.750	99.482
1929	6	2	Ray Keech	Simplex Piston Ring/Ragle / Miller / Miller	114.900	5:07:25.420	97.585
1930	1	4	Billy Arnold	Miller-Hartz / Summers / Miller	113.260	4:58:39.720	100.448
1931	13	23	Louis Schneider	Bowes Seal Fast/Schneider / Stevens / Miller	107.210	5:10:27.930	96.629
1932	27	34	Fred Frame	Miller-Harry Hartz / Wetteroth / Miller	113.850	4:48:03.790	104.144
1933	6	36	Louie Meyer	Tydol/Louie Meyer / Miller / Miller	116.970	4:48:00.750	104.162
1934	10	7	Bill Cummings	Boyle Products/Henning / Miller / Miller	116.110	4:46:05.200	104.863
1935	22	5	Kelly Petillo	Gilmore Speedway/Petillo / Wetteroth / Offy	115.090	4:42:22.710	106.240
1936	28	8	Louie Meyer	Ring Free/Lou Meyer / Stevens / Miller	114.170	4:35:03.390	109.069
1937	2	6	Wilbur Shaw	Shaw-Gilmore / Shaw / Offy	122.790	4:24:07.800	113.580
1938	1	23	Floyd Roberts	Burd Piston Ring/Lou Moore / Wetteroth / Miller	125.680	4:15:58.400	117.200
1939	3	2	Wilbur Shaw	Boyle Racing Headquarters / Maserati / Maserati	128.970	4:20:47.390	115.035
1940	2	1	Wilbur Shaw	Boyle Racing Headquarters / Maserati / Maserati	127.060	4:22:31.170	114.277
1941	17	16	F. Davis-M. Rose	Noc-Out Hose Clamp/Moore / Wetteroth / Offy	121.100	4:20:36.240	115.117
1946	15	16	George Robson	Thorne Engineering / Adams / Sparks	125.540	4:21:16.700	114.820
1947	3	27	Mauri Rose	Blue Crown Spark Plug/Moore / Deidt / Offy	120.040	4:17:52.170	116.338
1948	3	3	Mauri Rose	Blue Crown Spark Plug/Moore / Deidt / Offy	129.120	4:10:23.330	119.814
1949	4	7	Bill Holland	Blue Crown Spark Plug/Moore / Deidt / Offy	128.670	4:07:15.970	121.327
1950	5	1	Johnnie Parsons	Wynn's Friction/Kurtis-Kraft / Kurtis / Offy	132.040	2:46:55.970	124.002 c
1951	2	99	Lee Wallard	Murrell Belanger / Kurtis / Offy	135.030	3:57:38.050	126.244
1952	7	98	Troy Ruttman	J.C. Agajanian / Kuzma / Offy	135.360	3:52:41.880	128.922
1953	1	14	Bill Vukovich	Fuel Injection/Howard Keck / KK500A / Offy	138.390	3:53:01.690	128.740
1954	19	14	Bill Vukovich	Fuel Injection/Howard Keck / KK500A / Offy	138.470	3:49:17.270	130.840
1955	14	6	Bob Sweikert	John Zink / KK500C / Offy	139.990	3:53:59.130	128.213

Indianapolis 500 Winners

USAC SANCTIONING

Year	St. Pos.	Car #	Driver	Car Name & Sponsor Chassis/Engine	Qualify Speed	Race Time	Race Speed
1956	1	8	Pat Flaherty	John Zink / Watson / Offy	145.590	3:53:28.840	128.490
1957	13	9	Sam Hanks	Belond Exhaust/George Salih / Salih / Offy	142.810	3:41:14.250	135.601
1958	7	1	Jimmy Bryan	Belond AP/George Salih / Salih / Offy	144.180	3:44:13.800	133.791
1959	6	5	Rodger Ward	Leader Card 500 Roadster / Watson / Offy	144.030	3:40:49.200	135.857
1960	2	4	Jim Rathmann	Ken-Paul / Watson / Offy	146.370	3:36:11.360	138.767
1961	7	1	A.J. Foyt, Jr.	Bowes Seal Fast/Bignotti / Trevis / Offy	145.900	3:35:37.490	139.130
1962	2	3	Rodger Ward	Leader Card 500 Roadster / Watson / Offy	149.370	3:33:50.330	140.293
1963	1	98	Parnelli Jones	J.C. Agajanian/Willard Battery / Watson / Offy	151.150	3:29:35.400	143.137
1964	5	1	A.J. Foyt, Jr.	Sheraton-Thompson/Ansted / Watson / Offy	154.670	3:23:35.830	147.350
1965	2	82	Jim Clark	Lotus powered by Ford / Lotus / Ford	160.720	3:19:05.340	150.686
1966	15	24	Graham Hill	American Red Ball/Mecom / Lola / Ford	159.240	3:27:52.530	144.317
1967	4	14	A.J. Foyt, Jr.	Sheraton-Thompson/Ansted / Coyote / Ford	166.280	3:18:24.220	151.207
1968	3	3	Bobby Unser	Rislone/Leader Cards / Eagle / Offy	169.500	3:16:13.760	152.882
1969	2	2	Mario Andretti	STP Oil Treatment / Hawk / Ford	169.850	3:11:14.710	156.867
1970	1	2	Al Unser	Johnny Lightning/Parnelli Jones / P.J. Colt / Ford	170.220	3:12:37.040	155.749
1971	5	1	Al Unser	Johnny Lightning/Parnelli Jones / P.J. Colt / Ford	174.520	3:10:11.560	157.735
1972	3	66	Mark Donohue	Sunoco McLaren/Penske / McLaren / Offy	191.400	3:04:05.540	162.962
1973	11	20	Gordon Johncock	STP Double Oil Filter/Patrick / Eagle / Offy	192.550	2:05:26.590	159.036 d
1974	25	3	Johnny Rutherford	McLaren Cars / McLaren / Offy	190.440	3:09:10.060	158.589
1975	3	48	Bobby Unser	Jorgensen/All American Racers / Eagle / Offy	191.070	2:54:55.080	149.213 e
1976	1	2	Johnny Rutherford	Hy-Gain/McLaren / McLaren / Offy	188.950	1:42:52.000	148.725 f
1977	4	14	A.J. Foyt, Jr.	Gilmore Racing/A.J. Foyt / Coyote / Foyt	194.560	3:05:57.160	161.331
1978	5	2	Al Unser	First National City/Chaparral / Lola / Cosworth	196.470	3:05:54.990	161.363
1979	1	9	Rick Mears	The Gould Charge/Penske / Penske / Cosworth	193.730	3:08:47.970	158.899
1980	1	4	Johnny Rutherford	Pennzoil/Chaparral Racing / Chaparral / Cosworth	192.520	3:29:59.560	142.862
1981	1	3	Bobby Unser	The Norton Spirit/Penske / Penske/ Cosworth	200.540	3:35:41.780	139.084
1982	5	20	Gordon Johncock	STP Oil Treatment/Patrick / Wildcat / Cosworth	201.880	3:05:09.140	162.029
1983	4	5	Tom Sneva	Texaco Star/Bignotti-Cotter / March / Cosworth	203.680	3:05:03.066	162.117
1984	3	6	Rick Mears	Pennzoil Z-7/Penske / March / Cosworth	207.840	3:03:21.660	163.612
1985	8	5	Danny Sullivan	Miller American/Penske / March / Cosworth	210.290	3:16:06.069	152.982
1986	4	3	Bobby Rahal	Budweiser/Truesports / March / Cosworth	213.550	2:55:43.480	170.722
1987	20	25	Al Unser	Cummins-Holset/Penske / March / Cosworth	207.420	3:04:59.147	162.175
1988	1	5	Rick Mears	Pennzoil Z-7/Penske / Penske / Chevy Indy V8	219.190	3:27:10.204	144.809
1989	3	20	Emerson Fittipaldi	Marlboro/Patrick Racing / Penske / Chevy Indy V8	222.320	2:59:01.490	167.581
1990	3	30	Arie Luyendyk	Domino's Pizza/Shierson / Lola / Chevy Indy V8	223.300	2:41:18.404	185.981 *
1991	1	3	Rick Mears	Marlboro Penske Chevy 91 / Penske / Chevy Indy V8	224.113	2:50:00.791	176.457
1992	12	3	Al Unser, Jr.	Valvoline Galmer '92 / Galmer/Chevy Indy V8A	222.989	3:43:05.148	134.477
1993	9	4	Emerson Fittipaldi	Marlboro Penske Chevy '93 / Penske/Chevy Indy V8C	220.150	3:10:49.860	157.207
1994	1	31	Al Unser, Jr.	Marlboro Penske Mercedes / Penske/Mercedes Benz	228.011	3:06:29.006	160.872
1995	5	27	Jacques Villeneuve	Player's LTD/Team Green / Reynard/Ford Cosworth XB	228.397	3:15:17.561	153.616
1996	5	91	Buddy Lazier	Delta Faucet/Montana/Hemelgarn 95 Reynard/Ford Cosworth XB	231.468	3:22:45.753	147.956
1997	1	5	Arie Luyendyk	Wavephore/Spirit PCS/Miller Lite/Provimi G Force/Aurora	218.263	3:25:43.388	145.827
1998	17	51	Eddie Cheever, Jr.	Rachel's Potato Chips / Dallara/Aurora	217.334	3:26:40.524	145.155
1999	8	14	Kenny Brack	AJ Foyt Power Team Dallara/Aurora	222.659	3:15:51.182	153.176mph

a 1916 - 300 Miles (Scheduled)
b 1926 - 400 Miles (Rain)
c 1950 - 345 Miles (Rain)
d 1973 - 332.5 Miles (Rain)
e 1975 - 435 Miles (Rain)
f 1976 - 255 Miles (Rain)

* Track Record

Walt Disney World Speedway	January 29	Orlando, Florida
Phoenix International Raceway	March 19	Phoenix, Arizona
Las Vegas Motor Speedway	April 22	Las Vegas, Nevada
Indianapolis 500, Indianapolis Motor Speedway	May 28	Indianapolis, Indiana
Texas Motor Speedway	June 10	Fort Worth, Texas
Pikes Peak International Raceway	June 18	Colorado Springs, Colorado
Atlanta Motor Speedway	July 15	Atlanta, Georgia
Kentucky Speedway	August 27	Florence, Kentucky
To Be Announced	September 10	—, —
Texas Motor Speedway	October 15	Fort Worth, Texas